Future Tense

FUTURE TENSE

Australia beyond election 1998

The Australian, with Paul Kelly
and the national affairs team
Edited by Murray Waldren

ALLEN & UNWIN

Copyright © in the collection, *The Australian* 1999
Copyright in individual pieces remains with the authors.

All rights reserved. No part of this book may be reproduced or transmitted in any form or by any means, electronic or mechanical, including photocopying, recording or by any information storage and retrieval system, without prior permission in writing from the publisher.

First published in 1999 by
Allen & Unwin Pty Ltd
9 Atchison Street, St Leonards, NSW 1590 Australia
Phone: (61 2) 8425 0100
Fax: (61 2) 9906 2218
E-mail: frontdesk@allen-unwin.com.au
Web: http://www.allen-unwin.com.au

National Library of Australia
Cataloguing-in-Publication entry:

Future tense: Australia beyond election 1998.

Includes index.
ISBN 1 86508 034 9.

1. Australia. Parliament—Elections, 1998. 2. Australia—Civilization—1990– . 3. Australia—Social conditions—1990– . 4. Australia—Economic conditions—1990– . 5. Australia—Politics and government—1996– . I. Kelly, Paul, 1947– . II. Waldren, Murray. III. Title. IV. Title: Australian (Canberra, A.C.T.).

306.0994

Set in 11/14 pt Janson Text by DOCUPRO, Sydney
Printed and bound by Griffin Press, Adelaide

10 9 8 7 6 5 4 3 2 1

Contents

Introduction   vii
Acknowledgements   ix
Abbreviations   x
About the contributors   xii

1 THE PARADOX OF PESSIMISM Paul Kelly   1
  Australia today—and tomorrow

2 ADRIFT IN A TRIBAL TIDE Nicolas Rothwell   36
  Inside the psyche of the nation

3 THE VOTE THAT POLL-AXED TRADITION   48
  Dennis Shanahan
  After '98, elections are changed forever

4 FLUNKING LEADERSHIP 1 Dennis Shanahan   57
  The vacuum of a vision-free zone

5 THE BUSINESS OF BALANCE Mark Westfield   67
  How the corporate world plotted a tax reform coup

6 DEFUSING THE MINDFIELD Kate Legge   77
  Removing the oxymoron from Australian intellectualism

7 MAKING WORK WORK Ian Henderson ... 84
Tactics to employ for the jobless

8 TAX TRIUMPH IS A LEGACY LOST ... 97
George Megalogenis
Why the GST will be AWOL, PDQ

9 IS WEALTHFARE A SOCIAL HEALTH RISK? ... 109
Mike Steketee
The side-effects of a rationalist prescription

10 THE FOURTH R: RUINATION Catherine Armitage ... 124
In the Clever Country, education is withering

11 BACK TO THE FUTURE IS PASSÉ Michelle Gunn ... 139
Families, women and childcare

12 A NOTION FOR A NATION Mike Steketee ... 152
Exploring the republic of ideas

13 SILENCING THE IMMIGRANT SONG ... 163
Richard McGregor
Closed doors or open minds?

14 THE BLACK MARK ON OUR SOUL Stuart Rintoul ... 176
Reconciling reconciliation

15 BUSHWHACKED BY THE MARKET Asa Wahlquist ... 191
Why rural Australia is bleeding

16 STEALTH MISSILE FOR THE STATES Alan Wood ... 203
The rise and rise of Federalism

17 TOO MUCH TRUFFLE OIL Shelley Gare ... 217
Baby boomers and the generation war

18 MESSAGE FROM THE MELT-DOWN Robert Garran ... 231
What the Asian crisis has taught us

19 A STRATEGY FOR REVOLUTION Patrick Walters ... 244
Defence goes on to the front foot

20 THINK LOCAL, ACT GLOBAL Greg Sheridan ... 256
A return to Fortress Australia is no option

Index ... 268

INTRODUCTION

THIS BOOK EVOLVED FROM A PERCEPTION that became a conviction. As is the habit with newspaper news conferences at any time but more so during moments of editorial mayhem—say, a federal election—opinions and observations are launched, debated, developed, accepted, mutated or shot down. The perception at *The Australian* mid-way through the 1998 campaign was this: the campaign, ostensibly the last of the twentieth century and one in which so much was at stake, was a fizzer.

More than that, it was a campaign in which the major parties seemed to have signed a pact of omission, a non-proliferation agreement on issues other than the economic drivers of tax and unemployment. Certainly, they were accepted as the defining factors of the election, but many other issues of valid concern such as education, health, welfare, Aboriginality and native title, immigration, racism, the rural decline, even the republic, were largely ignored, or touched on only lightly, as was the more abstract but equally important philosophical debate over what sort of country Australia should be. Was our vision for the new millennium to be one of a country of each according to need, an egalitarian state outward-looking with unapologetic awareness? Was it of an inward-looking, shuttered nation, defined by the ethos of to each according to what they could win out of the system; a 'rationalised' society in which the adept prospered and the rest looked after themselves? Or was it something else entirely?

Despite the campaign coming alive in its last week, the conviction persisted that important issues were obscured on the national stage—not just the problems but also any attempts at solution. So we challenged our national affairs writers to investigate. Each is an expert in their field, with an added advantage of working for a national paper. Their rounds encompass the country, giving them a breadth of knowledge, access to information and overall experience second to none. The brief was this: using the campaign as a basis, give us a dispassionate overview of what is, demonstrate if and how 'vision' has become obscured, signpost the sectors requiring remedy and propose alternatives. The intention of the challenge was two-fold: to inform and to promote debate. For it is only through engaging in a lively exchange of ideas that we can hope to achieve any understanding and clarity. And it is only by being clear on what we want to achieve as a nation, only by understanding the needs and aspirations of our common wealth of people, that we will continue to develop as a nation. It has been a challenging project, and a privilege to be involved.

Acknowledgements

As always in a process that has involved a plenitude of contributors and a paucity of time, I owe thanks to many people. Prime among them are *The Australian*'s Editor-in-Chief, David Armstrong, and Editor, Campbell Reid, for their confidence in me and support of the project. I'm also indebted to the paper's National Chief of Staff, Peter Wilson, for his can-do enthusiasm, to electronic guru Warren Melksham for his patience, and especially to my wife Michelle Wright and my children for *their* patience and support. Special thanks too to all the contributors and bureau chiefs for accepting the brief and cooperating with my editorial provisions and cajolings. Finally, to Patrick Gallagher, John Iremonger, Rebecca Kaiser and the team at Allen & Unwin, my appreciation for their unfazed professionalism and minimal furphies.

Murray Waldren
January 1999

ABBREVIATIONS

ACCI	Australian Chamber of Commerce and Industry
ACOSS	Australian Council of Social Services
ADF	Australian Defence Force
AEW&C	Airborne Early Warning and Control
AIFS	Australian Institute of Family Studies
AIHW	Australian Institute of Health and Welfare
ALP	Australian Labor Party
AMA	Australian Medical Association
ANU	Australian National University
APEC	Asia Pacific Economic Cooperation
ASEAN	Association of Southeast Asian Nations
ATSIC	Aboriginal and Torres Strait Islander Commission
AVCC	Australian Vice-Chancellors Committee
BCA	Business Council of Australia
CARE	Centre for Agricultural and Regional Economics
CEDA	Committee for the Economic Development of Australia
CGT	Capital Gains Tax
CHOGM	Commonwealth Heads of Government Meeting
FECC	Federation of Ethnic Community Councils
FPDA	Five Power Defence Arrangement

GATT	General Agreement on Trade and Tariffs
GDP	Gross Domestic Product
GST	Goods and Services Tax
HECS	Higher Education Contribution Scheme
HREOC	Human Rights and Equal Opportunity Commission
IMF	International Monetary Fund
NFF	National Farmers Federation
NNTT	National Native Title Tribunal
OECD	Organisation for Economic Cooperation and Development
OPEC	Organisation for Petroleum-Exporting Countries
RDA	Racial Discrimination Act
RMA	Revolution in Military Affairs
WTO	World Trade Organisation

About the Contributors

PAUL KELLY is *The Australian*'s international editor. In a Canberra-based career that spanned Whitlam to Hawke, he was the chief political writer for *The Australian*, the *Sydney Morning Herald* and *National Times* before becoming editor-in-chief of *The Australian* in 1991. His books include *The Unmaking of Gough*, *The Hawke Ascendancy* and *The End of Certainty*. Married with two children, he lives in Sydney.

NICOLAS ROTHWELL has worked for *The Australian* as a foreign correspondent in the US, the Pacific and Europe since 1981. For the past three years he has covered stories in all states and territories of Australia. He writes the Reportage column in *The Weekend Australian* and is infrequently based in Sydney.

DENNIS SHANAHAN is *The Australian*'s political editor. In a 28-year career he has worked in Melbourne, New York, Bathurst and Sydney. He was briefly an adviser to NSW Attorney-General John Dowd, has a master's degree in journalism (Columbia University), is married with nine children, and lives in Canberra.

ABOUT THE CONTRIBUTORS xiii

MARK WESTFIELD has been a journalist for 27 years, 18 as a business writer and editor. He has been a business columnist for *The Australian* for four years and business editor before that. He has also worked for the ABC's 'Four Corners', the *Sydney Morning Herald*, *Australian Business*, the *Launceston Examiner*, the *Melbourne Sun News-Pictorial* and a number of British newspapers.

KATE LEGGE edits *The Australian's Review of Books*. One of the most experienced journalists in the country, she has covered industrial relations and federal politics, been *The Australian*'s Washington correspondent, a columnist and feature writer. In 1994 she was named Australian Journalist of the Year.

IAN HENDERSON has been economics correspondent for *The Australian* since 1995. A BA in economics, he joined the *Canberra Times* in 1994 after 16 years working for the ALP and as an adviser to Opposition leader Bill Hayden (1978–83) and Resources Minister Peter Walsh.

GEORGE MEGALOGENIS has covered national politics and economics from the Canberra press gallery since 1988. A Melbourne University graduate, he joined *The Australian* in 1991. His scoops include John Hewson's secret GST review ahead of the '93 election, and details of John Howard's GST ahead of the '98 campaign.

MIKE STEKETEE has been national affairs editor of *The Australian* since 1994. After eight years in the Canberra press gallery, he became Washington correspondent for the *Sydney Morning Herald* in 1977. In 1981 he was made state political correspondent before returning to Canberra as bureau chief and political editor. He co-wrote *Wran: An Unauthorised Biography*.

CATHERINE ARMITAGE is a senior writer for *The Australian* specialising in education issues. Formerly a business writer at Australian Consolidated Press, she completed a BCom with merit at the University of NSW before joining the *Sydney Morning Herald* in 1987. With *The Australian* since 1994, she has won awards across several fields, including law, science, health, human rights and education.

MICHELLE GUNN, a journalist for more than a decade, has for the past three years been *The Australian*'s social affairs writer, specialising in childcare, demographic trends, women and work, aged care and youth affairs.

RICHARD MCGREGOR is *The Australian*'s chief political reporter in Canberra. Prior to this, he was the paper's correspondent in Tokyo, Hong Kong and Beijing. Sydney-educated, he was a reporter for the *Sydney Morning Herald* and the ABC before joining *The Australian*.

STUART RINTOUL is a Melbourne-based senior writer with *The Australian* and former Victorian editor of the paper. The author of two books, *Ashes of Vietnam: Australian Voices* (1987) and *The Wailing: A National Black Oral History* (1993), he is married with three children.

ASA WAHLQUIST, *The Australian*'s rural business writer, is a graduate in Agricultural Science who ran a vineyard and worked as a proofreader before entering journalism. As a rural journalist she worked for ABC radio and television and the *Sydney Morning Herald*. In 1996 she won a Walkley Award for best suburban, country or rural report and in 1993 the European Community Journalist Award.

ALAN WOOD has been economics editor and an associate editor of *The Australian* since 1990. A graduate of ANU, he entered journalism in the 1960s with the *Australian Financial Review* in the Canberra press gallery. He is a former European correspondent for the *AFR*, economics editor of the *Sydney Morning Herald*, the *National Times* and the Seven Television Network, and managing director of Syntec Economic Services. He is based in Melbourne.

SHELLEY GARE is a consulting editor/columnist for *The Australian*. A former deputy editor of the paper, she was founding editor of *The Australian's Review of Books*, for which she won a Walkley Award. She has worked for the *Sunday Times* in London and is a previous editor of the *Good Weekend* magazine.

ROBERT GARRAN is *The Australian*'s foreign affairs and defence writer. He was the paper's correspondent in Japan and Korea (1995–98) and before that its economics correspondent. His book *Tigers Tamed: The End of the Asian Miracle* traces the factors behind the rise and fall of Asia's 'miracle' economies.

PATRICK WALTERS, *The Australian*'s Canberra bureau chief, established the paper's bureau in Jakarta in 1993, remaining in Indonesia until 1998. He entered journalism at the *Sydney Morning Herald*, where he specialised in defence and foreign affairs, and from 1988 to 1993 was senior adviser to Kim Beazley.

GREG SHERIDAN, *The Australian*'s foreign editor, has also been its diplomatic correspondent in Canberra, chief editorial writer and Washington and Beijing correspondent. His work has appeared in the *Sunday Times* (London), *Asian Wall Street Journal*, *Quadrant*, *South China Morning Post* and numerous anthologies. The author of *Tigers: Leaders of the New Asia Pacific* (1997), he is married with three children and lives in Sydney.

1

THE PARADOX OF PESSIMISM

Australia today—and tomorrow

Paul Kelly

AUSTRALIA IS BESET BY A PARADOX. In the late 1990s, our economy and standards of living have never been stronger or higher. Yet our mood, by and large, is that of apprehension and uncertainty amid growing wealth and opportunity. Often Australia seems to be a confused, insecure nation, pessimistic about its future. This pessimism has deep roots in our history but is overlaid by contemporary stresses. Australia has become a display laboratory where the symbols and afflictions of modernity are accentuated—rapid consumer take-up of the latest technology, mobile phones and the Internet amid deepening lines of drug addicts, youth suicide victims and broken families.

The evidence still abounds of Australians as an energetic, practical and adaptive people. Yet there is an unmistakable pent-up frustration at chronic high levels of unemployment; at the growing inequality of income and assets; at globalisation which is dividing the nation along a new class fault of winners and losers; at the rise of social fragmentation; and, above all, over the sense that the often-unspoken but common values we have shared for a long time are being eroded and contested.

There are many symptoms of the malaise—that 25 per cent of the population is on welfare today compared with 10 per cent a generation ago; the relative decline of services and income within rural Australia; high levels of marriage break-up and dysfunctional families; the decline of respect for institutions including church, company, union, media, banks, the ABC, the RSL, the rugby league and Parliament; hostility towards our political leadership; the collapse in support for a strong immigration program; the myopia of the media who spent much of the past two years falsely declaring a 'race-based' 1998 federal election; confusion over whether Australia should be a nation of one culture or many cultures; an intellectual divide between opinion-makers and the people; a shrinking of the middle class with its polarities breaking off to join, in turn, the wealthy and the working poor; fresh uncertainty about our history and our identity; spectacular failure of critical utilities relating to water, gas and electricity; and the rise of Hansonism such that 900 000 people voted for One Nation at the federal election—a party that did not exist at the previous election.

Australia's rites of passage into a more baffling, contradictory existence are unique for each person. But some events are community turning points. The 1996 Port Arthur massacre where 33 people were murdered was representative of the community's vulnerability to acts of solitary recklessness. The incomprehension of such evil provoked a remarkable opening of hearts, a unity in the sharing of grief, a sense that the nation, ultimately, was a community of people whose capacity to reach out to each other for support was an essential ingredient in a caring and civilised society. There was a political response—a Commonwealth–state agreement on uniform gun laws, an explicit decision that Australia would choose another path to the armed libertarianism of the American household. That choice, led by Prime Minister John Howard, won both overwhelming support and abiding hostility from a minority.

Another incident in 1998 did not claim lives but symbolised the changed nature of Australia. It was a drive-by semi-automatic weapon attack on a suburban police station at Lakemba in Sydney's south-west. As an assault upon the law enforcement authority by an assumed ethnic gang, it represented a new form of social violence in Australia's cities. The NSW Premier, Bob Carr, attributed the crime to an ethnic gang. NSW Police

Commissioner Peter Ryan said that 'apart from places like Northern Ireland and other war-torn countries, I've never seen anything like this in my career'. The police resorted to bullet-proof armour. Most Australians had never seen anything like it either—an unprecedented symptom of the crisis relating to values, safety and authority which worried so many people.

Qualitative surveys published by sociologist Hugh Mackay in the late 1990s have been stark, almost frightening in their pessimism. In his July 1997 overview, Mackay said:

> It is tempting to call us The Disappointed Country. On the evidence . . . we are feeling neither particularly lucky nor particularly clever: the mood is decidedly bleak and there is a growing sense that relief is not in sight. We are even becoming somewhat embarrassed about ourselves. More than any other single factor, the uncertainty of the job market has finally worn us down to the point where we no longer seem to believe that anyone has a serious solution in mind.

In his 1998 overview, Mackay reported:

> The big theme is insulation. We are looking for ways to distance ourselves from too much preoccupation with the national agenda . . . We see Australia as a country in trouble . . . We no longer expect politicians to keep their promises, tell the truth or do what they say they will do.

This suggests, at face value, a community that is close to losing confidence in its leaders, its institutions and itself.

There is, however, another wider and bigger picture which sharply contradicts much of these impressions. Australia's economy grew at an average of 3.8 per cent during the 1990s. That is distinctly superior even to the US, which has undergone such a famous 1990s economic renaissance off the back of its 3 per cent average annual GDP growth. Australia has outperformed the US on the indicator that matters most. Our growth, in fact, has been at the top of the OECD range through the decade.

Australia is in the seventh year of a sustained recovery. Our inflation rate and interest rates are at a generational low. Our federal Budget is in surplus. Our banking system, having undergone the 1980s boom and bust, has performed more reliably than banks in Japan, Asia and the US. At the close of 1998, our economy had weathered the Asian crisis far better than most forecasters had predicted. For 1997–98, the economy grew at 4 per cent with Australian exports showing a quick re-gearing to stronger European and US markets. The Treasury still forecast 1998–99 growth at 2.75 per cent while admitting a volatile outlook in the international economy. The Asian slowdown on the rest of the world, including Australia, will impact in 1999. But this is now part of a wider global crisis of finance whose lesson is the need for nations to run sound, transparent, accountable financial and corporate systems backed by quality economic policy management—areas where Australia, so far, rates well this decade.

All these are genuine achievements, and they did not occur by accident. They result from the lessons learnt and the reforms made in economic policy over the past 15 years under the governments of Hawke, Keating and Howard. These reforms relate to the internationalisation of our economy, more competitive pressures, a far more flexible and diverse economy, an unprecedented degree of structural change, the conduct of fiscal and monetary policy and Australia's growing corporate, technological and financial sector strengths. Meanwhile, US President Bill Clinton has called the late 1990s the most dangerous economic period since the Great Depression. Japan, the originator of the Asian economic miracle, is undergoing its deepest post-war crisis. Southeast Asia is in a profound recession. Indonesia is in a depression so deep it constitutes one of the greatest tragedies of the century, with an estimated 70 million people in the process of falling below the poverty line. The idea of Australia as the lucky country has never been more apt than it is today.

Do Australians grasp, however, that this time we have made our own luck? Our progress in the 1990s is the result of our own genuine achievements, not some fortunate event. We can't insulate ourselves from the world but the stronger our economy, the better we can handle the turmoil abroad. This is not the full story. Australia has a highly educated workforce, a rapid take-up rate of new technology, a deep attachment to the rule of law, a diligence about democratic practice, a sophisticated financial system, vast natural resources, a political tradition of adaptation and pragmatism, a balance between individual initiative and state support. It is a society remarkable for its diversity and for its multicultural reinvention, and a community increasingly identified by overseas Chinese as a place where they want to immigrate with their money.

There are three further remarkable opportunities for Australia. It will vote in 1999 to realise its evolving re-definition as a republic with a new constitutional preamble that embodies our unifying values. It will host the Olympics of the millennium and, in the process, become the showcase of the world in 2000, an event of vast potential in terms of message and image. It will commemorate in 2001 its centenary as a nation—a young nation but an old democracy. These are opportunities for dramatic self-realisation. When set against the reality of the decade's progress, they prompt a further conclusion. It is as irresistible as it is unfashionable—that the late 1990s had the potential to be a Golden Age for Australia.

It isn't, of course, because such ages are the creation of their society and time, and Australia doesn't interpret its current existence in this way. That is obvious. The reality, however, is that the potential for a golden age does exist. The greatest problem is manifest—it lies in our own minds and hearts. The gulf in Australia between our objective strengths and our psychological pessimism is very wide. It is a remarkable feature of our current existence. The repeated impression left by senior overseas visitors to this country is their admiration for our achievement and astonishment at the complacent devaluation of this achievement by the host community. Australians are trapped in a contradiction—too reluctant to grasp their successes outside sport, too willing to overlook genuine national progress as a role model, too ready to cut down tall poppies and too susceptible to the appeal of egalitarianism to justify mediocrity. It's enough to make you think that Australians are just plain unhappy about having so much good fortune and opportunity. And it highlights a nasty feature of Australian life today, the culture of complaint—brought to a zenith via the medium of talkback radio. It is a variation of the old-fashioned Australian gripe magnified, as distinct from an intersecting and healthy practice of robust self-criticism as the necessary prelude to constructive action.

In absolute terms, the overwhelming majority of people are better off than they were before. Per capita income, GDP and real wages have risen steadily during the 1990s. The nostalgia for the Australia of 30 years ago overlooks one key fact—the great lift in material conditions since then. If people were transported back to the 1950s with no television, direct phone dialling, wines, jumbo jets, mini-skirts or freeways and limited refrigeration, contraception and sewerage they would be shocked and horrified. But time capsules aren't available to create this consciousness. The revolutionary improvement in living conditions post-World War II now runs into a third generation that has no connection with either depression or war, and no frame of reference beyond an expectation that things are supposed to get better, and a resentment when this process is frustrated.

However, the complexity of modern society has driven a wedge between economic growth and quality of life. A pressing issue that arises from the 1990s is why increasing wealth has not produced a more satisfied society. There are two answers—because the distribution of wealth is so unequal and because economic growth no longer equates with living conditions. Income levels are critical but income levels don't always off-set traffic jams, urban congestion, environmental degradation, aircraft noise, psychic angst, domestic overload in work and family management, crimes of violence, fear for personal safety, sickness, lack of education and mid-life career termination. A strong economy within a global framework is a necessary condition for an enhanced quality of life but it is no longer a sufficient condition. Political leaders underestimate this point, but it will increasingly shape the politics of the next generation.

There is a dimension to the current pessimism, however, which transcends politics and is more an affliction of the spirit or inner life. In a 1998 interview with *The Australian*, the Treasurer, Peter Costello said:

> People might be unhappy for a host of reasons: because their marriage has broken up; because they feel they have never got

the recognition in life they deserve. You know this business is not religion. Within limited boundaries politics can make a difference but it's a limited science. Politics can't fill the vacuum of a family or religion or community.

Australia in the 1990s mirrored all the moral dilemmas that arise from the evolution of the Western cultural tradition. The nation achieved a level of material success during the 1950s and 1960s that meant younger people put a premium on personal satisfaction. Some baby boomers, despite their success, feel a sense of disappointment as they enter their 50s. They want life to offer more. This dissatisfaction with self translates into a disappointment with society and nation. The search for individualistic fulfilment was to be realised in life, typically through recreation, music, travel, marriage, career, religion and relationships. Personal fulfilment became a focus of life in a fashion inconceivable when a tolerable material existence was a lifetime struggle.

Many people think today that personal fulfilment is not merely an aspiration but a right. There is no such right; the right relates to the pursuit of happiness. But the pursuit has become confused with the objective. This is a recipe, ironically, for endless dissatisfaction since personal fulfilment remains an elusive condition. Its politicisation dooms our society to chronic dissatisfaction with our institutions. It is now the norm to expect more progress, better health, worthwhile careers, new technology, happy relationships, lifestyle of our choice without penalty and, ultimately, the right to self-fulfilment. And if we don't get this, then somebody is to blame. Sometimes it is a politician—an absurd confusion of cause and effect. Herein lie more seeds of our contemporary culture of complaint.

This decade has been dominated by an over-arching theme—the clash between the economic imperative of globalisation and the community's demand for security and safety in a mesmerising world. This was the underlying theme, though not the issue, of the 1998 election. But the political chemistry of the decade was shaped initially by two events—the early 1990s recession when unemployment exceeded 11 per cent, its highest for 60 years, and the defeat at the 1993 election of the radical market-orientated blueprint of new Coalition leader, Dr John Hewson.

The recession led Australians into a gradual but visceral suspicion of the 1980s era. This encompassed not just the financial excesses but many of the policies of the era, a resort to markets, trade liberalisation, deregulation, privatisation, user-pays, more efficient institutions and greater competition. The irony is that Hewson became a purist champion of such policy at the 1993 poll while a reinvented Paul Keating moved to construct a new position for the ALP, a synthesis between the market-orientated reforms he pushed as treasurer and a revival of the ALP social justice tradition.

Despite community apprehension about change, a cogent alternative credo to the economic liberalism of the 1980s was not devised as the 1990s advanced. This, in turn, created distrust between the people and the political class. While politicians had to offer concessions to public sentiment to win elections, they also had to govern in the real world where rapid change, globalisation and financial markets were a reality. The upshot is that only Pauline Hanson and the Australian Democrats threatened a decisive break from economic liberalism. The Kim Beazley-led ALP went part of the way towards a break in the 1998 election but it was also the essence of fiscal and monetary responsibility. In truth, mainstream politicians struggled and juggled during the decade, offering a range of piecemeal, populist and 'caring' responses to win votes while trying to manage their societies and economies within the framework of a market-orientated, more open, and financially ruthless global climate which, by its nature, destroyed some of the past in its rush to the future.

The 1993 election was dominated by the Coalition's pledge to introduce a 15 per cent GST. Hewson declared that 'if we can't win with a GST, then we don't deserve to win'—an insight into his economic evangelism. His Fightback! plan was based upon the calculation that the recession would cost Labor power—but Hewson misjudged, though narrowly. He was oblivious to the signs of voter unease about market economics, though a pre-election remodelling of Fightback! had exempted food from the GST.

Despite the ferocity of his assault upon Hewson, Keating still backed an internationally open and competitive marketplace. He merely pledged a more compassionate setting—no GST, no hard-line deregulated labour market and fiscal pump-priming to help job creation. His victory in the so-called 'unlosable' election demoralised the Coalition, doomed Hewson's leadership and destroyed the aggressive pro-market position Hewson had championed. It left the Liberal Party with few choices—Hewson had to be removed and the party had to moderate its position and march back to the centre ground. The enduring legacy of the 1993 election was that Australians wanted economic reforms limited by a social compassion not sharpened by a tough ideology.

But Keating, a masterful mythmaker, spun the story that 1993 was a win for Labor's 'true believers' rather than a bunch of cynical swinging voters. He insisted the result was more a vindication of him than a vote against Hewson. Herein lay the origins of the hubris, alienation and reclusion that infected him in the 1993–96 term when he succumbed, eventually, to voter perceptions that he was too arrogant and 'out of touch' with mainstream opinion and the ALP base.

While riding the business cycle to a successful economic recovery, Keating, an ambitious innovator, sketched what he fancied as his 'big picture'. He dedicated his prime ministership not just to economic recovery but to a vision of Australia that inspired many—a multicultural republic reconciled with its indigenous people and integrated into the Asia–Pacific region. In typical fashion, Keating pursued these ideas with the passion of a man who had discovered them for the first time. He had strong support from elite opinion-makers for his vision, which was founded in a realistic appraisal of our national life. But he failed to carry a majority of people with him. His mistake was to think he could be prime minister on his own terms rather than those imposed by the voters. His divisive personal style, breach of trust arising from failure to honour his 1993 tax pledges, his flirtation with sectional groups and self-projection as social justice crusader rather than national economic reformer left him deeply vulnerable.

Keating, in fact, had gone too soft, moved too far Left, allowed the Coalition to occupy the middle ground and had grown impatient with the keys to success in the 1980s. This was apparent to his close aide Don Russell when he returned from Washington to advise on the 1996 re-election strategy. There was a position for Keating in his final term—follow the Clinton revival tactic post-1994 after the Congressional election wipe-out. This meant tackling welfare reform, readjusting the personal rights and responsibility equation, promoting jobs through structural change and not just growth, a bold national interest agenda.

Such a reform-driven repositioning would have kept the momentum with Keating, and forced the Liberals out to the Right, the Coalition's losing ground. It was the tactic Hawke and Keating had used so successfully in the 1980s. The Coalition won the 1996 election only when Labor allowed it to occupy and hold the middle ground.

The pivotal point in the decade for the Liberal Party came in early 1995 when it returned in desperation to John Howard's leadership. He responded with a disciplined, practical and modest campaign program. His tactic was to ensure that the Keating Government and not the Coalition was the issue at the 1996 election. He completed the burial of the Fightback! ethos, accepted Medicare, rejected any GST, appealed to Middle Australia and denied Keating the target he wanted. Unlike Hewson in 1993, Howard pledged reassurance, not change; he spoke like a benign uncle offering to clean up the house.

The campaign was a study in leadership contrast. For Keating, the essence of leadership was to lead, to stride forward, to uphold a vision and damn the heretics. But Howard talked of the leader's need to listen and respond to the people and to absorb their message. Long underestimated as a campaigner by both his own side and Labor, he got his pitch just right. The 1996 election returned the Coalition to power for the third time since the war. Howard's victory, with a 44-seat majority on a 5 per cent swing, fell between those of Sir Robert Menzies in

1949 and Malcolm Fraser in 1975. Menzies polled 51.3 per cent of the two-party preferred vote, Fraser 55.7 per cent, Howard 53.6 per cent. All the historical indicators suggested he would have two terms on the back of this margin. Howard was in a Senate minority outnumbered by the ALP–Democrat–Green anti-Coalition alliance, a situation partly relieved by the defection of Labor's Mal Colston shortly thereafter.

The re-elected Coalition had been out of power for 13 years, the longest exile in its federal history. Its return to office was troubled and undermined by inexperienced ministers drawn from a limited talent pool. The story of Howard's remarkable 1996–98 term is dominated by a turbulent struggle to adapt to globalisation in its economic and social dimensions. The Government was strong on economics, inept on social policy and deficient in communicating either a vision or coherent program to the people.

Howard gave the economy priority; it was his strength. And it was critical to his survival. Having inherited a growth economy from Keating, he moved decisively towards fiscal consolidation with a tough inaugural Budget in 1996–97. This in turn reinforced the Reserve Bank to a series of sustained interest rate cuts that became the political ballast for the Coalition. Howard's sustaining lifeline was the economic 'circle of virtue'—low inflation, low interest rates, solid growth, strong investment, a Budget surplus and a falling public debt economy. Unemployment dropped slowly but stalled above 8 per cent, proof that more structural reforms were needed. But Howard's reforms were limited to his modest 1996 agenda—an industrial relations bill that weakened the central wage tribunal and the award system and the sale of one-third of Telstra.

Howard believed Labor faced an historic crisis arising from the gulf between its middle class 'chardonnay' set and its working class base. Flushed with his success in winning much of Labor's base vote—known as the 'Howard battlers'—he tried to govern with a mixture of social conservatism, calculated populism and sensible economics. It was a tricky combination that demanded greater political skill than he possessed.

While expectations about his Government had been low,

Howard incurred a backlash from three overlapping defects. There were a series of ministerial scandals and resignations that left the impression of systemic ineptitude. There was a loss of trust and then rising hostility across a range of constituencies, notably ethnics, Aborigines, tertiary students, nursing home clients, trade unionists, welfare recipients, churches, working women and environmentalists—sometimes because of new policy directions but often due to poor management. Finally, there was a sense of disappointment in Howard's leadership, in his tendency to 'mind the shop' rather than shape and articulate a national strategy or 'plan of action', a feeling that he was hostage to events and not their master and that, unlike either Bill Clinton or Tony Blair, he was unable to emotionally engage the people in an overall vision or just persuade them to his view.

The psychological turning point for Howard's leadership came in 1997 at the nadir of his fortunes. With the extra burden of his hospitalisation from pneumonia, he decided, on reflection, to strike out. He didn't have to put his ear to the ground to hear the leadership whispers. It was his weakness that begat boldness. So Howard declared that his Government would tackle tax reform. This meant seeking a mandate at the next election for a comprehensive tax package—including a GST and a new federal–state tax compact. It was a risky decision, a gamble, given the Hewson legacy, but it was a calculated decision he believed would help his re-election and define his prime ministership.

This was a personal decision taken with a minimum of consultation. Howard acted out of the self-preservation instinct; he was true to himself since tax reform had long been his refrain. In moving from caution to audacity he accepted the logic of his position—parliamentary majorities are political capital that can be mobilised for action or merely erode over time. He also concluded, correctly, that his approach to that point was failing in a strategic sense.

Despite Howard's House of Representatives majority, he had protracted difficulties in other power centres. He never carried much of the opinion-making elite, rarely won a fair deal from the ABC, sustained damage from the Senate, gained generally only lukewarm enthusiasm from business, and faced a surprise

High Court decision on Wik which advanced native title and caused an upheaval within the Coalition's constituency. Most of all, Howard forfeited much of his moral authority over his initial response to Hanson. The new independent elected for Oxley at the 1996 election erupted onto the stage with her own party, One Nation.

Howard's response to Hanson was a study in leadership failure. From the start it was manifest that she threatened to derail Australia's modernisation. She gave voice to a vast range of grievances, harnessed protest votes against immigrants, Aborigines, foreign capital, gun laws, Canberra, crime and multiculturalism. Her technique was to put into words the unspoken sentiments in the hearts of many about Aborigines and Asians, thereby earning kudos as a 'non-politician' prepared to talk truthfully. Hansonism was founded in resentment at the rapidity of globalisation-induced economic change, as well as being a cry from the Anglo-Celtic heartland against cultural diversity and the methods of Aboriginal reconciliation. She had no answers for any of Australia's national problems but her so-called solutions, if ever implemented, would mean a socially divided and economically debilitated nation.

Yet Howard seemed unable to grasp initially the moral threat Hanson posed to our politics. He appeared to interpret her emergence as part of the wider disillusion with Keating's values that was instrumental in his own election. He was reluctant to challenge Hanson on principle because he was less convinced that great principle was at stake. He failed to draw the critical distinction between genuine social grievance and the explicit introduction of racial chauvinism into our politics. He misjudged the lethal threat Hanson posed to the National Party, the Coalition and to non-Labor politics. His decision to try to ignore Hansonism may or may not have helped One Nation but it certainly weakened his leadership. It was only after One Nation won 11 seats in the Queensland state election that he moved into a sustained assault. His deputy and National Party leader, Tim Fischer, by contrast, had long been involved in a 'life or death' struggle with Hanson over policy and grassroots support.

Hansonism had two consequences for Howard. First, it weakened his authority across the board and was used by opinion-making critics to delegitimise his prime ministership. Second, it meant that Howard was under assault on two fronts—and history suggested this could be fatal for him. Labor attacked from the Left and Hansonism was a revolt from the Right within the National Party heartland. One Nation drew voters overwhelmingly from the Coalition and failed to return them via the preference system. It was a mechanism by which votes were transferred from the Coalition to Labor. In the prelude to the 1998 federal election, the Liberal Party finally agreed to direct its preferences against Hanson. This was a critical move. It ensured that she was denied political oxygen in the campaign, rarely became an issue (despite the best efforts of some of the media), and was neutralised as a threat to Coalition unity.

The Labor Party had its longest period of federal rule terminated at the 1996 election and faced a serious challenge as it returned to opposition. Kim Beazley, largely unknown to the community, was elected unopposed as Keating's successor. Like Howard, he was initially underestimated by colleagues and opponents. He brought to the task an unusual but wide mixture of experience and character. The son of Kim Beazley Snr, a minister in the Whitlam Government, Beazley had a religious childhood, won a Rhodes scholarship, served as a minister throughout the Hawke–Keating years, was a Hawke protege and was inspired most by fellow West Australian, John Curtin. Although a fully paid member of the ALP right wing, he had three qualities that would assist him in keeping the party united. His entire political experience had been in a marginal seat and Beazley, a veteran door-knocker, believed in grassroots politics. He was a natural 'people person' with an affable disposition, a genuine rapport with others and no trace of the megalomania of so many of his predecessors. Finally, he was a Labor traditionalist whose intellectual discipline—international relations—disposed him to believe in government intervention and who retained a deep scepticism about the pro-market policies of the 1980s.

From the start, Beazley set out to regain the ALP base vote

lost at the '96 election. This saw Labor revert to a more traditionalist economic policy that was a part-repudiation of the Hawke–Keating era. Howard's spending cuts, industrial reforms, privatisation plans and economic liberalism were attacked. But Beazley also strove to retain much of Keating's social vision. Labor took a pro-native title position on the Wik bill, kept its commitment to the republic and savaged Howard for his retreats on multiculturalism and Aboriginal reconciliation.

The 1998 election, in the shadow of the millennium, was dominated by taxation and economic credibility, not the broader more turbulent agenda of community angst. This triggered criticism that the campaign was 'boring'. But taxation had been an unresolved issue for a decade; it was Howard who chose this issue; it was Beazley who chose to fight it. Every household would be affected by the plans put by Coalition and Labor. It was a model of how democracies are supposed to resolve issues through the ballot box.

The Howard reform involved an overall cut in the tax burden; a 10 per cent GST with few exemptions; the abolition of the wholesale sales tax; the return of all GST revenue to the states; a cut in business costs; an estimated rise of 1.9 per cent in the CPI with compensation for fixed-income earners; personal income tax cuts with a 30 cents rate for 80 per cent of taxpayers. Howard's aim was to make virtually everybody a winner. But the package was vulnerable on equity grounds—the biggest proportionate gains were among the middle class, not the lower paid.

The Beazley package was more modest, rejected any GST and offered a new targeted system of innovative tax credits. Labor's aim was to convert the Howard battlers into Beazley battlers. Beazley beat Howard's tax cuts for people under $50 000 a year but the reverse applied above $55 000. He sought a conjunction between fairness and Labor's electoral needs. There were three risks in Beazley's approach—by refusing to broaden the indirect tax base, Labor courted criticism from welfare and business that it was spurning real reform; that the tax credits scaled out too fast so Labor was ignoring too many families that weren't rich; and that by opening up capital gains pre-1985, Labor was giving Howard a 'scare bonus'.

Both Howard and Beazley folded their tax messages into grander election themes. Howard's over-arching pitch was his reliability as an economic manager during a period of profound international crisis. He depicted himself as a reformer, a patriot, a realist and an economic manager prepared to take tough decisions for the nation. The Coalition television message was not to trust a return to Labor because it hadn't learnt from the past.

The campaign involved the electorate's 'discovery' of Beazley as a personality, but Labor's profile, by necessity, was more defined by negatives than positives. Beazley, however, did unveil a 5 per cent unemployment target over two terms but singularly failed to explain the policies by which the target would be met. At the industry level, he fought further Telstra privatisation and sought to reverse Howard's moves to a freer industrial system.

Howard won the election but paid a high price. His '96 majority of 44 seats was cut to 12. Howard's election-night sentiment was sheer relief—he had come to the edge of defeat and indeed, had feared on election day that Labor would prevail. His re-election meant he averted the humiliation of being the first 'oncer' PM since Labor's Jimmy Scullin in the Great Depression era. Howard won the 1998 election on his own mandate yet he was weakened politically. His majority is small; the Coalition is reduced to an ongoing Senate minority position from July 1999 when the new Senate is constituted; and the voters have come to the brink of rejecting a Howard Government after only one term. There is certain to be a debate within the Liberal Party over whether to stick with Howard or install a new leader this term. The Coalition primary vote was only 39.4 per cent, the worst since Menzies founded the Liberal Party, the basis of the modern Coalition. The Liberal primary vote was the worst since the McMahon Government lost the 1972 poll. The Nationals' primary vote at 5.4 per cent was the worst since the 1920s. In two-party preferred terms, Labor outpolled the Coalition. Yet Howard carried a GST, a unique feat in global politics. His post-election challenge is to legislate and implement the tax package.

It is significant that Howard won on a reform program—a more reformist program than he dared to put to the people in '96. While his position is weaker, his mandate for economic reform and economic liberalism is stronger. The moral Howard will draw from his victory is that policy boldness was rewarded. There is little point with a 12-seat majority in now retreating to caution. There is no route to salvation in 2001 in that tactic. The further lesson is that, despite the community apprehension for change and for the GST, it still voted for Howard rather than Beazley. There is a message here for both sides—the voters are suspicious of change but recognise there is no future in any return to the past.

Kim Beazley claimed a moral victory, with Labor polling 51.2 per cent of the two-party preferred vote, greater than that of Hawke when he won the '87 and '90 elections. Recriminations that Labor could or should have won miss the point: a year earlier the party would have 'killed' for this result. The test for Labor is whether this poll is like '69 or '80, a prelude to the victories of '72 and '83, or whether like '61, it is a false dawn. The ALP primary vote was only 40 per cent, a modest swing of 1.4 per cent. Labor won only a minority of the primary vote defection from the Coalition. The bulk went to One Nation. The test for Labor is whether it assumes victory next time or decides to compete in the ideas marketplace in a fast-changing debate.

Contrary to excessive pre-poll speculation, it was not a 'race-based' election. There was no significant issue of tolerance or race dividing Labor and the Coalition, despite differences of tactics and emphasis over Hanson. This situation was assisted by the eventual passage of the Wik native title bill through federal Parliament before the poll.

In an achievement for the major parties, Hanson lost her seat although One Nation polled strongly overall. It won 8.4 per cent of the primary vote, outpolling the National Party. The key to preventing One Nation translating this strength into seats was the decision of other parties to preference against One

Nation. Its vote was far below the 23 per cent it recorded at the Queensland state election and this was the key to Howard's victory. But One Nation still won a Senate place in Queensland. Despite Hanson's own defeat, One Nation will remain a significant force and a threat to the main parties. Yet the campaign revealed its flaws—its defective internal structure and the perception that it had no answers, just complaints.

The 1998 election offers new opportunities and risks for Australia in its transition through the millennium. While Howard prevailed, disenchantment with both major parties was manifest. The real lesson is that globalisation and scepticism about politics demands a new approach. The need is for a new politics based upon a reappraisal of policy and community sentiment. This involves a better integration of economics, social policy, values and leadership. It demands a strategic redefinition of the role of government and the relationship between government and the people of Australia. Globalisation in the late 1990s is manifestly a new challenge for democracies and for society and it will demand, eventually, a new politics.

The central lesson is that there is no hope in a flight to the past. Internationalisation will reward those nations that adapt and punish or crush those that succumb to nostalgia. Australia has no successful future but as an open and competitive economy. There is no salvation in a return to Fortress Australia. The great myth is that we can prosper by re-regulation of our economy, reinvention of protection barriers and a retreat from the ground made in the 1980s. This is the agenda of the Greens, the Democrats, sections of the ALP and parts of the media, in both its elite and populist dimensions.

There is an associated myth—that Australia can prosper by bringing economic change and reform to a halt. We can't. The issue is whether we wish to be engaged with the global economy, and win more investment and trade and revenue as a result, or whether we wish to disengage and win less of these.

The 1990s in its turbulence and confusion is ripe for the mythmakers and great deceivers. They occupy influential positions in the media and politics, and are busy pushing their barrows each day. They push the myths gaining currency today—that protection saves jobs; that Australia is exploited by other nations when it opens its economy to the world; that re-regulation of the economy will promote growth; that a market-based wages system isn't basic to creating new jobs; that governments can run competitive businesses better than the private sector; that free and expanding health, welfare and education services are sustainable within the current tax structure; that Australia can decline to judge itself by international standards and still prosper; that a pro-market economy is incompatible with a caring society; that an Australian refusal to take more of the world's population won't compromise our future; and that Australia can take the economic gains from Asia but discriminate against Asian people.

Australia's economic growth in the 1990s has been strong precisely because the nation had the courage to open its economy, embrace reform and improve its public and corporate performance. This was a singular enduring achievement of the Hawke–Keating era. Viewed in the longer term, the world economy has seen unprecedented prosperity since 1945 precisely because the post-war compact was based upon economic liberalism and the gradual opening up of international trade and finance. Australia's 1997 foreign and trade White Paper pointed out that average tariff levels in developed nations have fallen from 40 per cent when GATT was formed in 1948 to under 4 per cent when the Uruguay Round commitments are completed. Australia has been a beneficiary of this process.

Claims that market-based reforms have run too far in Australia are sadly out of touch. The contrast between Britain and Australia illustrates the point. British Telecom was privatised 15 years ago; Britain already has an indirect tax; the British labour market is highly deregulated compared with Australia's and the result is much lower unemployment, even with a growth rate below Australia's. Issues over which we are squabbling today have previously been settled in Britain.

The purpose of the domestic campaign to erect an Australian bogy of 'economic rationalism' is to secure a return to government guarantees—for client groups and producers. It involves a rewriting of history about the Hawke–Keating years. We are being told, believe it or not, that Bob Hawke and Paul Keating were free market ideologues who undermined our economy. Hawke and Keating, in fact, were intelligent pragmatists. Most of the time they specialised in winning elections by finding pragmatic solutions to the problems of the age, unburdened by the dead hand of the past. Their market-orientated economic reform agenda combined with social justice themes won more elections for the federal ALP than any other policies in any other era in federal Labor's history. A smart ALP will learn from them, not repudiate their achievements.

Having won the '98 election on a pitch of superior economic management, Howard knows he must redeem this pledge or face electoral liquidation. He has a dual purpose—he wants to govern successfully and he wants to win elections. While Howard's economic performance so far has been a variation of 'stop-start', there are distinct signs he believes a bolder approach offers the best political prospects. (Whether he is able to implement such an approach is another issue.) The omens are that in his second term Howard, after taxation policy, will incline to policies designed to improve employment. Indeed, this may be imposed upon him by a growth slowdown. He seems more disposed to the view that regressive economics, while convenient as an occasional electoral sop, won't work as a long-run policy for a government. It won't work because it isn't a solution to real world problems.

The politics of economic reform, however, have changed decisively in the 1990s from the 1980s. The central difference is that last decade there was a bipartisan agreement between Labor and the Coalition on the direction—though differences of detail. In the 1990s, the ALP has grown increasingly sceptical of market-based change in its own quest for re-definition.

The Beazley-led ALP is caught in the conflict between democratic socialism and globalisation. It is an epic struggle both politically and intellectually. Globalisation is destroying the post-World War II 'mixed economy' compact which successful labour and social democratic parties of the Left struck with capitalism. The tools that made this compact work are no longer available—central banks now run interest rate policy; financial markets impose regimes of fiscal austerity as national economic sovereignty declines; freer trade has destroyed government-imposed tariffs to design industrial structures; the imperative of jobs growth drives more flexible labour markets; a competitive world makes government ownership of industry increasingly unsustainable; the failure of the 'passive' welfare state is forcing governments to get people off welfare into work; and pressure for devolution in decision-making means the authority of central governments, the vehicle of democratic socialism, is in retreat. It is idle to pretend these forces don't constitute a crisis for social democracy.

This crisis can be stated precisely—the risk is that parties such as the ALP will be striking at its trade union constituency and destroying its class base if it embraces the policy agenda of globalisation. That is, it will cease to be Labor and become something else, a liberal party or US-style Democratic Party. This is the issue raised by the ascendancy of Tony Blair in Great Britain. He has tried to devise a new position for British Labour which accepts the Thatcher settlement. Previously, British Labour spent 15 years attacking Thatcher's policies and driving itself towards electoral extinction. Blair imposed a clean break. Yet in his part-Thatcherite family background, his education, his values and his policies, Blair can be seen as a bridge between Labour and the old British Liberal Party eclipsed earlier this century by the rise of class politics, the unions and the Labour Party itself.

Blair champions constitutional reform—the old Liberal passion—keeps most of the Thatcher restrictions on the unions, and has opened a dialogue with the Liberal Democrats to explore an alliance to marginalise the Tory Party. The symmetry is striking; the issue is epic. Does Blair believe that globalisation, certain to weaken the unions, means a reversion of politics to the early twentieth century structure before the rise of the labour parties when the contest was Liberal versus Tory? His answer, probably, is more 'yes' than 'no'.

That issue will be determined in the future. For the moment,

Blair pursues what is branded 'the third way'—a position whose local champion is the ALP's Mark Latham, who went to the backbench in disgust after the 1998 election. Latham's critique of Beazley's destination may prove to be right or wrong: the jury is out. But his analysis defines the issue. Latham argues that globalisation accentuates the usual choice that faces oppositions. Labor can prosper by 'scab lifting', which means exploiting the 'change process', or it can engage in genuine 'agenda setting', which means defining new policy solutions.

Latham asserts that Labor in Opposition, so far, has adopted the McEwenist technique and 'backed in producer interests, whether in the car, footwear clothing textile, music, sugar, chicken meat or pork industries' and mounted a scare campaign against change. Latham's message is that Labor can no longer achieve a growth economy by relying upon the post-war social democratic tools. This means recognising that the market can't and won't be abolished but that new policies are needed to combat its anti-social legacy. The decision Labor takes about its future direction under Beazley and Simon Crean will be important for Australia's future since Labor has been the primary party of innovation over the past 30 years.

The ultimate issue is not whether globalisation is good or bad. It is that globalisation has arrived and is here to stay. An international debate is underway about how to curb the worst excesses of an open global financial system. The result is uncertain. But it is more likely to focus on disclosure and limited new controls rather than sweeping re-regulation that turns back the clock. The technological dynamic has gone too far. The chief executive of Visy Industries, Dr John White, notes that 'at the heart of our emerging global economy is an information technology that doubles in capability every 18 months and almost halves in prices'.

Cross-border capital flows have created the most fabulous fortunes in history, and destroyed Asian economies in the past year on a scale and at a pace never seen before. The task is to channel these forces, globally and domestically, for the benefit of people and society. That constitutes a new politics whether it is called the 'third way' or 'progressive liberalism' or something else.

Market-based policies are the key to growth. But they are destructive as well as creative. In the late 1990s, it is apparent that globalisation runs deeper than understood in the 1980s. Its challenge must be met at different levels. In the political domain that process is under way. The pure free-market zealots who believe their nirvana is nigh are as misguided as the re-regulators. They grasp neither the dangers inherent nor its potential threat to democracy. The task ahead is to cofashion new policies and attitudes that make globalisation work for people. The journey is unpredictable but it is a time for ideas. Not all will work but new solutions must be tried. Australia's path will be tested against many signposts.

First, politicians must recognise their task is to deliver better government. That means working out what the state should do and what it should not do—and teaching the public those limits. This is integral to devising a new strategic role for government. The old role is being supplanted. A new strategic role is essential to restore faith and confidence in government without which the 1990s pessimism will be prolonged and democracy itself will be jeopardised.

Many people remember the enthusiasm surrounding the election of John Kennedy in the US, Gough Whitlam in Australia and Harold Wilson in Britain. It was a very different age. The chief difference was the belief that governments could solve any social problem—that the combination of leadership, money and government intervention was a masterful answer. This was the exact assumption of Whitlam's famous 1972 policy speech. It was an age of idealism and, in retrospect, of innocence. The high tide of faith in government was that remarkable Keynesian age after World War II. It has gone forever. It won't return.

Governments are not the effective problem-solvers they were once. Yet the public is equivocal about governments. It holds them in contempt but expects them to solve too many of its problems and politicians often pretend that they can.

Globalisation has undermined the role of government as problem-solver. And globalisation is only in its early phase. Governments must adjust to having less power just as nations must adjust to having less sovereignty. Governments should not try to run businesses in competitive markets. They should leave business to the private sector whether it is a bank, airline or telecommunications company.

The aim is to bring the expectations of people into harmony with the more limited capacity of government. The lesson of the Fraser era in Australia was that government intervention had strict limits on its success. It was also a lesson from the Whitlam period.

More recently, Bill Clinton defined a new position for the Democrat Party after its 1994 congressional election debacle. His own political remaking was described by Bob Woodward in his book *The Agenda* when an angry Clinton was told by his economic advisers that his ability to do things as president would be determined by the money markets. But Clinton learnt. Since 1994 he has been masterful at recognising the limits to government and carrying people behind this realism. Americans have spent most of the 1990s dosed on optimism—but this derives not from decisions or scandals in Washington but from realising personal opportunity.

The conclusive case for bringing the government expectations/capacity equation into harmony is Asia's financial crisis. Global capital exposed the fallacy of the Asian economic miracle, starting with its flagship Japan and moving through the rest of the fleet. The domestic defect was the idea that financial systems could be run as an extension of industry policy. Corporatism was the basis for allocating capital, often degenerating into a 'crony capitalism' for family, supporters and mates. The Asian revival will require a withdrawal of government from this process and the creation of strong central banks, firm prudential supervision, transparency and accountability. Asia's crisis has destroyed the much-vaunted role of government in allocating capital in favour of market-based risk assessment. The government's future role is to define the rules and monitor the system's integrity.

Second, integral to the new strategic role of government is a values-based re-definition of the rights and responsibilities of the individual and the individual's relationship to the state. John Howard calls this 'mutual obligation'; Tony Blair calls it 'reciprocal responsibility.' The point is that the day of the 'passive' welfare state is numbered. There are two moral concepts here which work in political terms. A civilised society will keep a social safety net for the disadvantaged; but many welfare recipients must accept responsibilities, namely, to work to get off welfare, as a trade-off for the welfare payments they enjoy. Social security budgets are threatening to become unsustainable. In Australia, social security constitutes 38 per cent of federal spending compared with 20 per cent a generation ago, though family payments contribute a hefty slice.

The principle here has a wider application. Tertiary students can't expect taxpayers to fund all their costs; retirement incomes must increasingly be funded through the working life rather than from a retirement pension; the unemployed must accept obligations in relation to training and job application.

The same argument applies to corporations. A 1998 Clemenger survey exposes the gulf between shareholder and customer interests. The survey finds that business is seen as a 'largely self-serving entity driven by short-term interests and quick gains for the benefit of a priveleged few'. Howard intimated post-election that business would be included in his 'mutual obligation' net—an important step. But the debate about how to reconcile the drive for profits with community support in the global age is just starting in Australia. For Howard this tension will be played out in the issue of bank mergers, a difficult post-election test.

Getting people to take responsibility in individual, family and work life is a core requirement for a better society. Responsibility and liberty are bedmates. What is liberty? Is it the right to do whatever you desire or is it the right to act to achieve a better society? We should be honest enough to admit that liberty is too often corrupted and interpreted without a moral or social compass. Yet if greater personal responsibility is accepted then society is stronger and liberty is enhanced.

Third, the government needs to define far better its relationship with markets. Markets are valued for their ability to create wealth efficiently, but they possess no inherent morality and must operate within democratically sanctioned rules. By their nature, markets are amoral; markets share no democratic legitimacy; markets can't be automatically trusted to deliver for the public good. The market is not necessarily an honest broker. The mistake governments sometimes make or have hoisted upon them is the perception that they are investing in the morality of markets. But markets can't be a religion any more than Keynesianism, social democracy or Marxism could be a religion. The market is something we live with while trying to harness its utility. Markets undershoot and overshoot, sometimes on a vast scale.

It is the sheer volume of funds in the financial system combined with massive leverage and rapidity of movement that is so potentially dangerous. The debate about market supervision and safeguards, globally and domestically, is being renewed. This is a good thing. Governments must revise and revive the rules of the domestic marketplace. The aim should be to keep markets open, honest and competitive. Market operatives will conspire, invariably, against such aims. Authorities such as the Australian Competition and Consumer Commission are basic in promoting market competition. The Productivity Commission is critical in providing a transparent analysis of economic resources and performance. Its former chairman, Bill Scales, after listing the scope of the Commission's public inquiries—including cars, telecommunications, textiles, computers, private health insurance, public housing, dairy, meat, education and industrial relations—said 'in each of these areas we have found Australia is not achieving anywhere near its full potential'.

Even where governments define effective rules for the marketplace, there will still be market failures. Australia's financial system in the late 1980s is a classic example with banks overlending to reckless entrepreneurs. The crisis in international finance in the late 1990s is the most spectacular contemporary example of market failure. John Howard reflected the reassessment of the crisis when he declared in October 1998 that 'The global financial system also failed us'. The upshot is that governments and international institutions are trying to address these issues. It is a fine judgment—it involves letting markets work; creating a framework to curb and control the excesses of markets; and being prepared to intervene in cases of serious market failure. It means talking frankly to voters about the philosophy and the rules.

Fourth, it seems that globalisation, while creating great wealth, distributes that wealth on an increasingly unequal basis that threatens the social compact. Market forces have helped to promote inequality of wealth in Australia. A recent study by Access Economics shows that the top 10 per cent of Australian income units owned 48 per cent of the wealth in 1998, compared with 43.5 per cent in 1993. The top 1 per cent of income units had 15 per cent of the wealth, up from 12 per cent over the same period. The cause of this rising inequality is share price surges and escalation in the value of expensive houses.

While share ownership in Australia is rising, the real story is that share wealth is highly concentrated. The top 10 per cent of income units retain 90 per cent of the shares held by private investors and two-thirds of that is held by the top 1 per cent. There are many more millionaires in Australia, but at the same time the welfare bill is expanding rapidly. Wealth is far more unevenly distributed than income, yet income is taxed where much wealth is not. A society that offers incentives to excellence, achievement and hard work is a sensible society—but the reward system is distorted and the public sector is struggling as a result.

Wages across most income levels remain relatively compressed in Australia compared with other democracies. Over the past decade, however, there has been an increase in income inequality because of increases in the incomes of the top 10 per cent of Australians. This is an inevitable result of a market-orientated economy. The top decile enjoys a lifestyle of expensive cars, wine, cleaning services, overseas holidays, restaurant meals, private school fees and health insurance. It is noteworthy that rural National Party electorates have lower than average incomes, and that farm districts dominate the list of ten postcodes with the lowest average incomes. Globalisation is creating new divisions in which 'knowledge workers' are able to leverage their skills into high income at an early stage of professional life. The much publicised multi-million-dollar chief executive scales—and their separation from performance—is a source of growing community resentment.

There is a special political pressure in Australia to try to reconcile market forces with ongoing support for a degree of wealth redistribution and to balance equity and incentive. This is a good thing. It is one of the great strengths of our democracy. It is guaranteed by our system of compulsory voting.

But no nation, so far, has been able to reconcile satisfactorily market-oriented growth with limits to wealth inequality. It is a challenge Australia and other democracies still face. If the idea takes hold that globalisation means a form of economic Darwinism, there will be a revolt against globalisation. Democracy itself will be under assault if this dilemma cannot be addressed. If the disparities only grow—and where will they be on current trends 25 years from now?—then people will disengage, revolt or despair. This is where the new and still evolving 'stakeholder' concept is relevant. The idea is that individuals and families win a sense of stakeholding in globalised economies through shareholding, pension and superannuation funds, enterprise deals and other innovative instruments.

One priority is the need to attack Australia's 8-plus per cent unemployment more aggressively. Unemployment is a major source of inequality and the problem is political, not intellectual, since the solutions are known. Several years ago, the head of the Australian Treasury, Ted Evans, said that unemployment was largely a matter of choice. After the 1998 election, five prominent economists advanced a realistic proposal to achieve a 5 per cent unemployment level while putting a premium on equity. The details of their proposal—freezing Living Wage adjustments and using tax credits to assist the low paid—can be disputed. But their approach in seeking a mid-path between the European social regulation and American pro-market models is the right method for Australia. Unless Australia tackles its unemployment problem, there will be more disillusionment with the political system, deeper opposition to economic reform and more support for One Nation. A freer labour market, a further move to limit the award system and a move away from the central wage tribunal are by-steps in this process.

The three central economic challenges facing the second Howard government—tax reform, a job strategy and a better national savings effort—all demand a synthesis of efficiency and equity. In each case the policy—and political task—is to design reforms that are not just beneficial to the economy, but helpful to people. Inevitably there will be losers. This is where substantial funds for social and economic restructuring (which means helping people to re-make their lives) is essential.

Another lesson in the equity debate is that market forces will split different regions into winners and losers. Parts of rural Australia have been adversely affected by low commodity prices, loss of services and structural changes. The moral is the need for local planning on a government–industry basis to adjust to change, for regional development strategies, and for governments to again commit to sizeable social and economic adjustment funds.

Globalisation suffers from two public relations disasters well evident in Australia. Job losses from either tariff cuts or corporate change are identifiable; the job gains aren't because they are economy-wide. Second, people are aware of import penetration into Australia's market; they never see the great success story of rising Australian exports. The two go hand-in-hand.

Fifth, the pressure will intensify for a greater emphasis on national technological, transport and educational infrastructure. This will require a deeper collaboration between government and private sector across a range of industry. For example, alarm about Australia's transport infrastructure has re-entered the mainstream political debate. There are serious proposals to upgrade rail, push ahead with very fast train proposals and, belatedly, more action is under way to improve our airports and aviation infrastructure, notably at Sydney, the nation's main gateway. Australia will need to put a premium on transport and communication efficiency. Another lesson from the US in the 1990s is that economic success is intimately tied to value-added high-technology development. This demands a combination of skill, financial resources and technological companies.

Integral to this process is a renewed commitment to education and learning. The issue was best put by Melbourne University Vice-Chancellor, Alan Gilbert, at the 1998 Australia Unlimited conference:

> The simple relentless truth is that even the very best funded Australian university is resourced in 1998 between a fifth and a half as well as the best North American, Japanese and European universities are. In most cases those universities actually teach fewer students than Melbourne does. Without a seat at the table of first world intellectual discourse and knowledge creation, synthesis, dissemination and application, the future is going to be very dark indeed in the knowledge based international economies of the twenty-first century. Is it arrogance or innocence or simply a 'she'll be right' hoping against hope that makes Australians somehow believe that we can match the rest of the world at a discount?

This issue of knowledge based industry needs to be put honesty on the political table—it means a new approach to university education, communications and technology.

Sixth, the societies that succeed in the twenty-first century will be those that can combine diversity with harmony. This is a mission for Australia. One of our greatest achievements has been the substitution of the original Federation belief of White Australia with a multicultural Australia. White Australia was the essence of our nationalism and central to our Federation. The policy was abolished only in the 1966–73 period. The first major subsequent influx of Asian immigrants in this century under the new policy came only in the 1970s.

The foundations for the transformation of Australia's culture lay in the post–World War II immigration program. A total of 5.5 million people have come to our shores through this program. It was a deliberate exercise in nation-building. It ranks, along with that of Israel, as one of the most successful exercises in population growth and national development in the century. Of course, not all the consequences were foreseen. In politics, you have to back your judgment. The task now is to manage this society successfully. It is a vast undertaking that must be underpinned by essential principles.

The guiding philosophy must be that of social inclusion since there is no other satisfactory basis for a twenty-first century society. There is no place for the leader who refuses to champion social inclusion. Such leaders are obsolete and will only promote divisions within their society. Social inclusion relates to individual opportunity, how people feel, whether they are appreciated, the values the leader wants to promote in the community by example, and the ability of new arrivals to find work, friends and a satisfactory existence.

Social inclusion is tied to the idea of inter-dependence. It is no good just arguing that social inclusion is a moral requirement. It is something that transcends altruism. The truth is that society is more inter-dependent than ever which means social inclusion is a requirement to hold society together and preserve the common good. It is a condition for successful globalisation.

Social inclusion also involves the separate but related process of Aboriginal reconciliation. You can't have one section of the community alienated and expect to have a harmonious society. Aboriginal reconciliation involves a formal recognition of the prior occupation of the continent by the Aboriginal people, a recognition of their unique culture and an acceptance that history and deprivation mean that special programs for Aboriginal advancement are needed. It also means, however, that such action must occur within the spirit of a united Australia. In this respect, I think it means an implicit acknowledgement that a full restoration of past injustice cannot be achieved, and will never be achieved. It is important to say this because it is at the heart of much of the current misunderstanding.

Finally, social inclusion is realised through a recognition that diversity must operate within firm limits and social balance. This point is best grasped in the notion of multiculturalism whose worst advocates are those who refuse to recognise its limits or to draw that balance. When in 1989 the Commonwealth Government embraced a National Agenda for Multiculturalism, it endorsed three principles of multiculturalism and three principles that limited multiculturalism. This is the formal compact;

it is the essence of the idea. Unfortunately, one rarely hears much about this today. Yet this 1989 definition of multicultural policy was bipartisan and followed wide consultation. It is a very good definition, and should be spelt out. Multiculturalism was seen as a policy 'to manage the consequences of this diversity in the interests of the individual and society as a whole'.

It had three dimensions. The 'right of all Australians, within carefully defined limits, to express and share their individual cultural heritage'; the right of all 'to equality of treatment and opportunity and the removal of barriers of race, ethnicity, culture, religion, language, gender or place of birth'; and the 'need to maintain, develop and utilise effectively the skills and the talents of all Australians regardless of background'.

Yet there were limits to multiculturalism and they were given equal weight. There were three defined restraints. The 'premise that all Australians should have an overriding and unifying commitment to Australia, to its interests and future, first and foremost'; a requirement that all Australians accept 'the basic structures and principles of Australian society—the Constitution and the rule of law, tolerance and equality, parliamentary democracy, freedom of speech and religion, English as the national language, and equality of the sexes'; and finally, acceptance that multicultural policies 'impose obligations as well as conferring rights: the right to express one's own culture and beliefs involves a reciprocal responsibility to accept the right of others to express their views and values'.

If this definition of multiculturalism had been consistently put, its critics would have been much weakened. In fact, it has rarely been put. The notion of rights and responsibilities has typically been ignored. Few people in our community have a view of multiculturalism that corresponds with this official policy, surely a serious problem. What is the explanation? It is partly because our politicians have not advanced the cause the right way. But there is a deeper reason. It is because the word multiculturalism fails itself to convey the balance in its intended meaning. It is a confusing and divisive word, undermining of unity and inadequate as an over-arching symbol. 'Many races: one Australia' is clearer since it captures diversity and unity.

The issue is important not just for community values but for immigration.

Our immigration program has been basic to national development. Immigration has helped to expand our small population base, assisted over time our economic growth, and confirmed the sense of Australia as a young country prepared to renew itself. But in recent years support for immigration has slumped dramatically. This is not unique to Australia and different leaders have responded in different ways. For example, in 1998 President Clinton went to Portland and delivered an inspiring declaration for the US program, pledging that America will continue to take just under a million immigrants a year, and nominating America, in effect, as the nation for the next century because of this faith. There are risks in this approach. But this is what Clinton said:

> Let me state my views unequivocally. I believe new immigrants are good for America. They are revitalising our cities. They are building our new economy. They are strengthening our ties to the global economy . . . because of immigration there is no major race in Hawaii or Houston or New York City. Within five years, there will be no major race in our largest state, California. In a little more than 50 years, there will be no major race in the United States.

Clinton's policies or rhetoric can't just be translated to Australia. But he offers a model of the commitment required.

Reviving support for immigration in Australia will not be easy. The ethnic lobby has made a disastrous mistake by pushing for policies that have only made immigration unpopular. The future of immigration goes to the nation's sense of mission. But immigration cannot be revived in isolation; its revival will occur only in the context of other changes. This means getting not just social inclusion right but further re-casting economic policy. A stronger immigration intake can only be sustained when the unemployment level is reduced far below its current 8 per cent; when there is a greater sense of economic confidence; when the program is geared more to the national interest and such nation-building is seen as necessary; when the wages market is more deregulated and better regional policies are in place so that immigrants can be attracted to particular regions and jobs where there are competitive advantages based upon lower costs or higher skills; and when a new generation of politicians emerges that believes in the renewal of the program.

The major directions that characterise Australia's recent history are economic liberalism and social diversity. There are many problems with these policies and directions. But the essential element should not be ignored—that these policies have been right for Australia and that our broad national directions have been sound. This is the critical point because Australia has displayed courage in recent decades in confronting the challenges of a global era. It has moved from economic nationalism to economic liberalism and from a social mono-culturalism to social diversity. The past 20 years of Commonwealth government policy under both Labor and the Coalition has represented a strong movement along these lines. The course is never even and the progress is never easy.

It is no surprise that there are complaints, grumbles and protests. It is no surprise that Pauline Hanson's One Nation opposes both economic liberalism and social diversity. It is a party with a true nostalgia for the past and no answer for the future. There are many phoney prophets peddling the message that Australia is on the wrong track. Their message is false, but it falls on a field of pessimism, confusion and fear of change and it is often taken up.

This highlights the biggest and most dangerous myth in our current political dialogue—that economic efficiency leading to economic progress and social inclusion leading to a more caring and tolerant society are incompatible. This assumption has almost become an article of faith in some quarters. The slogan is entrenched—if you believe in the market, you don't believe in society. It is damaging because it is false and its consequence is to weaken economic liberalism or social inclusion or both.

Economic liberalism and social inclusion are more likely to reinforce each other than they are to fight each other. The stronger our growth economy, the more compassionate we can become as a society. On the other hand, the path of economic decline will multiply our social divisions and disorder. Our economic and social polity must become twin companions on the path of globalisation. But this isn't an easy task.

It is why new policies, new responses and a new politics are needed. The task is to make globalisation work for Australia. The aim is to reconcile a market-orientated growth economy with a caring, diverse and interdependent society. Some of these needed responses are clear and require only political will; for others, the details are still a relatively open policy book. Yet the agenda is apparent. It is about the role of government, the rights and responsibility of the individual, the need to reduce unemployment, to secure genuine equality of opportunity, a greater national commitment to education, technological advance and career re-training, ways to reinforce social inclusion within a growing community, an ongoing drive to a stronger economy leading to greater national income, a renewed sense of national mission and an informed self-confidence that matches Australia's potential. Globalisation, above all, means that life changes faster on a permanent basis and that demands a cultural adaption. This book attempts to grapple with the issues.

2

Adrift in a Tribal Tide
Inside the psyche of the nation

Nicolas Rothwell

Almost a century since that inspiring figure of Federation Alfred Deakin spoke of a nation whose members share 'the same ideals, the same general cast of character and tone of thought', how many ways there are today to speak of division!

Australia seems a tribalised nation, split into classes of affinity. One can speak of the divides of economics, geography, age and education. The rhetorical emphasis on unity has, in the past three years tinged by One Nation's shadow, become acute. But the truth is that this decade has been one of ever greater focus upon individuals, upon their differing needs and rights and satisfactions. Diversity and multiplicity have been the catchwords of public imagination.

But if Australians in this post-modern age form many subtle, self-defining tribes, does the constitutive bedrock of national vision and identity provide an anchor strong enough to hold them together? Such, at times in the first term of the Coalition Government under Prime Minister John Howard, was the crucial, unstated question at the heart of Australian politics.

Tribes aplenty. Geographic tribes: for the Australia of inner-city Sydney, Brisbane or Melbourne, with its styles and flavours, its kaleidoscopic, fast-paced, fluid life, has little in common with the unleavened, tranquil symphony of the suburbs, or with the still, depopulated bush, or the regional centres and semi-rural zones—those magnets of new population and new political loyalties.

Age tribes: for the youngest groups of voters, devoid of the allegiances of the baby-boomer generation, operate by maps of susceptibility quite different from those followed by the commentators and explainers of the nation, lost upon their commanding media heights.

Social tribes: blue-collar workers, for instance, especially those between 45 and 60, have proved unusually sensitive to the unquiet messages of Pauline Hanson's crusade, while retired Australians find themselves troubled by financial concerns and life prospects far distant from those animating the majority of a young nation.

Knowledge tribes: for there is an unseen tribal division, perhaps the most profound of all, now opening between the information-rich and information-poor; broadly, between those who are gainers from the transformation of the Australian economy, those who are losers. The gainers are an intriguing coalition of interests: not just the members of professions and the prospering cultural intelligentsia but also the new, successful working class, the support workers, members of the hospitality and tourism sectors, and the entrepreneurs of the service and construction industries.

A very different fate confronts those workers left behind by change, and unsure how to modify their life-courses: rural workers, factory employees, men and women pushed out of the workforce with 20 years of active labour still to give. These groups may live in the same towns and cities, see the same movies and watch the same television, but their respective social capacities and economic potentials are very different.

How to bind together such varied aspirations and outcomes? A nation like Australia, with its high component of communal spirit, its sense of fairness, sharing and mateship, should be well placed to manage such social and economic turmoil as is now upon us, and as threatens in a period of global downturn and regional readjustment. Not for nothing is this country threaded together by community and volunteer organisations, with all its bushfire brigades and surf lifesaving clubs; not for nothing is it a high taxation, high welfare society.

Governments and political parties have many techniques to bind atomised individuals into a collective destiny—but perhaps the most important of these, the articulation and promotion of a shared set of goals and values, is the one people feel most strikingly absent from the pre-millennial public stage.

The nation's political forces have reacted in intriguing ways to the challenge of diversity—the problem of sharply divergent economic prospects across different regional and social groups. Almost imperceptibly over the past decade, the two dominant party groupings—Labor on the one hand (with its occasional, informal allies in ideology, the Democrats), and on the other, the ungainly coalition of Nationals and Liberals—have all but changed their stripes.

Labor, once a class-based party, retains something of that original flavour but has been substantially remade as a collection of special interests: the academic and intellectual elites, the welfare community and their administrators, many in the newly-arrived ethnic communities, the more embattled elements of the trade union movement. These are the fundamental consumers of the Labor gospel, and they form a rainbow of competing priorities and beliefs, yoked in tandem until 1996 by the heady Keating brew of economic thrust, symbol-laden national quest and the politics of triangular identity: Asia, republic, reconciliation. Through a second parliamentary term of Beazley-led Opposition, the party's guiding vision-cocktail may well be modified further into an economic conservatism based upon assertion of community spirit and grandly-invoked idealisms. A project definitely still under development.

The condition of the Liberal-National camp is rather different, after three years in office. Howard's Liberal Party had reconceived itself by 1996 as one that spoke not just for the interests of the middle classes and above, but one that also wooed, and won, the battlers—the conservative in heart and mind, those voters most suspicious of what was airy and elusive in Labor's dream of a multiplicit Australia. Yet during the first Howard term, this marriage of convenience between high Liberals and low came under almost as much strain as the formal arrangement binding free-market Liberals with Nationals from a rural sector eviscerated by economic rationalism. The schizophrenic aspect of the modern Liberal Party was plainly on display on the night of Howard's greatest triumph, October 3 1998, when he claimed victory at Sydney's Rydges-Wentworth hotel before a mingled crowd of partisans—equal numbers of sleek establishment power-brokers and 'new Liberals', the brash working men and women from the suburbs. It's too simple to say that both main party groupings have simply changed their markets and muffled their respective visions in the process, or to say that the Liberals now have no national perspective, and Labor hardly any policies.

For the first time in a political generation, a third force has appeared. One Nation's performance in the federal election may have appeared unspectacular: its great figurehead was dismissed unceremoniously from the House of Representatives, and its grassroots campaign failed to elect a single member of the Lower House. Its prospects without Hanson may well be bleak, for such parties rely strongly on the prominence and the aura of invincibility that attaches to the wise, high-tempered leader.

Nevertheless, One Nation, a party not even dreamed of two years ago, secured the votes of close to a million Australians. It held 15 per cent of the Queensland vote. It had stronger backing across the country than the Nationals and Democrats. This is more than backblocks protest. The sources of Hanson's brief, spectacular initial passage through the field of national politics have begun to emerge. It was not a question of guns or of immigrants: she spoke to those Australians who felt left behind, not just economically but emotionally, by the brave new projects and beliefs the elites and intelligentsia of the city centres promoted. There is a regional component to Hansonism, and a cultural component. Above all, it has been an ideological phenomenon—Hanson had a vision of sorts, and shared it in her fashion.

In the eyes of the judging, impatient public, the two main

parties seemed peculiarly alike in their proposals, their style and their contempt during much of the last parliamentary term for their new rival. Indeed, it was only the Liberals' GST and tax reform package that separated Left and Right sufficiently to polarise the electorate and, perhaps, to reduce One Nation's campaign support so decisively. Hanson's crusade failed in the end to catch fire and reshape the political landscape at the first try—but only just. A skilled and gifted conviction politician, faced with such an opportunity, might have fared better. Vision, in a nation deprived of publicly articulated purpose, can be a most seductive thing. Hanson's distinctively demotic, drawlingly delivered perspective had a well-founded demographic appeal.

Who were the million or so voters? They were not all racists and haters of Aborigines, despite the denunciations of columnists and protesters across the capital cities of the south-east. They formed, and doubtless still form, a sharp core group, surrounded by a much larger nimbus of half-approving fellow-travellers—those who admired Hanson's guts and outspokenness, who disliked the pervasive, saccharine-flavoured culture of political correctness, who loved One Nation's discomfiting effect upon professional politicians but who were unwilling, in the privacy of the ballot-box, to support a ramshackle party with half-thought-out policies.

One Nation's strongholds were those areas of Australia, and Australian society, that seem on the fringes of the picture, the edge-cities and semi-rural strips of unconstrained development that cluster on the coastlines and around the capitals: the stretch of regional centres running north from Brisbane to the Sunshine Coast, Wide Bay and beyond, or inwards towards Ipswich; the fast-growing coastal towns of northern NSW; the western suburbs of Sydney and the eastern surrounds of Melbourne; the prospering south-western corner of Western Australia; the declining towns of the bush.

One Nation's voters include the youngest electoral generation, and the retired as well, but the party's chief strength is among men between 28 and 45, unskilled or semi-skilled, living in the outer suburbs and regional towns. One Nation sympathisers are social conservatives. Often they have not, until now, been involved in, or much cared for, party politics. They reject both the main parties, feel abandoned by the state, are disillusioned by social priorities that cut against their interests. What most troubles them? Jobs and health care, and the conviction they are not as well treated as other clearly defined minority groups. Perhaps just as significant as their number and opinions is the fact that their concerns are shared more widely across Australia—a nation of anxious individuals, confronting change and feeling quite without a guiding hand or common sense of goal. As much as it needs to be viewed as a direct political phenomenon, One Nation can be seen as a symptom of disquiet, a lightning conductor of protest and revolt.

Any sketch of the national psyche cannot help but be impressionistic. Mine represents the sediment of countless conversations and interviews I had in compiling *The Australian*'s Reportage series throughout 1998 with people in all states, from most walks of life: the young and the retired, the struggling and established. Amidst the baffling range of divergences you would expect to find within a society straddling a continent and a hundred different micro-cultures some constants. And some repeated themes did emerge. Those Australians—the great majority among those encountered—who would class themselves as unquiet and dissatisfied express unusually strong feelings about certain things in their lives and their society. In Victorian towns and Sydney suburbs, in the newly sophisticated communities of knowledge workers clustered in such regions as the Adelaide Hills or Blue Mountains, in Queensland's regional cities and West Australian mining camps, the concerns are similar. Close to the top of every agenda is that familiar bugbear—economic rationalism. This was the term people used to label the sweeping structural changes in their lives, and their sense of a lack of control over their own surrounds. Job insecurity, price changes and cutbacks in state-provided services are all seen as symptoms of a new and much-resented overriding government philosophy.

Economic rationalism represents the opposite of the old,

decent life-course of Australia where there was work aplenty, things were slower and more personal. Above all, Australians seem to view economic rationalism as something being done to them by the political and corporate elites, and by the broader world. It benefits special interests, not identifiable individuals. Even economically literate people who well understand the policy dictates of governments have become greatly concerned at the destruction of small communities in the name of efficiency. This overall dissatisfaction undoubtedly translated into the spectacularly low combined primary vote for the two major parties at the last federal election, associated as they are with the cause of economic reform.

Alive in the thoughts of the broad community is a related concern: that the general wellbeing of the nation is being neglected in favour of aggressive attention to special groups. All Australians accept the need for welfare and a social safety net but there is a growing conviction that the system has been rigged and that it is being exploited by minority interests. This angry sense that 'fairness' has been subverted lies behind the low-level annoyance freely expressed over funding supposedly available to new migrant groups and Aboriginal organisations. There is a feeling that difference is being rewarded, that those who are 'the same' get nothing. These are emotional concerns, played out at the level of individual communities, where small disparities in benefits are visible. They are easily extended into the conviction that Australian society has become unfair, that some are less equal than others, that 'we' are being ripped off by 'them'. And in a climate of free-floating discontent, such ideas drift naturally towards the scapegoating of particular community groups.

What is perhaps most striking is not how much but how little cultural resentment and bitterness can be detected. Visit small Queensland towns like Maryborough, in One Nation's Wide Bay heartland, and you will find an appealing, multicultural sort of place, with no signs of public intolerance. If there are tensions and strains across any divide in rural Australian society—as undeniably there are in certain isolated towns of Western NSW with high Aboriginal populations—these seem caused chiefly by high crime rates and a crisis in maintaining law and order. In the Australian collective consciousness, the resentment of difference is most important as another tribal phenomenon. Younger, urban Australians, the cappuccino culture, adore the styles of multiculturalism: it is theirs. Older, less metropolitan people are wary, uncertain: they fear its 'difference' will swamp them.

The politics of reaction plays, in a half-articulated fashion, upon these anxieties. The different, the special, the foreign, these are the categories that trouble many Australians. They love their solid country, and its values, even if they might have trouble saying precisely what those values are. They want to keep them. They know, even if they've never been abroad, that theirs is the best, most peaceful, most democratic country in the world. They want to be proud of it, and are enraged by people who run it, and its historical track record, down. They know they and their world are not racist: indeed, almost everyone has direct experience of the bonding effects of immigration, and is prepared to give any incomer a hand and a fair start. Let these new arrivals, though, join the team. This is a widely-based, pan-Australian attitude, deeply held.

Tellingly, perhaps, there is significant opposition in the community to high levels of immigration—a sharp, almost instinctual connection is being drawn between today's high unemployment and the recent years of strong immigration flows. Many Australians have made this link even though they may dislike the politics of the Right and regard Hanson's occasional anti-Asian outbursts as intolerable.

There is, then, a sophisticated mental map that large numbers of these disquieted mainstream Australians have in common: they are patriotic, rather than nationalistic. They have certain core values, including a sense of fairness and fellowship. They believe society should be run for their collective benefit, not for that of special interests, whether minorities or giant companies. The people who hold these views dislike seeing Australia made less. They don't want it homogenised and internationalised, even if they like the 'add-on' of multiculture. They treasure the old bush myths, even if they go to the beach for holidays. In fact, they love Australia's particularity—Mambo and Violet Crumble, Kakadu and Arnotts.

If they think much about today's politics, they become frustrated. They feel curiously disenfranchised, for all the splendour of Australian democracy. They see the constant sound and fury of national and state election cycles, they hear the cries and shouts of Question Time, and sense obscurely that none of this is being done for them, though it is played out in their name. The level of hostility expressed in the community towards politicians and figures of public authority these days is probably greater than at any time in Australia's disorderly history. This seems caused not just by anger at the direction of the nation, but by the sense that it has none.

Drift, stagnation, loss of purpose—these are the impressions the past three years' conduct of national affairs has left in the minds of many everyday Australians, those who cordially dislike their remote-seeming politicians and who may well, even if they were worlds apart from the One Nation camp, have nurtured a soft spot for Hanson's anti-political message. In this light, it is intriguing to note the success—across class and political lines—of state leaders who tap a sense of regional pride and economic prowess, principally Victoria's Jeff Kennett and Western Australia's Richard Court.

The federal Government, with its stern economic programs, may simply have steered too harsh a course for these unclear times: the aims of good financial management and providential housekeeping have failed to set the national community alight. Instead, there was a slow-growing disappointment in the Prime Minister and the Government elected in 1996 to effect a return to stability. Not only has it delivered, in the name of common sense, economic austerity, it has conspicuously failed to win over hearts and minds. Its lacklustre return to power is arguably as much an index of the deep-seated popular dislike of Paul Keating's politics as it is an endorsement of the Coalition's own first-term initiatives.

This, of course, is the paradox of the re-elected Prime

Minister. John Howard, more than most of his ministry, seems personally in tune with many of the sentiments that make up the bedrock values of the broad cross-section of the Australian community. Yet he cannot reflect these sentiments; he has not framed them and clad them in eloquence. No vision of any substance has been offered, and in that absence has bloomed the lush, intoxicating flower of Hansonism: a reactive, negative brand of politics, criticising but rarely advocating; a kind of super-democracy responding chiefly to frets and resentments, exalting a harmonious dream of the past yet, in the present, building nothing, accentuating no positives.

The surreal consequence: a Government, just returned to power, that stands for very little beyond a tax; an Opposition with a mouldering legacy of causes and no prospect of advancing them; and an intellectual and moral vacuum, a serious state of affairs for a nation as much under construction as this one. Serious, too, because the virtual mental abdication by the conservative side of Australian politics, the decision to quit the battlefield of ideas, has its effect. The realm of thought becomes the preserve of the Left, and by extension of the ALP. Social prescriptions, civic ideas, concepts of national identity, all the cultural–symbolic issues become politicised and lose their unifying appeal. In an ideal society, there should be a constant flux of dreams and visions for the public to choose between.

No surprise, then, if all through the interviews and discussions that made up *The Australian*'s Reportage series over the past year a constant theme was a longing for direction, vision, national vector. However, this longing was not for anything as vulgar or definite as a goal or ideology, but for rather more than the comfortable and relaxed first-term atmospherics Howard put on offer.

Significantly, Howard used his victory speech on re-election to inject a more elevated tone into his public persona. He spoke of reconciliation and of Australia's diversity. But there remains a need for a distinctive vision statement to be put forward. It needs to be one that balances the priorities of an open, modern, internationalising nation and a sense of cultural particularity; one that marries those core Australian values—fairness, love of personal freedom, and even-handedness; and one that exalts the sense of community without lapsing into an exclusive, inturned, brand of national obsession.

These are hardly implausible things to parade before a public that craves a national story, a national script. Yet aside from the Governor-General, Sir William Deane, few in national office seem inclined to respond to that need. It is as if the clear desire of many in Australia's far-flung, disparate communities for a unifying, clarifying vision—that desire for something grander than efficient economic progress so obvious in interviews and discussions of public affairs—was invisible; or as if the Government somehow lacks the confidence to articulate the values and principles that animate its work.

This reluctance to spell out a vision, this suspicion of dreams, has a corollary: almost the entire media and academic elite regard the Government's cultural credentials as illegitimate, and disapprove of its—or the Prime Minister's—core positions on such key symbolic questions as Aboriginal reconciliation and the nation's progress towards a republic. There is a consensus of ideas in the grand broadsheets and high-value media, in professional circles and in the realms of enlightened discussion, and that consensus points away from the world-view of the Government. Such conformity has something about it of sterility. It is uncharacteristic of other Western nations, where rival schools of political and cultural thinking contest and thrive.

Here, by contrast, something like systemic failure holds. It is hard not to draw the conclusion that the sheer lack of argument about national priorities is a grave problem; and that the Government's reluctance to engage with its critics concedes the entire field, and leaves it to silence. It is hard, too, not to feel the intensity of the public yearning for overt debate of these matters; and hard, in the end, not to assume that the reactive, hectic, flag-draped nationalism of Hanson in her prime was a response to the sheer absence of anything remotely like a blueprint for the future of Australia.

In this multilateral, internationally-flavoured time, hybrid, migrant-built nation states such as this one badly need their specific sense, and they need it proclaimed. 'Out there', in humdrum, everyday Australia, that need seems surprisingly acute. Those generations and communities that value the old Australian compact of belief must be reassured that new directions need not cancel established principles; those who cleave to new influences and maps of life need to be reacquainted with the social substrate upon which their creative ferment works; those who wander, delighted by the diversity, between both realms need to have their subtle, intermingling efforts recognised and reaffirmed.

A delicate task, one that requires a leader of cultural openness, with an assured step and a willing heart, and responsive to the half-stated hunger abroad in a nation permanently inclined to speculation as to what it is. The place is here, the moment to unfurl these dreams and prospects of Australian futurity is now. But is there a leader suited for this challenge on the horizon?

3

THE VOTE THAT POLL-AXED TRADITION

After '98, elections are changed forever

Dennis Shanahan

WHAT HAPPENED IN THE '98 federal election? A John Howard-led Coalition was returned to government with a much-reduced majority; a Kim Beazley-led Labor Party performed well enough to restore a reasonable balance in the House of Representatives. That's what happened. Or rather, that was the result.

What really happened was more dramatic: a shift in Australia's political tectonic plates sufficient to change the electoral landscape into the next century and to lend weight to a fundamental change of course in the nation's rhetoric. The emergence of the new political force represented by One Nation, the change in voting patterns at the election, and the disposition of policy debate during the campaign have forced new directions and accelerated old trends that go well beyond the simple mainstream political result.

The nature and even the form of the major parties will change irrevocably. This is particularly true of the conservative parties. The debate, and what is not debated, has already changed. And in the result most directly linked to voting in the election, campaign strategies will change. It is inevitable that after the next election, which may be as late as mid-2002, there will be a realignment of the leading conservative forces of Australian politics.

For 'realignment', read the death throes of the National Party and its absorption into the Liberal Party. The National Party, in the form in which it went into the 1998 election, is doomed. One Nation is not the cause of the decline—it is more a catalyst that has accelerated the Nationals' inexorable slide into becoming a rump rural party on the fringe side of politics, just as it has become an irrelevant option on the mainstream side because of changing demographics.

The merger is not a short-term prospect, but it is a long-term certainty. And it is acknowledged as such by realists within the National Party. But while ever One Nation threatens to take a large slice of the Nationals' vote if that party is seen to surrender the rural and regional interests it has championed, no one in the hierarchy of either the Liberal or National parties will admit it.

Nevertheless, the balance of conservative politics has forever changed. The 1998 poll recast politics in this country when 900 000 people voted for a new, anti-establishment party that was not of the Left. While the Australian Democrats had until the last election dominated the scene for two decades as the only third force, it had in practice voted overwhelmingly with the social-democrat Labor Party. The Democratic Labor Party, which arose from the split between the right and left wings of the Labor Party and the labour movement in the 1950s and early 1960s, had held the balance of power federally in favour of a conservative government. The Democrats changed that emphasis to give the Labor Party the ascendancy or close to it in the Senate from the 1970s to the 1990s.

Then came the swooping arrival of the archly conservative One Nation. And ironically, perhaps, its influence through its impact on political thinking and campaigning could well outlast the party itself, and the overall rejection of its ideals. For of the 12 million Australians qualified to vote in the 1998 poll, almost one-twelfth voted for One Nation in the House of Representatives, and more than that cast primary votes in the Senate ballot for a party standing for restricted immigration and a cascading 2 per cent tax. The influence is not restricted to the accelerated amalgamation of the Liberal and National parties:

the Labor Party too has been hit, not only in votes lost to One Nation but also because of the change it means for political strategy and campaigning. One Nation challenged the ALP on two fronts: in its loss of direct votes to Hanson candidates from traditional areas of support (notably blue-collar males over 50) and, more importantly, in its inability to garner the Coalition's lost votes. There is no doubt that the bulk of major party votes for One Nation came from the Coalition, but there were some direct Labor losses. The party's real loss, however, was in its failure to convert One Nation primary protest votes into ALP second preferences in marginal seats. Marginal seat strategies and preferences will now have to be reviewed by all parties, including One Nation.

The poll also signalled the end of 'the electoral pendulum' as a tool and guide for electioneering. With a significant diversion of primary votes to a new minor party (8.3 per cent in the House of Representatives, 8.9 per cent in the Senate) and a highly unpredictable preference voting pattern, the simple arithmetic of a uniform swing sweeping aside a set number of seats held by margins below that swing to deliver government is finished. On the pendulum, Labor won more than enough of a swing in the two-party preferred vote, 4.75 per cent to take its total vote to 51.12 per cent, to claim victory if a uniform swing applied. It didn't, and Labor lost.

Even if One Nation's vote at the next election drops to 4 per cent, half its national level of support, it will still be a significant factor capable of determining results in marginal seats on preferences. It won't win a seat again but it could prove the king-maker (or breaker) in any number of regional and urban fringe, sand-belt seats. The demographic support for One Nation underlines its threat to the National Party. It is a threat of population erosion and change in the old Country Party's areas of traditional support that has been growing for years. Pauline Hanson has just given the momentum an extra push.

At the 1996 election, the Nationals lost the seat of Murray. Given that the party performed well overall and had reached a peak of representation, the loss was somewhat glossed over. The underlying message was far more ominous, however, because the

Victorian seat had been held by none other than legendary Country Party leader John 'Blackjack' McEwen for more than 20 years and then by another National for 25 years—and it was lost to a Liberal, Sharman Stone. That loss reduced the party's presence in Victoria to just two MPs and one Senator.

At the 1998 election, Stone was easily re-elected, partly because the Nationals could not contest the seat under the Coalition agreement on three-cornered contests not being conducted in a sitting Coalition member's seat. That helped establish a firm base for the Liberal Party in years to come. Even more disturbingly for the Nationals, the party lost one House of Representatives seat in Queensland to the ALP and a Senate spot to One Nation's Heather Hill. In NSW, the party's stronghold federally, the news was just as bad, with former transport minister John Sharp's seat of Hume lost to a Liberal in a three-cornered contest after Sharp's resignation. The Nationals also lost a NSW Senate seat to the Democrats. That's four losses to four different political parties. The Nationals are surrounded and succumbing.

For them, the natural, and probably only, solution is to become 'Liberalised', thereby appealing to the rural and regional business communities and effectively abandoning hopes of moving into the urban fringe territories, which have virtually been lost. National leader Tim Fischer is proud to have stared down One Nation, but for a leader unlikely to be at the helm by the next election the future of a realigned National Party with an even more dominant Liberal Party must be clear.

For short-term political reasons, Fischer will not own to such an outcome but it is inescapable. Another reason for not admitting to the impact of One Nation on the National Party vote—down 2.8 per cent nationally and just over half the Hanson party vote—is to deny the new party oxygen and protect Australia's international reputation. On election night, Fischer wanted the Asian newspapers to carry the story of Hanson's defeat—assuming she would lose as he expected. As Minister for Trade, he could call upon the Department of Foreign Affairs and Trade to issue a press release to reassure our Asian trading and tourism partners that the Australian people had rejected

One Nation. But the department was reluctant to have an officer near the tally room on election night, so the Deputy Prime Minister dictated a press release by mobile telephone as soon as the result was clear. For a trade minister, he demonstrated fine journalistic skills by calling the result and transmitting his release with enough time to reach the first editions of the Asian press.

The Liberal Party is similarly tied to highlighting National Party successes and playing down One Nation's vote as it tries to recapture the voters lost to the conservative fringe group. Party director Lynton Crosby has deliberately kept Liberal response to the One Nation threat as low-key as possible. Although his leader and Fischer have publicly declared that the threat of One Nation is not dead, Crosby is already in campaign mode for the next election, and denying One Nation oxygen at every opportunity. Liberal Party research found that every time Hanson received media coverage, or was put into the limelight by others—positively or negatively—her party's standing rose in the polls. As Crosby noted:

> For many Australians who did not agree with much, if anything, that she said, she earned points for sticking to her guns in the face of constant attacks.

Personal houndings gave her the publicity 'essential to her survival'. Crosby also accused Labor of hoping that One Nation would create a new Coalition 'DLP' that would drag votes away from the Coalition and then remain angry enough not to move back with preferences to either the Liberals or Nationals. The protest almost worked in this way, he believes, or at least it did in safe seats where more than two-thirds of One Nation voters had previously voted for the Coalition and barely half gave the Coalition their second preference.

For the Liberal campaign director, there is a dilemma in all these figures and trends. On the one hand he, Howard and Fischer must belittle the One Nation achievement and declare its polling in 1998 a failure. Yet with more than 8 per cent of the vote, with two-thirds of that coming from Coalition support, it cannot seriously be ignored. The One Nation threat to the

Coalition continues and yet in confronting it, the parties cannot afford to promote it or build on the martyrdom attraction for Hanson. As Crosby told the National Press Club in his analysis of the campaign:

> There remains an important task for the Government in engaging with those fair and decent Australians amongst One Nation supporters who gave that party their vote at this election.

That process has begun with the reshaping of the ministry to pay more attention to regional and rural voters, and in giving National Party ministerial portfolios more of a traditional 'Country Party' flavour with the explicit task of reconnecting with as many disaffected regional people as is possible.

The Labor Party responded to the One Nation result with a similar emphasis on regional issues. Labor's newest frontbencher and former Democrat leader Cheryl Kernot was given the frontline post of Regional Development, Infrastructure, Transport and Regional Services, with a special task of keeping in touch with those who feel so out of touch. But for the ALP, still in opposition, the election result should have more impact on the policies it takes to the next election, and on the tactics it adopts in marginal seats, than on how it performs on the ground in the electorate.

The last Labor campaign had an undertone of mood swings emanating from leader Kim Beazley and federal national secretary Gary Gray, which varied according to how optimistic or pessimistic one or the other was feeling. From the outset, Labor faced a practically impossible task in attempting to win government because it needed to snatch 27 seats off the Coalition. No other Opposition had succeeded in such a task. Although this time it was within the realms of possibility because of Howard's determination to stick to an unadulterated GST, few Labor hardheads believed it likely.

Labor's tax package was sharply defined and aimed directly at its heartland. Low-income earners were the beneficiaries, the 'rich' the targets. The practical effects of the package were to appeal to the 'Howard battlers' who had deserted Labor in the

Coalition landslide in 1996. The rhetoric was designed to attract those who felt disenfranchised, abandoned and 'hurt' by government decisions in the pursuit of globalisation and economic management. Tax credits were directed at those re-entering the workforce; overwhelmingly, the benefits were for those families with incomes of less than $50 000. The 'nasties' in the package were directed against caviar, four-wheel drives—'Toorak tractors'—and exemptions for capital gains tax. The appeal and flavour were plain. The problem was, the package lowered the definition of 'wealthy', and the Coalition was able to score off the fact that many two-income families with an annual income of $55 000 to $65 000 did not consider themselves rich.

And a fair percentage of four-wheel drive owners were Labor voters—especially in those vital marginal seats—as were those who would feel the impact of capital gains tax in the Sydney real estate market. In reaching out for traditional Labor voters, the ALP policy had succeeded, but at the same time it had disaffected potential middle class supporters.

After the election, arguments over how adversely the capital gains tax and four-wheel drive policies had affected the campaign divided the NSW and national ALP offices. NSW was the key state for Labor and given the gains in other states, it was blamed for not getting the party across the line. Ultimately, there was little point in arguing over seats Labor leaders had long thought impossible to win anyway. This sentiment was the source of the strategy for Labor's campaign and the changes in outlook for Beazley and Gray.

Long before the election was called, Labor's strategy was to go for a two-election win—that is, get within reach in 1998 and then pick up government at the next election. Apart from those who openly admitted this approach, there is clear evidence of this blueprint in the party's negative campaign of opposing government policies rather than producing substantially new Labor policies. As the campaign unfolded and the polls indicated that the Coalition and Labor were neck and neck, sentiment and outlook shifted accordingly. Despite no numbers person on the Labor side being able to nominate the 27 seats necessary for victory, hope welled. That hope, so often based on a lack of reality, proved forlorn. One Nation preference factors, Labor's inability to move voters in marginal seats—not just in NSW—and the Government's unwavering message of economic competence meant it could not bridge the improbable.

For the ALP, the challenge is to hold the heartland vote while offering policies that will attract swinging voters in the marginal seats of urban Australia. This is no easy task. Labor should not assume that at the next poll the electorate will automatically decide it has spent sufficient time in the wilderness. The electorate, no matter how reluctantly, has re-elected a government that has promised tax reform, including a GST, and no retreat from globalisation. Voters have demonstrated they are sceptical of easy solutions or suggestions that the world tide can be turned back.

This is not to say that the mainstream parties did not avoid particular issues during the campaign to ensure that One Nation remained irrelevant and without publicity. In what had threatened to be a 'race election', issues of Aboriginal affairs, immigration, foreign aid, competition and globalisation were effectively sidelined by both the Coalition and Labor. The potential for political gain by either party in exploiting differences on immigration—not large in either case—or their records on delivering health and education services to indigenous Australians was ignored. Ironically for Howard, who campaigned before the election about the censorship of the politically correct, there was a tacit acceptance not to tread in the areas where One Nation could profit.

Since the election, he has begun to edge the debate back to tax reform and the need for continued economic reforms to stave off the threats of regional financial crises. But the rhetoric has changed; instead of talking specifically about the need for economic reforms or of assisting Indonesia in a time of crisis because it is good for regional stability, the Government now talks about children being denied schooling, the malnutrition of families and the burden of massive unemployment.

These are all terms the disenfranchised of Australia can recognise. They also acknowledge that the human costs of competition and international financial reforms have claimed greater tolls outside Australia. In time, the 1998 election will prove to be an electoral watershed that changed the shape of political campaigns, parties, policies and rhetoric. Indeed, the process has already begun.

4

FLUNKING LEADERSHIP 1
The vacuum of a vision-free zone

Dennis Shanahan

As AUSTRALIA MOVES TOWARDS a new century and a new millennium, there is an almost universal, decidedly heartfelt view that what the nation needs most is leadership. Electoral disenchantment and ennui have created an atmosphere of uncertainty about our political system, and a lack of trust in it. The 1998 federal election merely confirmed the dearth of enthusiasm about political alternatives. And while the Coalition can claim an electoral win, no party can claim a positive victory—a national negativism towards politics, politicians and party leaders sullenly rose towards the end of the campaign to mar every result.

For all politicians and governments heading into the new era, this raises serious and fundamental questions: How can faith be restored in the political system? How should a sceptical, even cynical, electorate be led during times of difficulty? And have the rules and demands of leadership and political management changed so drastically and permanently that all the old qualities of leadership have lost their currency?

The 1998 millennium poll also accentuated evidence from earlier federal and state elections that raises even more fundamental questions about the electorate's demands for leadership. Does the electorate *know* what it wants from its political leaders?

And has Australia's enviable record of parliamentary democracy and stability led to a dangerous combination of ignorance and apathy which is playing into the hands of highly-organised, populist fringe groups and the marketing managers of the major parties?

The latter questions bear on how politicians should respond to the former; and on how they should shape their leadership to a changed political environment. The election experience suggests that some time-honoured leadership qualities may now be timeworn. Vision has become the prime requirement for a leader, followed closely by the need to stand against threats (external and internal), to exemplify a personification of the national ethos and social values, to express a common touch and to demonstrate political and moral authority. Such qualities were claimed by all the leaders, to greater or lesser degree, during the last campaign, yet the electorate still appears dissatisfied. And cynicism towards parties, politicians and policies—and the demand for change—was not restricted to any one group: all sides lost something, somewhere.

The Liberal–National Coalition suffered an electoral beating, their comfortable 40-odd seat majority of the '96 landslide more than halved, with Liberal casualties in every state. John Howard has publicly declared that many losing Liberal MPs did not blame the GST for the loss but 'other' factors, suggesting that all the conservative losses cannot be attributed to an unpopular tax. If the electorate was not ready to re-elect a Labor government after only two and half years in Opposition and the GST was not the cause for electoral defeat in a significant number of Liberal losses, what was? An unprecedented protest and a loss of faith.

The National Party, despite withstanding the immediate threat of One Nation for seats in the House of Representative, still polled at historically low levels and lost two seats and two senators.

Labor, despite coming within a few thousand votes of victory, failed to convince people outside the ALP's heartland seats that it was ready to govern again. While Kim Beazley was credited with winning the election campaign, voting gains were patchy.

Overall, the Australian Democrats' vote was down, although nearly getting the scalp of Foreign Minister Alexander Downer in the South Australian seat of Mayo will probably confirm a strategy of running high-profile Democrat candidates in safe Lower House seats. Again, though, the Democrats' campaign was essentially a negative one. They wanted people to lodge a protest vote with them rather than with One Nation, allowing them to continue their role as spoilers and negotiators in the Senate. Party leader Meg Lees milked the possibility of negotiating food as an exclusion from a GST for all it was worth, and a savvy electorate responded, turning to the third force in the Senate, as it has for decades, as a check on the main parties.

No sign of an appeal to leadership here. Quite the opposite. One Nation's success in gaining only one senate seat is tempered by the loss of Pauline Hanson's own place in the House of Representatives. From its Queensland base, One Nation remains a smouldering reminder and symbol of disenchantment with our political leadership.

In the face of this rejection, Howard has admitted some regrets, some mistakes and promised to be a different prime minister. Beazley has tried to convince voters that he learnt from the Labor thrashing of 1996 and has adjusted his party's policy accordingly. But swings against the parties, the lack of a swing to other parties and an electorate more interested in sport and holidays than political rhetoric signal an indifference at best, an active dislike for politicians at worst. The answer to this electoral malaise, which was bruited about by both sides during the campaign and by others since, is succinctly put as leadership. A lack of vision from Howard was Labor's common refrain. As Beazley said in his main policy speech: 'Historians 50 or 100 years from now will write of this last election of the 20th century as a contest between a vision for the whole nation, and a plan for a tax.' Howard's riposte was to suggest, with telling effect and sails set close to the wind of personal abuse, that Beazley 'didn't have the ticker' to be prime minister.

Leadership into the future, for national security and to

provide vision, was a constant issue in the campaign. Both sides recognised it as a potent weapon to foment voter dissatisfaction, yet neither succeeded in making it produce convincingly for them. The simple reason is that while everyone yearns for and recognises leadership, no one can define what is actually expected from our political leaders. It is possible to identify where people feel leadership has failed, but suggesting what the electorate actually wants is a different matter. For when the inhabitants of the pond are given the choice between King Log, who offers uninterrupted and unchanging tedium, and Tommy Tadpole, who offers certain and radical change, the vote divides. There is resistance to all change in some quarters, and a lively embrace of challenge in others.

Successful political leadership is the ability to convince, cajole, persuade and even frighten as many as possible from both camps to follow the leader into a consensus. The Coalition Government failed in several areas of changed policies to prepare the electorate before the changes were made, so that the need for reforms and their benefits were never recognised. The debate was lost. Leadership has to mould opinion ahead of action so that decisions which may be resisted but have to be made are launched upon a receptive audience, and not into a hostile atmosphere. Modern leadership has to demonstrate the need for change, not thrust it upon an unprepared and uninformed public.

Recent political experience suggests certain qualities of leadership are taken for granted, or rather are expected to be fulfilled without thanks on the one hand, grievously punished if not delivered on the other. Economic management and delivery of services are why governments exist. But why should voters reward a political party simply for doing its job? It may be enough to keep returning King Log when there isn't an alternative, or at least even a slightly palatable alternative, but it's not enough to keep a government in power if the opposition can offer something better. Certainly, as *The Australian*'s economics editor, Alan Wood, pointed out at the time, the Keating Government presided over an economic recovery but it was a 'voteless recovery'. Poll support for the ALP remained much lower than for the

Coalition, even as the economy recovered and interest rates dropped. Labor's rout was disproportionate to the economic conditions of the time, and to what the Coalition was offering as an alternative. Clearly, maintenance of the economy is not enough. Voters, like the biblical master who gave talents of gold to his servants to use in his absence, do not reward those who merely keep the gold hidden: the kudos is given to governments that use the taxpayers' gelt to do something.

The first Howard Government used its credit on economic management at the last election, but the voters were in no mood to give Howard a second chance merely on the strength of Treasurer Peter Costello's surpluses. The 1998 election also made it clear that a large section of the population believed the Government was out of touch with ordinary people, their experience and their hardships. Rebellious Coalition MPs and One Nation candidates made much of change brought about by competition policy and globalisation. Simple mantras that world markets dictated what had to be done did not satisfy regional areas and demographic pockets of retirees who were alarmed at all change. Which is why party leadership needed to be seen to have a common touch, and common sense.

Labor, the first burned by being out of touch in '96, was the first to be seen to be listening to the people. Beazley's consumption of 'humble pie' became such a consistent and persistent theme that it highlighted a Labor belief that it had to distance itself from the arrogance of the Keating Government. Less than two minutes into his formal policy launch speech in Brisbane on 23 September, Beazley had made three references to 'listening' to the people. It was a theme he returned to in the closing minutes, repeatedly 'listening and learning' from the people 'who have been disappointed (and) hurt by government decisions'.

Disappointment and hurt are the themes of the breakaway One Nation Party, and of the protest voters who feel betrayed by government and other familiar and comforting institutions such as the churches, the banks and the media. This is particularly so in regional Australia where the effects of economic and social change were probably felt last but, because of isolation, were probably felt the hardest. Howard touched on the same theme in his policy launch three days before the Labor campaign centrepiece:

> My friends, rural Australia continues to suffer very great challenges. And I know all of us who've grown up in the city regard the bush and all that flows from it as being permanently part of the Australia that we love. And we feel for our fellow Australians in rural Australia who continue to go through difficult times.

This appeal encapsulated Coalition fears about a backlash from the bush, which had already dealt a devastating blow to the Liberal and National parties in the earlier Queensland state election and had caused rebellion on the Coalition backbench, particularly among the Nationals over the sale of Telstra. Punishing the federal Labor Government in 1996 or the Queensland Coalition in 1998 had not assuaged a smouldering hurt in regional electorates. The punishment continued as One Nation picked up a large percentage of primary votes—and the National and Liberal vote slumped, with Labor picking up only the scraps. On a personal front, the leaders pushed all the traditional buttons yet party performance and individual popularity did not suggest any won a clear advantage.

In the 1993 election, the disclosure that John Hewson had left his first wife and family on Christmas Eve was deemed to have had a negative impact on his image. In this campaign, the leaders of the major parties appeared often with their families—particularly on stage for the campaign launches—and Beazley's close relationship with his two daughters from his first marriage was highlighted in Labor advertising by his mother. Mrs Beazley declared her son a good family man, and that his daughters were his treasures. The Howard family appeared with the Prime Minister on stage as a similarly clear declaration of his embodiment of family values. Hanson's clear distress at her son's suggestions that she had been too busy to take an interest in him was seen as both a disruption and negative to her campaign. Given she was a single mother, an image that appealed to many disenchanted voters, the disclosures may not have been so damaging, although the credence her son's allegations were given suggests that the personal life of the leader is still a powerful symbol.

Voter identification with a leader goes beyond the embodiment of social values to the extent of having a common touch, a feeling that no matter how high a politician may aspire, there is still an 'ordinariness' in their lives that allows them to understand the day-to-day existence of the citizens. This extends to asking an American president the price of a carton of milk, or a prospective prime minister the price of a loaf of bread.

Beazley—clearly no ordinary person—reinforced his own portrayal as an 'ordinary bloke' at every opportunity, while a homely Labor video of him as a part-time grave-digger reinforced his 'common touch'. The same promotional material paradoxically made a reference to his Rhodes Scholarship and Oxford education as a reminder of his intellectual abilities and equipment for leadership. On the negative side, he made pointed references to Howard as being unaware of the impact on people's daily lives of his decisions to cut government services. Howard's image needed little to reinforce a sense of his suburban ordinariness, but he did underline his 'proud state government' education—the first Liberal PM not privately educated. He too made the point, though, that it was a 'selective' high school education. Both just ordinary, decent blokes but bright with it.

However, the honours for the common touch, the representation of the feelings of real Australians, went to Hanson. One Nation single-mindedly appealed to what the 'real people' were suffering and wanted. Wrapped in the same nationalism that had Beazley and Howard talking of their pride and love for Australia, Hanson's support grew on the disenchantment in the electorate and the resistance to change. And her party skilfully manipulated the perception of a gap between the major parties and the people which had been filled by lobby groups and media machines. While he constantly identifies the suffocation of debate by the 'politically correct' and a lobby industry representing sectional interests, Howard was unable to convince One

Nation supporters he would be able to listen directly to the people.

Hanson, on the other hand, made a strategic leadership mistake by attempting to go beyond being a voice of protest and complaint towards assuming a role as an alternative government. The electorate rejected her party's cascading tax plans partly because it had no record and no hope of providing economic management, security or stability. Its leadership had stepped beyond its bounds of credibility, but the party still provides succour for hundreds of thousands of Australians dissatisfied with the leadership of the main parties.

It is the people who demonstrated their lack of faith in the system through their One Nation protest vote that have to be brought back into contact with the political mainstream. If almost one million Australians feel disenfranchised enough to seek comfort in a stigmatised alternative, the stability of our political system is under threat. A permanent pool of discontent cannot exist without damaging the political fabric; and 'communication' programs and marketing gestures are not the answer. The political leadership has to 'reconnect' with the electorate. People need to be informed, truly convinced, of the need for changes in direction, the imperatives of global pressures, and then helped through the process. This is a leadership imperative not restricted to Australia.

Which brings the argument back to what the electorate wants and expects from its political leaders. All parties offered policies at the election designed to appeal to enough people to allow the political leadership to actually govern and carry out those policies. But policy—past, present and future—which involves further challenge and reform is not popular. The Coalition has a mandate, if a grudging one, for tax reform. Its basic offering to the electorate was economic management, based on a record of turning a $10 billion Budget deficit into a surplus, against the backdrop of financial uncertainty in Asia. As Howard noted at his campaign launch:

> I said when this election campaign was called that the major issue was that of economic competence. The major question

to be asked was which side of politics was better able to manage and lead the Australian economy in these difficult times into the twenty-first century.

The Coalition's main vision for the future was its tax reform plan, which was 'good for Australia'. The emphasis was on contrasting Labor's record with the Coalition's economic management, rather than any forward-looking agenda: 'We have given Australia stability and predictability and prosperity in the management of the Australian economy.'

Beazley derided Howard's 'plan' and offered his own vision and plan for an Australia with job creation and equity at its heart: 'Australians can vote for a plan for a nation, a plan for jobs, or they can vote for a plan for tax.' He also appealed to the electorate to take Labor on trust—as he said all political parties must be taken on trust—because he would try to reach an unemployment target of 5 per cent in two terms:

> When Australians elect a government, they do so on trust. They have to. They have to trust how their government will handle the thousands of tiny decisions that go on in the daily business of governing.

But trust did not appear to be forthcoming for an Opposition leader who was seen to be committed, trustworthy, likeable and popular; polling showed that the electorate treated the target sceptically, just like every other political promise.

Apart from trust, the other traditional commodity of leadership paraded in the election was the basic quality of courage. The Prime Minister attempted to turn the great political risk of a GST—which indeed it was and which cost the Coalition dearly—into a positive display of strength. 'I've seen political courage displayed on issues, I've seen political cowardice displayed on other issues,' he declared as he committed himself to the tax plan as the most important reform in his public life. Howard's thrust at Beazley's perceived lack of ambition and 'ticker' had to be countered during the Labor campaign. Again, it was Beazley's mother who reassured the public that her boy 'had grit'. Grit, courage and risk are all qualities clearly sought in the personalities of our political leaders because of their need to deal with unforeseen circumstances. It is also a measure of a government's ability to pursue an agenda, despite voter resistance.

Yet the electorate has refused in recent years to embrace any government so wholeheartedly as to give it an unfettered mandate—hung parliaments, hostile Upper Houses are now the norm. Leaders are shackled by having their agendas and policies nip-and-tucked from all sides, and then criticised and punished at the ballot box for not delivering. If the negative cycle now ascendant in Australian politics, which threatens to solidify into a permanent core of begrudging and reluctant support for our leadership, is to be beaten, it must be addressed now, well before the first election of the new millennium.

Leaders of all parties have to hold fast to those values of public duty, national interest, personal courage and the embodiment of social values that still hold sway with a large part of the electorate and are necessary for good governance. Simple maintenance of a secure economic atmosphere will no longer be enough to hold government. Action leading into new areas, after proper engagement and enfranchisement of the electorate, is necessary to regain respect and support for the democracy that has served Australia so well for a century.

Political leadership is a two-way street: leaders must listen, through their followers, to the electorate. But the act of leadership is by definition not just to follow what is being said in a simplistic, populist fashion swayed by raw numbers and marketing; it is to change the way people think before changing what they think about. The rise of One Nation has provided the major parties and leaders with an opportunity to change their patterns of operation, style and substance, to ensure they regain a relevance in Australian life that can revive a national purpose.

5

THE BUSINESS OF BALANCE
How the corporate world plotted a tax reform coup

Mark Westfield

THE 30-SECOND TV ADVERTISEMENT was simple but effective. Aired over the weekend of 15–16 August 1998, it opened with a still shot of an orange saying to itself 'I hate the apples'. Then an apple complained about tomatoes, and a tomato declared that strawberries were ruining the neighbourhood. Next, a strawberry reckoned pineapples had funny skin, a pineapple expressed horror at a lemon/lime 'mixed marriage'. Finally, a lemon/lime accused oranges of being 'bludgers'. Then the words 'Intolerance in people is just as stupid' appeared on the screen.

The ad ran for a week while the main parties were testing each other and the looming issues of the forthcoming campaign before John Howard formally called the October election on 30 August. It did not endorse or criticise any party or any party figure. Rather, it took a direct shot through lighthearted ridicule at the crude and provocative statements of One Nation's Pauline Hanson, which were starting to divide the electorate and cause considerable harm to the fabric of Australia's multiracial society. Party leaders John Howard, Kim Beazley and the Democrats' Meg Lees were having very little effect with their denunciations of One Nation, due perhaps to the electorate's extreme cynicism towards politicians. The ad did.

'Our research discovered it had had considerable impact,' says the person who devised and paid for it, Melbourne businessman Doug Shears. A noted pastoralist and investor in food businesses, Shears controls the Berri fruit juice company, although he is best known as the founder of the Uncle Tobys cereal and snack foods company, which he sold in 1992 to food group Goodman Fielder Ltd. He won't say how much the ad cost him and his company, only that it was 'seven figures'. It was unusual in its concept, and it was unusual too for a company to commit itself in an election campaign.

Business leadership has not exactly been a feature of the Australian political process. Analyst Phillip Ruthven of IBIS Corporate Services believes this is because companies here, with some notable exceptions, are such mediocre performers that they are in no position to give advice or support: 'Compared with the US where corporations take a "can do" approach, Australia is still more of a "can't do" country.'

Another prominent businessman believes Australian companies and their leaders are too scared to speak out in support of principles because they fear offending their shareholders or customers. Companies can also be accused of self-interest if they publicly support a policy that might benefit them commercially, even though it might also be in the national interest. And they aren't prepared often to criticise governments or opposition parties because they never know when they may have to deal with them. The prime example of repercussions from this was Kerry Packer's mild endorsement in an interview on his own Nine Network in February 1995 of then Opposition leader John Howard as 'an honest and decent man' who would make a good prime minister. His comments drew a ferocious attack from Paul Keating, who went on Nine's Sunday program a few days later to accuse Packer of trying to force a multi-billion-dollar 'scam' on his Government in relation to pay television. Keating used the colourful language to describe a proposal put to him by Packer's interests to have Telstra and Optus limit their cable-laying to regional monopolies rather than force the carriers to undertake expensive national roll-outs.

> The last scam I had run past me that was ever this large, to transfer seven or eight billion from the Commonwealth public purse to an industrial company ... was when I saw reported Murray Farquhar's reported attempts to take the gold reserves from the Philippines National Bank.[1]

Keating backed up his extravagant remarks by freezing out Packer and his lobbyists from important decisions on telephone and cable pay TV until Labor lost the ensuing election in March 1996. The public humiliation of Packer for such a seemingly innocuous remark stunned the business world. It was every corporation's nightmare.

Besides, business is rarely monolithic on issues like tax. In political attempts to bring on tax reform in 1985 and 1993, business was divided. Miners, farmers, retailers, financiers and the housing industry have not been able to agree once the debate on tax change gets down to detail. Accordingly, opponents of change have seized upon the differences between these groups on the extent of variation, the reach of any new tax and definitions of fairness to defeat any meaningful reform.

The 1998 campaign was different. Hanson's divisive racism had provoked Shears into taking her on publicly. Establishment business groups such as the BCA and the ACCI also realised that unless they came out publicly to support and explain two crucial issues of the campaign, they would lose once-in-a-decade opportunities to promote what they regarded as crucial reforms: tax, and the even more complex issue of globalisation and international competitiveness.

Tax has been a battleground twice in the past two decades when Labor treasurer Keating (in 1985) and Liberal leader John Hewson (in 1993) attempted to win acceptance for fundamental changes in the system. Keating's change of heart and subsequent destruction with a scare campaign of Hewson's Fightback! package in the last days of the 1993 election campaign were still burning in the memories of BCA chairman Stan Wallis and ACCI executive director Mark Patterson in the lead-up to the 1998 poll. These two would play business's leading roles in trying to win public support for tax reform, although Wallis and his deputy chairman, John Ralph, kept a generally low profile.

Tax was destined to be the main issue in 1998 from the moment Howard declared in August 1997 that his Government would contemplate fundamental tax reform in the lead-up to the next election. His Treasurer, Peter Costello, ended months of expectation and speculation on 13 August 1998 by announcing a reform package with a 10 per cent GST as its centrepiece. The Government would win the election only if it could persuade the electorate that tax reform was a necessity. If it failed, it would lose. To compound his difficulties, Howard had also made the unfortunate promise during the 1996 campaign that he would 'never, ever' introduce a GST. Businessmen such as Wallis believed, however, that tax reform was so important, and that an indirect tax would more than likely be part of that reform, that Howard would have to swallow his words.

According to Wallis, a former chief executive of the paper and packaging group Amcor Ltd and chairman of the financial system inquiry named after him, 'The present system has had it.' Says Patterson: 'The case for reform is compelling.' Few would disagree, even the welfare and church groups who have fought reform in the past. The vexed issue has always been how the tax cake would be cut. Although it was always up to the Government to make the political judgment on tax, proponents of reform were forced to conclude that unless they did the groundwork and prodded the politicians into action, reform would not happen.

Self-interest eventually drove business into this role. Despite the costs to it of being collectors of any indirect tax, the benefits flowing from a broadening of the tax base would ultimately benefit most businesses. In the absence of reform, the alternative for a conservative government was either to increase the burden on the narrow base from which it draws 75 per cent of its taxation revenue—pay-as-you-earn taxpayers and companies[2]— or to continue to cut spending on welfare. Fear of the alternatives led to the first meeting of big business and the Australian Council of Social Services. ACCI president Graeme Samuel rang ACOSS president Robert Fitzgerald in April, a month after Howard won government in 1996. Although there was greater awareness in business of the need for reform of the tax system, it also realised it would get nowhere unless it won some consensus on the issue from influential welfare groups and the churches.

Samuel suggested a meeting to talk about tax. Their discussion led to the Tax Summit sponsored by the two groups in Canberra over the October long weekend, with ACOSS publishing a paper in which it did not rule out a broad indirect tax. The summit gave the churches, academics, community groups and business an opportunity to air their divergent views. And they agreed that three areas needed further study: the adequacy of the tax base, interaction between the tax and social security systems, and an improvement to the tax mix in a revenue-neutral way. The summiteers also agreed to set up a Tax Reform Forum, which would further examine these issues.

At this point, the ACCI brought in the BCA, which represents chief executives of 101 corporations. Both groups recognised the need for business to iron out any disagreements before going into any debate on tax. Apart from ACOSS, the other key welfare sector group on this forum was the Brotherhood of St Laurence. Not surprisingly, with groups as diverse as these there was considerable disagreement as to the best way to achieve an improved tax mix. The welfare groups did not want a shift away from income towards consumption, preferring an attack on the exploitation of tax loopholes. The forum deliberations also exposed differences between the various business groups.

Once the Prime Minister signalled the Government's readiness to revisit tax reform in August 1997, however, the interest groups were forced to focus on producing realistic outcomes. Fitzgerald said that if tax reform were officially on the agenda, he would rather be part of the deliberations than being sidelined. For business, which was preparing to take the initiative in encouraging the Government to pursue reform and perhaps in educating the wider electorate, it was essential that it talk with a unified voice. The BCA and ACCI called a meeting of all business lobby groups in Melbourne on 19 October 1997.

The 37 industry groups which met in the offices of audit firm Arthur Andersen included retailers, miners, farmers, bankers, accountants and the housing industry. The audit firm's managing partner, Fergus Ryan, who would become a key figure in articulating the business position on tax, chaired the meeting. At this conference, Wallis put to the 50 or so in attendance that if they were to succeed in promoting tax reform, they had to win broad support for the need for change, rather than raise sectoral issues that would only cause division and invite criticism from non-business interests. The meeting decided there was no point in arguing for hard-edged reform—business would have no chance of winning popular support for any change unless the reforms were seen to be fair to the bulk of the population.

It also had to decide whether to break with business's usual role as a backroom lobbyist, and take its campaign to the public. This would risk alienating the Labor Opposition, and it made it even more essential that some form of consensus was won from the welfare sector. If the churches and welfare groups attacked any business tax proposals, it would mean the end of any reform.

The BCA had already played a key role in 1991 and 1992 by committing money and staff to help Hewson and his advisers put together their Fightback! package. But the organisation then stayed in the background while the Liberal leader attempted to 'sell' the reforms to the public. For 1998, however, the business alliance decided to declare itself and publicly promote the cause of reform. In a surprising move, the Business Coalition for Tax Reform, as the group now called itself, appointed the former ALP advertising agency, John Singleton Advertising. This followed an equally surprising move when Labor had earlier ditched Singleton for Saatchi & Saatchi, the agency which made its name internationally as the Conservative Party's image-maker during Margaret Thatcher's British rule of the late 1970s and early 1980s.

Agency principal John Singleton was aware of the wide, but suppressed, support within the Labor Party for meaningful reform, and the cynicism within the party towards Keating's 1993 election scare campaign, given his previous support for a consumption tax. Singleton recruited former ALP secretary Bob Hogg and former Liberal Party executive director Andrew Robb for the business-backed campaign. Timing was critical. Once the group decided to back a campaign to promote tax reform, it needed to create a series of television advertisements before the Government announced its own package. Says Wallis:

> We wanted to convey a simple message that the present system was stuffed, and that it was important the country got a decent tax system. But we felt it was essential to have the campaign finished before June/July to be well clear of the Government's own package. We wanted to put our position, to argue the need for reform, without getting caught up in the party political debate of an election campaign.

Wallis and Patterson were anxious to lift the level of debate on tax. Previous attempts at reform had been howled down by senseless and selective attacks on one element of the reform packages, the GST. In the days immediately before Howard called the election, BCA opinion polling showed far less public hostility towards changes to the tax system, and in particular towards a GST. Once the campaign got under way, however, Labor leader Kim Beazley focused his political attacks almost entirely on the GST. It was a repeat of the scare campaign of 1993, and it nearly worked. As Wallis reflected later: 'Unfortunately, the whole campaign degenerated into a mindless debate about the GST. There was no discussion about the need for reform.'

Globalisation and our national competitiveness is an even more complex topic. It is an extension of the taxation debate, and involves numerous issues relating to national and business competitiveness. Few in business attempt to explain it to anyone beyond their own shareholders. Essentially, it boils down to a debate on where Australia stands internationally with its taxation, regulation and industrial relations. Champions of globalisation argue for less of all three. Critics of globalisation lump it in with the term 'rationalism'. And politicians run a mile from the debate because it so readily attracts criticism politically and from those in the community who would be inevitably affected by any government attempt to reduce tax and regulation. Instead, the major parties spend the greater part of election campaigns making extravagant promises that will have entirely the opposite effect.

Those corporations that dare to venture offshore find a dog-eat-dog environment. There are no rules, and the penalty for failure is very high indeed, as demonstrated by BHP's fall from favour after it paid about $1 billion too much for a copper refining and mining company in the US. But if corporations compete effectively overseas, the rewards to them and their shareholders are huge. Companies like Brambles Industries, Lend Lease and National Australia Bank and their shareholders have enjoyed remarkable increases in wealth from astute investment decisions and good timing. Companies who have been unlucky or unwise in their offshore forays, such as BHP, MIM and Pacific Dunlop, have slumped dramatically.

For companies that do decide to expand overseas, it becomes essential for them that conditions in Australia do not place them at a competitive disadvantage with their competitors based offshore. Yet once their senior executives try to argue for more amenable tax or industrial relations treatment, they are branded as self-interested. The inevitable consequence is that some of the more successful companies are moving more and more of their business offshore, and may eventually relocate completely, as NAB's chief executive Don Argus threatened on 5 November 1988 when he unveiled the bank's $2.51 billion net profit for the year. Argus has become the corporate sector's most outspoken proponent of globalisation and critic of the government. And he has paid a price for this. He is disregarded by his rivals and largely ignored by Canberra, which with typical lack of vision sees him as self-centred.

In a speech to CEDA on 13 August 1998, the same day Costello was announcing the Coalition's tax policy, Argus spelled out the potential costs of governments failing to acknowledge the process of globalisation. As the head of a bank with total assets of $251 billion, half of them based offshore, Argus is acutely aware of the impact on all economies of the trillions of dollars of stray money that trawls the world's markets looking for good returns and/or safe havens:

Globalisation is not optional. For governments, the cost of not running responsible or sustainable economic policies in a world of integrated capital markets can be very high, be that through a gradual but prolonged decline in living standards or by more dramatic events such as we have witnessed to our north in recent times.

The riots in Indonesia and Malaysia and the economic turmoil in Thailand and South Korea are largely the result of governments failing to heed the signals of the international marketplace. Their banking systems were corrupt and lacked credibility; cronyism was rife, and their media largely government-controlled. Australia knows only too well the pain of falling into disfavour in international currency markets, having suffered brutal sell-downs of its dollar in 1986 and 1998. At a United Nations Association award ceremony in New York on 29 October 1998, US Treasury Secretary Robert Rubin summed up the system of 'carrot and stick' meted out to countries choosing whether or not to tune their economies to global capital and trading flows: 'The global capital markets reward countries that pursue sound policies and punish those who do not far more than used to be the case.'

Ruthven, who advises many of Australia's largest corporations, also laments the willingness of politicians to sacrifice living standards in order to buy votes. Australia's slide down the international table of countries in terms of income per capita to number 20 is an irresistible pointer to the failings of successive governments:

> If one looks at the 20 most prosperous countries, 12 have populations less than Australia's. These countries, like Switzerland, the Netherlands and Singapore, are great traders. They are part of the global marketplace and generally doing very well.

Now that the long-running contest between capitalism and socialism is dead, Ruthven says, the next ideological battle is between humanists and rationalists. 'It is a struggle between those who say let's do what works, and those wanting to take a softer more humanist approach.'

In other words, politicians will prefer to buy votes rather

than promote policies that will benefit an economy in the longer term. It will be a battle of the head versus the heart. Clearly, Australia's politicians are tugging at the electorate's heartstrings in their quest for votes, preferring polemical abuse over reasoned debate on important issues such as taxation and globalisation. Unfortunately, those in business who will argue the case for rationalism over irrationalism are few—most corporations would prefer to take their business elsewhere rather than try to reason with vote-driven politicians.

When Argus called in mid-1997 for a relaxation of the so-called 'four pillars' policy of blocking mergers between Australia's big four banks, he and the banks generally were savaged by both Howard and Costello when a rational response would have been adequate. The politicians merely fed the simmering distrust of banks. And much of that distrust has been caused by ill-informed comments by politicians. When Howard and Costello abused Argus again after he repeated his abolition call in November 1998, he noted that the NAB might move its domicile offshore where it could grow.

There was nothing spiteful or malevolent about his suggestion. It was driven solely by commercial considerations. But the warning signals are sounding. And it is doubtful that the politicians are listening.

Notes

1 *The Australian*, 20 February 1995 p. 1
2 Budget statement No. 1, pp. 5–3

6

DEFUSING THE MINDFIELD
*Removing the oxymoron from
Australian intellectualism*

Kate Legge

'OH, HEAVENS,' BEGAN POET LES MURRAY in a postcard to explain that he could not possibly write a piece for *The Australian*'s *Review of Books* while we remain on the Australia Council drip:

> I vowed in public never to take money from that body again because of its political bias, and because it privately called me its Token Fascist. I'm sorry.

American poet Archibald MacLeish once observed 'There is nothing worse for our trade than to be in style' and Murray is prepared to bite the hand which he thinks feeds intellectual fashion by promoting ethnic diversity and gender balance at the expense of merit. In his 1996 *Subhuman Redneck Poems*, he voiced feelings of displacement and public anger over special rights for minority groups in verses written before Pauline Hanson shook us up.

> Our one culture paints Dreamings, each a beautiful claim.
> Far more numerous are the unspeakable Whites,
> the only cause of all earthly plights,
> immigrant natives without immigrant rights.
> Unmixed with these are Ethnics, absolved of all blame.

As literary editor of *Quadrant*, the poet plunged into a nasty feud with Melbourne-based writer and commentator Robert Manne, then editor of the conservative journal, when Murray complained about sympathetic commentary on Mabo, Wik, the meaning of Hanson and the question of Stolen Children. Manne resigned in 1997 claiming Murray had attacked him 'for what he called my opportunistic capitulation to the Left on Aboriginal matters'.

'Not indigenous, merely born here,' Murray harrumphs in a poem. Odd that such a proud mocker of correctness should turn his blowtorch on another for not toeing a line—still, these battles, bloody at times and intensely personal because of our small population, are the stuff of culture building.

How we manage reconciliation on the cusp of a new century goes to the core of our national identity, hence John Howard's post-election commitment to make this a priority. Just as Ronald Reagan was driven in his second and final term of office to push disarmament talks with Mikhail Gorbachev, our PM caught a whiff of posterity after hanging on to power in the 1998 poll which elected an Aborigine to the Senate for only the second time in history. Balanced budgets and economic growth are necessary scaffolding for national confidence, but they do not illuminate a shared vision for the future.

In a tribute to American poet Robert Frost who died in 1963, President John F. Kennedy celebrated 'a man whose contribution was not to our size but to our spirit; not to our political beliefs but to our insight; not to our self-esteem but to our self-comprehension'. The men who create power, Kennedy went on to argue, make an 'indispensable contribution to the nation's greatness. But the men who question power make a contribution just as indispensable, especially when that questioning is disinterested'.

For me, this speech comes closest to articulating the ideal of intellectual leadership. Manne, an associate professor of politics at La Trobe University who writes a weekly newspaper column, and Murray are both practitioners of this honorary public role for the way they prod at our national soul, and in the process contribute to our spirit, insight and self-comprehension. Plenty of players fight for space on the stage of national debate. We have the strident voices of talkback radio hosts venting public spleen and inner-city stress who would compete for the leadership title on the size of audience. Yet influence is only one of many qualifying conditions for this heavyweight crown.

There are tireless activists for different causes, all of them worthy—from Ian Kiernan of Clean Up Australia to photographer Peter Dombrovskis, who with a single stunning image of Tasmania's wilderness awoke generations to the idea of conservation, to scientist Tim Flannery, whose writing has forced us to reappraise our continent and its history.

There are tireless advocates on behalf of the dispossessed— from Melbourne Baptist minister Tim Costello with his campaign against casino culture and hands-on pastoral care in the grit of St Kilda's streets, to Jesuit priest Father Frank Brennan, a veteran mediator between indigenous communities and governments. There's the Dodson brothers, Father Pat and his younger brother Mick, who have served at the frontline of Aboriginal politics for more than 20 years, or Queensland historian Henry Reynolds, who has recast the narrative of white settlement.

There is Malcolm Turnbull, the merchant banker who made a republic his personal mission following the 1988 Bicentennial celebrations, or the former lawyer and entertainment entrepreneur Steve Vizard, a fellow foot-soldier in the fight for an Australian president. There are artists, writers, fashion designers, chefs, film directors, actors, painters, musicians, athletes, academics and scientists working here and overseas to build Australia's profile and enrich our sense of identity. Their work showcases the brainpower and creative talent drawn from a relatively small pool undernourished for the first half of this century, its growth stunted further by distance, the colonial cringe, depression and war. A cultural swagger has elbowed the inferiority complex aside.

Author Robert Dessaix in his recent book *Speaking their Minds*, a study of intellectuals and public culture in Australia, recalls the mistrust of the intellectual in English-speaking societies, an attitude embedded in pre-Whitlam Australia. Dessaix believes we still shirk the label intellectual: 'Any Australian whose name was included in a "Dictionary of Australian Intellectuals" would very likely sue for libel.'

This cultural preference for one-down-man-ship and the desire to retain life membership of the ordinary persons' club is slowly disintegrating. Intellectual capital is being heralded as the most sought-after export in the new century as nations compete for this valuable currency in the global marketplace. Furthermore, the American tradition of self-promotion and assertiveness is being absorbed here as corporate culture rewards individual strengths over egalitarian principles and encourages pride in original ideas.

Australia is coming alive. Only 30 years ago there were so few active publishers in this country that Frank Thompson, former manager of the University of Queensland Press, recalls he had difficulty hiring trained staff and 'there were actually not many young talented writers' looking for outlets. Today, as editor of *The Australian*'s *Review of Books*, I am amazed by the volume of publications produced in this country, from non-fiction anthologies to personal memoirs that examine our place in Asia, the idea of the republic, immigration and environmental questions about sustainable population growth, the recasting of our history from an Aboriginal perspective, with many stories being told for the first time, and the dramatisation of white settlement through explorers' diaries and letters home.

It is impossible to overestimate the importance of these voyages of discovery as evidence of a healthy and energetic national psyche. We are having conversations with each other about the past in a way that will shape our future. Americans have long celebrated their history and agonise still over their sorest legacies with countless books on race, civil rights and affirmative action. We are just beginning this process.

How then does one voice prevail, and prevail authoritatively? Leadership by its nature demands a following. Dessaix maintains that performance is every bit as important as independent thought. In his tick list of what makes an Australian intellectual, he includes an 'outstanding ability to communicate with many publics'. We live in an age of celebrities where institutional voices of authority are losing clout. Hugh Mackay in a recent summary of the national mood spoke of a rising cynicism in the community towards everyone from politicians to priests. People are less attached to church or workplace, political party or even neighbourhood. They operate increasingly as independent corporate units, perhaps more inclined to make up their own minds on everything from personal philosophy to public policy, given new access to information in a wired world.

In a new book called *The Good Citizen: A History of American Civic Life*, sociologist Michael Schudson argues that modern citizens engage in environmental surveillance more than information gathering: 'They are perhaps better informed than citizens of the past in that somewhere in their heads they have more bits of information but there is no assurance that they know at all what to do with what they know.' Most of us skim across the surface of public debate. Samuel Coleridge, who lived in the early nineteenth century, is said to be the last man to have read all that mattered in his time. This is impossible for modern citizens who are time-poor and information-rich, which is why we need public thinkers such as Manne and Gerard Henderson—they can provide us with a moral compass through careful judgments based on solid research, a sense of history and extensive reading.

Manne was an early critic of economic rationalism and distinguished himself during the furore over Helen Demidenko/Darville's book *The Hand That Signed The Paper*, which he condemned along with Henderson for its historical untruths and moral corruption. He subsequently wrote *The Culture of Forgetting* to expose what he found to be a dangerously low level of political and historical understanding in Australian intellectual culture. Since the release of the Stolen Children report, Manne has read widely in the field to familiarise himself with the history of this policy in a detailed and rigorous way. In his newspaper columns and in public forums, he is arguing strongly for a national apology, insisting that the Prime Minister is wrong to present the removal of Aboriginal children as an unfortunate incident in our past that does not carry the significance of a premeditated government policy. Echoing his argument during the Demidenko affair that support for this young writer was born of ignorance, he has urged Howard to read the reports, the transcripts of evidence, the historical documents so that he can properly brief himself on the issue. Here is a man of reason and gentle persuasion who appeals not with strident opinion but by quietly setting out the facts.

In his examination of public culture, Dessaix considers different definitions of what constitutes a public intellectual—from the editors of the *Dictionnaire des intellectuels Francais* and their description of someone who 'offers society as a whole an analysis, a direction, a moral standpoint which their earlier work qualifies them to elaborate', to the American intellectual Stanley Fish, who applies the label to 'someone who takes as his or her subject matters of public concern and has the public's attention'. Prominent Australians interviewed by Dessaix interpreted matters of public concern to mean social issues. And if you look at the public record here, very few of our thinkers stray far beyond the realm of gender relations, race, tolerance, individual rights, censorship, poverty, national broadcasting, land rights and the republic.

Although Manne published a series of articles in *Quadrant* in the early 1990s questioning economic rationalism, this discourse does not occur often enough. We are literate enough in the language of economic reform but perhaps not confident enough to critique the orthodoxy. Reconciliation captures the national imagination. It is a story of people and their past. Unemployment with its complex economic causes fails to stir us in a sustained way. Voters always name this problem as a top priority, but it is also one that then gets dumped in the too-hard basket. Economics commentator Ross Gittins recently called on us to get behind the plan put forward by a group of leading economists to reduce the jobless rate, particularly for young Australians. Can the economists be called to account? Perhaps they are not distinguishing themselves as intellectual leaders.

Physicist Paul Davies has shown how to brighten dark zones of public ignorance in the same way Robert Hughes popularised art appreciation. Science writer Margaret Wertheim seeks to do the same with articles in mainstream publications on maths and genetic engineering. Simple interpretation of subjects previously above a general audience's reach is not exactly leadership, but it's a start. Manne says he takes a long time to get into issues, which is why when he speaks on them it is so worth listening to, and why he is reluctant to debate issues that require knowledge outside his expertise. The economists need to engage a wider audience.

Kennedy's tribute to Robert Frost in the 1960s focused on the poet's contribution to national insight, spirit and self-comprehension rather than the indices of size, political beliefs and self-esteem. In the 1990s, optimism about the future is at a lower ebb—the more practical measures should not be discounted by thinkers helping us to contemplate who we are, and where we are headed.

7

MAKING WORK WORK
Tactics to employ for the jobless

Ian Henderson

IT IS DIFFICULT TO BELIEVE that any credible plan to solve Australia's unemployment crisis would fail to capture the public's imagination. Survey after survey during the past two decades have reported overwhelming public concern at the nation's chronic and acutely high jobless level. The community consistently rates unemployment as the main issue demanding government attention.

Yet with apparently little improvement in the situation despite politician after politician promising to do something about it, voters could be forgiven for abandoning hope. As the eminent American economist Paul Krugman wrote in his 1994 analysis of US economic policy:

> Why does unemployment matter? Partly because high unemployment means that potentially productive workers are not being used, preventing the economy from producing as much as it might; partly because high unemployment breeds persistent poverty.

Australian research compiled by the Brotherhood of St Laurence highlights the even more disturbing impact of unemployment on affected individuals, their families and the wider community. Unemployment has long been accepted as the main cause of poverty yet policy analysts Alison McClelland and Fiona Macdonald have found that its personal and social consequences embrace other equally serious costs such as high levels of homelessness and ill health; family stress and family breakdowns; boredom and alienation from society; an increased incidence of crime and behavioural problems among children; and the erosion of personal confidence and self-esteem.

Just as important for the longer term future of society, unemployment adds to the already alarming divisions between the well-off and the disadvantaged. The crisis suffered by individuals gradually engulfs communities and regions, damaging their societies and ultimately their economies. Economists have contributed some insights into the problem's causes and possible solutions but offer no simple or universally acceptable answers. Moreover, the entire world of work continues to undergo change at an accelerating pace that:

- drives more and more people from full-time employment into part-time and casual jobs;
- abolishes traditional jobs, and jobs in long-established regional centres;
- fails to deliver enough employment opportunities to meet the needs of new entrants to the labour market;
- undermines job stability and security for household breadwinners.

What many people are finding increasingly disturbing is that the revolution at work—for that description fits the rapid pace of change—has failed to make life noticeably easier, even for those in jobs. The promise several decades ago that working hours would be slashed and leisure time expanded as labour-saving technology transformed the factory, the shop and office has proved hollow.

Australian Bureau of Statistics figures show that between 1989 and 1995, the average hours worked each week by full-time male workers increased by 3 per cent, by full-time female workers by 2.4 per cent. Separate and more detailed ABS figures show that between the early 1980s and the mid-1990s, there was a slight rise in the 'ordinary' hours worked by full-time non-managerial employees, with the average number of non-overtime hours almost reaching 38 a week across the full range of industries. On top of that, the average employee was working two hours of paid overtime in 1995.

The picture of a workforce putting in increased rather than decreased hours on the job was reinforced by 1996 Department of Industrial Relations research on enterprise bargaining. The study revealed that 66 per cent of employees said their weekly working hours had not changed between December 1994 and December 1995. More significantly, 25 per cent reported a longer working week while only 8 per cent said their hours had fallen. It mattered little whether workplaces were covered by state, federal or unregistered agreements or whether there was no enterprise agreement in place. What is more, some 29 per cent of employees reporting their hours had increased also said their weekly wages had remained unchanged; another 6 per cent claimed their wages had fallen.

The effect of a long period of change has not been, as many had hoped, that change has brought greater opportunities for relaxation. Nor has it delivered on a promise that work would be shared more evenly. Indeed, many observers have expressed concern that with rising hours at work for those in jobs co-existing with high levels of unemployment, the 1980s and 1990s have seen rising inequality and unfairness in the distribution of work and of work opportunities. A snapshot of the jobs crisis at the end of the twentieth century is cause for alarm. Despite what will be eight years on the trot of steady—occasionally heady—growth in economic output since the 1990–91 recession, official Treasury forecasts suggest the unemployment rate will be stuck at around 8 per cent in the middle of 1999. In the preceding 12 months, employment will have expanded by around 1.5 per cent—or 150 000 people—just fast enough to soak up the influx of new jobseekers entering the labour market. That prediction means some 800 000 people will be officially unemployed: out of work and actively looking for a job. On top of that, you can add in:

- some 120 000 or more discouraged jobseekers who are also out of work but who, because they have given up looking, are not counted as unemployed;
- a further 720 000 who would look for a job if their personal circumstances were more conducive, that is, if they had childcare available, were not regarded by potential employers as either too young or too old, were better trained, etc.;
- an extra 500 000 people who are in part-time jobs but would work longer hours if the chance became available.

In other words, the shortfall between the amount of work available and that needed to meet the demands of the population is in the region of 2 to 2.5 million jobs.

That is one dimension of the jobs crisis. A second is the scale of the long-term unemployment problem. In mid-1998, the number of people who had been out of work and looking for a job for at least 12 months began to turn upwards again after trending downwards for several years. A quarter of a million people fell into that category—the most disadvantaged in the labour market because they are among the least attractive to employers. That figure is bound to increase as the overall job market fails to improve.

Work experience programs like 'work-for-the-dole' give a small fraction of the jobless some familiarity with the normal routines of a job, but offer no solution to the real needs of the unemployed: a continuing job with at least some future prospects and a wage or salary that enables the person involved to live above the breadline. And while the unemployed struggle to find work, the employed also struggle with an increasingly serious challenge: that the jobs they hold are constantly under threat from the rapid pace of commercial, technological and economic change. Job insecurity has been the rising problem of the past decade: it will not disappear as the next century unfolds.

If it is the slightest slowdown in the pace of economic growth that undermines any hope of reducing the unemployment queue, it is the accelerating pace of change that has wrecked traditional expectations that once a man or woman had a job, their main worry was over. Economists see the issue a little differently from the perspective enjoyed or endured by most people. Macroeconomic policy—managing the economy with fiscal and monetary policy—is directed at keeping GDP growth as strong as possible in the short term, at smoothing out the peaks and troughs of the business cycle as far as possible.

In the short term, Treasury's research shows changes in the level of employment are determined predominantly by changes in output and in real wage levels. According to the department's analysis of figures accumulated since the early 1980s, a one percentage point increase in non-farm GDP in one quarter will boost employment by 0.8 percentage points after five quarters, with most of the jobs benefit coming in the first nine months following the rise in activity. On the other hand, a one percentage point increase in wages and salaries adjusted for inflation reduces employment by about 0.3 per cent after five quarters. And most of that impact comes within six months. The lessons for policy-makers are apparently straightforward: to generate as many jobs as possible, keep up the pace of economic activity and hold down the pace of wages and salaries growth.

Two important caveats attend that advice. First, no economist believes they have found a way to eliminate the business cycle that more or less regularly plunges the economy into downturns that end in recession and dry up the supply of jobs. Even in the short term, the best that sound macroeconomic policy can deliver is a mix of good times and not so good times for jobseekers. If policy-makers attempt the impossible—to drive demand faster than supply—they rapidly run into the inflation roadblock as growth reaches an upper limit imposed by the short-term availability of capital, trained workers or some other resources. The difficulty that constraint exposes for policy-makers and their technical advisers is finding a way to lift the upper limit to growth—the problem of the long term that is addressed by microeconomic policy and microeconomic change.

Treasury's cautious best estimate of the long-term trend rate of growth—the figure that averages the accelerations and decelerations of the business cycle—is at present 3.5 per cent. With labour productivity rising at around 2 per cent a year, that GDP growth rate is just enough to deliver the job opportunities needed to satisfy new entrants to the labour market. But a faster trend rate of growth is necessary if enough work is to be created to provide opportunities for at least some of the people now on the dole, as well as for those who would look for work if there was hope of finding it.

Macroeconomic management is about boosting effective demand for labour over the short term; microeconomic reform is about increasing the effective supply of labour by lowering its cost and/or improving its productivity—and hence lifting the 3.5 per cent growth rate lid. From an economic perspective, the price that must be paid for short-term employment gains is wage and salary restraint. The price that must be paid for sustained improvements over the longer term is widely regarded as the threat of insecurity at work. There are still sharply differing versions of both prescriptions, some less harsh, others more so on jobholders and jobseekers.

The final two decades of the twentieth century saw four largely distinct periods of experience on the unemployment front. After the economy suffered a large shock in the mid-1970s from the combined impact of surging oil prices and hefty wage increases, unemployment rose to a 6.7 per cent peak at the start of 1978, before declining to 6 per cent at the beginning of the 1980s. Within four years, unemployment had leapt to a new peak of 10.4 per cent as the economy suffered its worst recession for decades following the second OPEC oil price shock.

Fitfully and slowly, the unemployment rate fell to a trough of 5.8 per cent by late 1989 before that improvement was wiped out by the recession of 1990–91 which drove jobless numbers to almost one million—two and a half times the figure recorded 25 years earlier. The jobless rate rose to 11.1 per cent in August 1993, almost twice that registered in the late 1970s. Since then, progress has been slow, notwithstanding community desire and federal policies to achieve this.

Four phases of pro-jobs policy can be readily identified within the past 15 years. When the Hawke Government was elected in early 1983, its economic policies were built on its

Wages Accord with the trade union movement. One key element was union agreement to restrain aggregate wage and salary demands with a heavily centralised wages policy in a bid to help reduce then hold down labour costs. The aim was to encourage employers to hire more workers rather than force them to pay existing employees more as the economy recovered.

A second element was to put into practice a community-based, publicly-funded job creation scheme that would help ease the pain of high unemployment until economic growth generated by macroeconomic policy started to take up the employment slack. It was understood to be a short-term policy addressing the specific crisis facing the incoming government. And the initial Accord did work for a time to reduce unemployment—between 1983–84 and 1989–90, employment grew by 1.445 million. But the cost was falling real wages and low growth in labour productivity. Those conditions failed to prepare the ground for faster economic growth in the long term, or to satisfy the legitimate needs of the community for rising living standards.

As the 1980s wore on, policy-makers switched to an approach they believed held out the promise of longer term benefits. Wages policy was to become significantly more decentralised, with its focus on workplace change at individual enterprises rather than on economy-wide wage ceilings. The idea was that unions and managers would reach agreements that suited their individual circumstances and covered industrial conditions, pay and issues like new investment and training —commitments by both workers and bosses to boost productivity and competitiveness. Wage movements would be closely tied to changes in labour productivity. If that happened across industry in conjunction with other measures to boost market-based competition, so the argument went, it would help underpin a rise in the upper limit to the rate of sustainable non-inflationary growth. And the potential of faster economic growth opened the way for a faster pace of employment growth in the long term. As Krugman wrote:

> Productivity isn't everything, but in the long run it is almost everything. A country's ability to improve its standard of living

over time depends almost entirely on its ability to raise its output per worker.

If we jump forward to the second half of the 1990s, we find evidence of a steady, apparently entrenched rise in labour productivity to around 2 per cent a year, implying that the policy of emphasising productivity has delivered valuable gains. By contrast with the 1980s, that latter period has combined productivity and employment growth: between August 1992 and August 1998, some 939 000 jobs were added to the total.

Two predicaments dogged Labor's second policy approach: the 1990–91 recession and the fact that many workers were ill-equipped for the new jobs and opportunities becoming available. No plans to focus on the long term could abolish the business cycle; all the gains of the second half of the 1980s and more were rapidly wiped out by the economy's dive into negative growth. Recovery from that was slow, and it was not until well after the Keating Government's re-election in 1993 that policy-makers made real attempts to rethink jobs policy.

Phase three was not unveiled until May 1994 when the Government promised to spend $6.5 billion over four years on its Working Nation initiatives. This ground-breaking 'active labour market program' combined personalised help for the most disadvantaged jobseekers—especially those out of work for at least 18 months—with new job training and work experience as a condition of upgraded income support. It included spending on industry assistance and aid to depressed regions, and had the goal of reducing the jobless rate to 5 per cent by the turn of the twentieth century.

From an economic perspective, Working Nation was aiming to boost the effective supply of labour by improving the capacity of the unemployed to take up new jobs generated by economic growth. Without this stratagem, economists argued, faster growth and a consequent rise in the demand for workers was bound to run into labour shortages that would drive up wage demands. Decentralised enterprise-by-enterprise negotiations could not be relied upon to hold down aggregate wages as the centralised wages system had during the recovery phase from the previous economic trough. Post-1991, the result would be a rising cost of labour and attendant accelerating inflation as the economy picked up post-recession steam.

In economic terms, Working Nation was directed towards lowering the 'natural rate of unemployment'—the figure that represented the effective lower limit that could be achieved by economic growth alone. Economists were uncertain exactly what the natural rate was but agreed it had risen since the 1960s and 1970s and was a barrier to further improvement. Most estimates for the 1960s and 1970s were around 2 to 3 per cent; for the late 1980s and early 1990s, they were more like 8 per cent. In other words, economists believed that without microeconomic reform to better match the supply of jobs with demand, it was impossible to push the rate below 8 per cent. So many jobseekers had been out of work for so long that they were effectively no longer a part of labour supply—no matter how desperate employers were to hire new workers, they were unlikely to find those people attractive options.

Behind Working Nation was the idea that better motivated jobseekers would be more willing to take up job opportunities when they became available, and better trained jobseekers would be more productive when they did so. Provided other markets were competitive, that would also help to restrain the capacity of workers to demand and win earnings increases that would put their employers' businesses—and hence their jobs—at risk.

An alternative version of microeconomic reform of the labour market concentrates more intensely on the wages cost of newly-hired employees. Central to this is the view that labour markets should be as competitive as other markets, thereby keeping the price of labour at affordable levels. Bosses would lift wage rates only if workers delivered higher productivity, and hence the scope for increased profits. Pushing that policy to its limits would mean removing such anti-competitive devices as minimum wage and salary guarantees, and any role for trade unions and industrial tribunals in wage determination. Inherent in this policy is the view that for the unemployed virtually any job, no matter how low paid, is a better option than time on the dole queue. And surrounding the dole with tough eligibility conditions would make it an increasingly unattractive alternative to taking up a job, even a relatively low-paid job.

The Howard Government's industrial relations policies have moved significantly down that path, backed up by a more market-oriented approach to delivering help to jobseekers. The Industrial Relations Commission's role in wage-setting has been reduced even more than it was the early 1990s under Labor, while the capacity of industrial awards to provide a wages and conditions 'floor' has also been sharply marked down. The Government's labour market programs—delivered by its publicly-subsidised but predominantly private sector-provided employment service—more severely limit the help jobseekers can expect than was available under Working Nation.

Whether either Labor's or the Coalition's approach has been successful is partly a matter of fact, partly of opinion. Working Nation was tried for less than two years, during which time a little progress was made in reducing the unemployment rate—from 9.9 per cent in May 1984 to 8.5 per cent when the ALP lost the March 1996 election. How much of that could be attributed to what was a plan with a long-term focus is moot. And whether even those gains should be considered adequate is also a matter of judgment, some five years after the end of the recession. In the first two and a half years of the Coalition's federal stewardship, even slower progress was made, with the 8.5 per cent figure being reduced only to around 8 per cent.

The final federal election campaign of the century saw almost no Coalition promises that would hearten the jobless. Only a small amount of already-committed public sector spending was offered for the immediate future, and an unquantified but certainly minor boost to long-term economic growth from tax reform was proposed for those prepared to wait even longer. Labor's jobs plan fell well short of its ambitious Working Nation programs, despite its severe criticism of the Coalition's flawed Job Network arrangements. And one promise—to aim for a 5 per cent unemployment rate in six years—was challenged as unrealistic. Nearly eight years into the business cycle's growth phase, a pledge of further substantial growth in jobs without fresh policy ideas was deemed to defy reason. On reasonable assumptions about population growth and the labour force participation rate, getting the unemployment rate down to 5 per cent by 2005 would require at the very least the creation of one million new jobs, perhaps as many as 1.5 million.

Recent experience suggests a goal of that size is not unattainable. But the only times anything like that has been achieved in the past two decades have been in the first years of rapid cyclical growth after a recession. Adding a further complication, one of those circumstances included falling real earnings: not a recipe offering hope of sustained public support, regardless of public sympathy for the plight of the jobless.

The latest research and advice of the Paris-based think-tank for the industrialised world, the OECD, offers one sound starting point for a jobs policy for the next century. Even before the global economic crisis that had its origins in East Asia in mid-1997 began to take its toll, the OECD said economic growth could not be relied upon to generate big falls in unemployment. That conclusion served to emphasise rather than diminish the scale of the problem, with Australia being one of only six countries in which structural unemployment—basically the 'natural rate'—had eased during the 1990s.

The other frequently-touted but simple-minded solution to the jobs problem—the abolition of minimum wages—was also dismissed by the OECD. Its research showed that notwithstanding the passionate views of its advocates and opponents, both sides had overstated their cases:

> If minimum wages are set carefully, they can improve the material well-being of some low-wage workers, have some positive impact on work incentives and limit the extent of earnings inequality which has widened significantly in some (OECD) member countries.

The OECD also warned that 'minimum wages are not the solution for family poverty and low family incomes, and they can give rise to job losses, especially for young people.'

In the 1990s, the US has had the best record in generating jobs, although as Australian economists have pointed out, many of those were low-paid, the product of a system with little or no protection at the bottom end of the wages and working conditions scales.

At least three elements are essential in any policy directed to easing the personal, family and community burden imposed by high levels of unemployment:

- Ensuring that the unemployed have an incentive to work, with wages, salaries and other benefits higher than the incomes people receive by staying out of work;
- Ensuring that the unemployed have the capacity to take up available jobs, with adequate help provided to find work rapidly, develop the skills needed by employers, and to move if necessary to where jobs are; and
- Ensuring that employment opportunities are generated at a fast enough pace to meet more than the needs of new labour market entrants, with macroeconomic policy settings designed to drive output growth as fast as is sustainable.

A more comprehensive policy approach must include:

- encouraging employees and employers to seek new ways to boost productivity, by better training for workers, increased capital investment and improved management; and
- underwriting appropriate income, training and other guarantees for workers whose jobs are lost through the commercial and technological change that is at the heart of long-term growth.

Finally, it is difficult to imagine any successful employment strategy that does not embrace:

- wages policy that stresses and delivers rising incomes rather than giving increased prominence to the abolition of established protections for workers already enjoying little protection;
- tax and social security policies that judiciously mix incentives to work with income protections for the unemployed;
- education and training policies that encourage mature adults as well as younger people to upgrade work-related skills;
- industry and regional policies that facilitate rather than

impede efficient economic change, partly by providing generous support to the losers from change; and
- publicly-funded job creation schemes that fill in the immediate and short-term gaps with work on well-justified projects, while giving the unemployed at least the bare minimum of job-readiness training.

References

Fred Argy, *Australia at the Crossroads*, Allen & Unwin, Sydney, 1998
Australian Bureau of Statistics, *Labour Force* (monthly), and other statistical releases
Committee for Employment Opportunities, *Restoring Full Employment*, Australian Government Publishing Service, Canberra, 1993
Guy Debelle and Jeff Borland (eds), *Unemployment and the Australian Labour Market*, Reserve Bank of Australia and Centre for Economic Policy Research, ANU, 1998
Paul Krugman, *The Age of Diminished Expectations*, MIT Press, Cambridge, Mass., 1995

8

Tax triumph is a legacy lost
Why the GST will be AWOL, PDQ

George Megalogenis

If John Howard could have eavesdropped on the Canberra press gallery directly after the launch of Labor's tax package on 27 August last year, he might have allowed himself the sort of smirk Treasurer Peter Costello produces at the whir of a television camera. Journalists the PM considered Labor sympathisers could be heard complaining that Opposition Leader Kim Beazley had made a fatal error in not giving enough tax cuts to the middle class. It would have been music to Howard's ears, a tangible sign that his gamble to seek re-election with a new 10 per cent GST could pay off.

One comfortably-paid member of the Canberra press corps was aghast that Labor was offering him a tax cut of less than $5 a week. With an accusing finger he stabbed at the tax tables: 'I can't believe it, they've really stuffed it up. There's *nothing* here for the middle class.' Another extremely well-paid opinion-setter pontificated that Labor's tax scales would create 'a poverty trap for the middle class'. Fortunately this line did not appear in the next day's paper. He quickly realised that poverty traps apply only to people at the bottom of the income ladder, and it would take a pretty weird policy to force middle- or higher-income earners to give up their day jobs for a dole cheque of less than $10 000 a year.

By middle class, the reporters meant themselves, even though their $50 000-plus a year salaries placed them in the top 20 per cent of the nation's taxpayers. Nevertheless, their private judgments proved a telling omen for the campaign Howard would call three days later. The real middle class—the 30 per cent of taxpayers on between $31 000 and $50 000 a year—appeared to agree that Labor had sold them short. This target group cast its ballot where it mattered for Howard's tax plan on election day. Yet these voters would have received a better tax cuts deal out of Labor. And they had also told pollsters they did not personally support a GST.

Against this background, it would be tempting to read Howard's 1998 election triumph as the birth of a new era of altruism in Australian politics where the electorate placed national interest ahead of self-interest by endorsing a GST. Politics is never that simple. The key to understanding why voters finally accepted the GST after 24 years of tortured debate lies in a coincidence of personal obsession, political opportunity and a badly-prepared Opposition. The GST was not inevitable, despite what Howard and the tax reform cheer squad in business and academe would like to think. There was no pressing financial need for the Government to introduce it in its second term: Budget savings of the first term meant a substantial surplus had already been secured on the back of the existing tax system. Much of that bottom line had been built on bracket creep, where inflation pushes workers into higher marginal income tax rates without their living standards improving, but Howard did not need the GST to return some of that excess revenue to voters as personal income tax cuts. As his tax package showed, the cuts were paid for by raiding the surplus and fiddling with non-GST revenue sources. In short, he could have muddled through for another three years with the present mess of spending taxes.

If Howard had sat on his hands, a GST might have gone off the national agenda for ever because the states would have filled the vacuum by introducing their own services taxes into the twenty-first century. NSW had already broken the seal with its hotel bed tax in 1997. But the status quo was never a realistic option for Howard. For him, the GST was always much more than a tax—it was the Holy Grail of economic reform, the policy the nation's previous four prime ministers, Paul Keating, Bob Hawke, Malcolm Fraser and Gough Whitlam, had either failed to implement, or had vetoed those who tried.

Politicians, like moviemakers or rock artists, crave immortality. As fate would have it, Howard felt the GST would be what *Citizen Kane* was to Orson Welles, or *Blonde on Blonde* was to his favourite singer, Bob Dylan—a shot at making history. Howard and the GST have had more lives between them than Kenny, the kid killed off in every episode of the crass cartoon series 'South Park'. They arrived on the national scene in the same year, 1974, Howard as the new Liberal member for Bennelong in Sydney's inner north, the GST as the main recommendation of the Asprey inquiry into the taxation system, which the then Whitlam Government promptly ignored. Seven years later, Howard became the first politician to embrace the GST as treasurer in the Fraser Government, only to be rebuffed by his own leader.

John Howard has the memory of an elephant. And the stubbornness of a rhinoceros. The nature of his betrayal by Fraser meant the GST would be near the top of his list of political scores to settle over the next two decades. Yet he and the GST ran parallel lives of disappointment throughout the 1980s and into the 1990s. When Keating pushed his own consumption tax option as treasurer in the Hawke Government in 1985, Howard did the unfashionable thing for an opposition leader by offering support. But Keating, like Howard before him, could not get past his own leader. Howard then tried to make a consumption tax Coalition policy for the 1987 election, only to be thwarted by Queensland premier Joh Bjelke-Petersen.

Howard lost the Liberal leadership in 1989, was overlooked after the 1990 and 1993 elections, and again in 1994. By the time he resurrected himself at the beginning of 1995, the GST had become political poison, having cost the Coalition the 1993 poll. Always a pragmatist first and a policy wonk second, Howard declared the GST dead and buried on his return from the wilderness. It would 'never ever' be policy again, he told voters before the 1996 election. Of course, he did not mean it, but he had to become prime minister before he could start finessing the GST back onto the agenda. The irony is that it took a series of self-inflicted wounds in office in the first half of 1997 to give him the excuse to bring the GST out of mothballs. He floated the idea in May 1997, just days after his Government's second Budget had failed to excite the community, elevating it to the status of formal policy three months later after another of his ministers had resigned over conflict of interest charges. However, merely talking about the GST didn't stop the trouble Howard had brought on himself. He would have to wait until his tax package was finally released a year later on 13 August before the tide started moving his way.

It was somehow fitting that Howard, the nation's most underestimated and most ridiculed politician of his generation, could use the nation's most rejected tax to mount a political revival. The GST had brought Howard back into the contest after the traumas of 1997 and the first half of 1998 because it gave him the semblance of a vision. This did not mean the GST guaranteed him a second term: the Coalition's own research of swinging voters showed it rated as both a plus and a minus. It helped return to the fold those conservative voters who were flirting with Pauline Hanson's One Nation Party, but drove the blue-collar workers who had deserted Keating in 1996 back into the Labor camp.

On election night, an otherwise humble Howard boasted he had secured a mandate like no other in the Western world for a new tax. But it was a near-death experience. Internal polling for both sides showed the GST had become steadily more unpopular as the campaign wore on. Labor believes another week would have seen Howard out on his ear, while Coalition strategists admit that a better-focused Labor scare campaign would have been almost impossible to counter. As it was, Labor polled more than 51 per cent of the national vote after the distribution of preferences, repeating the result of 1993 when the electorate last said no to the GST. Against this background, it is clear that Howard's victory had nothing to do with any intrinsic merit in the GST.

He secured a second term because the Coalition had a

superior marginal seat strategy in his home state of NSW. Labor had lost 13 NSW electorates in its 1996 election debacle, 12 to the Coalition and one to an independent. If Beazley were to have any chance of grabbing the 27 seats he needed to form government, NSW had to deliver. It's history that NSW was the only state where Labor did not recover at least half the seats that had defected in 1996, wining just two of the 13 in 1998. Put another way, NSW was the only state where Labor could not convince voters to repeat their anti-GST ballots of 1993.

In the finger-pointing that followed the election, NSW Labor figures, like the self-centred journalists six weeks earlier, blamed Beazley's tax policy for underestimating the aspirations of the new middle class in Sydney's west. The argument went that the upwardly-mobile battlers who previously voted Labor all their lives felt Howard's tax package, with its tax cuts skewed to individuals and families earning more than $50 000 a year, was more appealing. And Labor had also upset NSW voters by extending the capital gains tax net to previously exempted assets bought before September 20 1985, and increasing the tax on four-wheel-drive vehicles. That combination of miserly tax cuts and an assault on the hip pockets of the elderly and the wannabe-yuppies was touted as the reason why the party went nowhere in NSW.

The problem with this self-serving theory is that neither the Coalition nor Labor had received any credit in the community for their competing tax bribes, according to their own internal polling. So it is hard to see why voters in NSW would be saying yes to the GST while the rest of the nation said no, just because they didn't like Labor's counter-offer of targeted tax cuts without a GST. Furthermore, Labor's tax cuts were actually more generous for single-income families earning up to $50 000 and dual-income families earning up to $65 000 a year, depending on the number of children. Labor outbid the Coalition for voters in 12 of those 13 seats in its former NSW heartland. And it reclaimed seats in Melbourne and Adelaide that were more prosperous compared to the ones that did not budge in NSW. The real reason Labor did so badly in NSW was it had pre-selected poor candidates at a time when it did not expect to win.

While the same could be said of other states, it hurt Labor the most in NSW because that was where the Coalition had its best local members from the Class of 1996. The Coalition out-campaigned Labor there. If it hadn't, Howard and the GST would be sharing the dustbin today.

Coalition strategists admit they were able to misrepresent Beazley's package as treating people on $50 000 a year as rich. Labor did nothing of the sort, of course—it still gave tax cuts to those above this threshold but its NSW branch didn't seem to know how to get this message across. Labor could have made itself a smaller target if it had put all its tax cuts in the one basket by extending its so-called family tax credit, rather than trying two forms of tax cuts. The $1.4 billion it had set aside to index the 43 cents in the dollar marginal income tax rate for people earning between $38 001 a year and $50 000 was wasted. The electorate did not buy it. If the money had been used instead to top up the tax credit, Labor could have eclipsed the Coalition's tax cuts for everyone earning up to $70 000 a year. Of course, Labor should also have avoided giving the Government an excuse to run a scare campaign on the CGT. Coalition insiders agree the ALP would have been hard to beat under such a scenario.

All this underlines the extent to which Howard's survival had more do to with his abilities as a political animal, and less to do with the GST. In the end he won because he had a near-record majority to play with following his 1996 success, because he called the election at a time when he knew people would be distracted by the Commonwealth Games, footy finals and school holidays, and because he would have lost without a plan for his second term.

The surest bet that can made about Howard's GST is that it won't live up to the hype. At various points during the campaign, he said it would be a $10.5 billion job creation scheme, a $4.5 billion export enhancement program, and the only way to guarantee public spending on hospitals, schools, roads and police into the twenty-first century. These promises will sound hollow at the next election because the first thing the GST will do is cause confusion as businesses and consumers adjust to the new regime. Any economic gains will be felt only over the long term; but as with lower tariffs, the electorate will probably be none the wiser.

The GST is a necessary repair to the nation's spending tax base, and will help some exporters. When future governments prepare their Budgets, they will be grateful Howard has replaced the narrow, and shrinking, federal wholesale sales tax with a broadly-based levy that grows in line with the economy. The GST reduces the risk that future governments will have to face the budgetary nightmares that confronted Keating after the 1993 election, and Howard after 1996. But that is all a GST is really good for. A GST is not the last word on tax reform. Taxes on spending account for roughly 30 per cent of the nation's tax pie; the other 70 per cent comes from taxes on the incomes of individuals and business. Howard's GST will replace about half the nation's existing spending taxes in dollar terms. It amounts to a major renovation of two floors of a ten-storey apartment block. It is hardly the stuff of nation-building.

The tragedy of Howard's GST fixation is that it risks stifling debate on the wider problem in the nation's tax base—the failure of successive governments to make people pay their fair share of income taxes. No government in its right mind collects more than 30 per cent of its revenue from spending taxes because they impose a bigger burden on the poor. Income taxes do the bulk of the work in funding government services because they can be varied according to one's capacity to pay. But the paradox of a progressive income tax system is that nobody has come up with a model that does what it is supposed to. Higher-income earners invariably find loopholes to reduce their tax bills; governments try to cover up this flaw through bracket creep. But this does not solve the problem, because low- and middle-income earners have that money returned in the form of regular tax cuts to keep governments in power.

Howard's GST will not make the tax system fairer, nor will the personal income tax cuts that accompany it. True fairness can be achieved only if the income tax scales are indexed to counter the effects of inflation. Then, and only then, will governments be forced to make higher-income earners pay more, not less, tax. Howard understands this point, which is why his tax package sought to create the impression that the rich will suffer by keeping the top marginal income tax rate at 47 cents in the dollar. It was a self-defeating gesture because it increased the gap between the top rate and every other rate, giving higher-income earners even more incentive to minimise tax.

The riddle the nation's leaders must solve is how to convince those who can afford to track down the tax loopholes to give up the search. If you asked Howard or Costello as private citizens whether they would be prepared to pay more tax if they knew the revenue went to a worthy cause, they would answer yes. Unlike Hawke or Keating, they do not appear to be in a hurry to make their first million. Howard has said that when he leaves politics, he will do some form of charity work. But neither he nor Costello has ever sought to project their admirable moral codes onto the political stage. Like Hawke and Keating before them, when they face the public at election time, they talk less, not more, income taxes. It is a pity neither seems to have the wit to get off the tax treadmill.

The public stopped trusting the tax cuts they were being offered a long time ago. This, perversely, is why Howard's tax cuts with a GST were judged as more credible than Beazley's tax cuts without one, according to the focus groups used by the major parties to judge community attitudes. Howard maintains that Keating is responsible for the public's cynicism towards politicians bearing gifts. Labor is, of course, still living down Keating's announcement after the 1993 election that one-half of the L.A.W. tax cuts he used to defeat the GST could not be afforded. However, Howard would also remember that the first election tax cheat of the modern era had come from his own side of politics. He was Fraser's treasurer when the fist-full of dollars promised at the 1977 election were subsequently dishonoured. He also held the record for the most dodgy tax cuts when his 1987 election tax platform was found to contain a humiliating double-counting error. (He must have been relieved when Hanson wrested this title with her so-called Easytax, the 2 per cent compounding tax that confounded a lot of One Nation sympathisers, and convinced the rest of the population that she was indeed half-crazy.)

Howard has set himself up to disappoint all over again by over-selling the GST to a tax-weary community. Several commentators pointed out during the 1998 campaign that if the relative fairness of Labor tax cuts could have been combined with the efficiency of the GST, the electorate would have had a decent tax blueprint to vote on. Labor's tax credit plan, which neither its leadership group nor its marginal seats candidates could explain, was actually a smarter method of delivering tax cuts to low- and middle-income earners. It was a tax cut calculated in another way, on the basis of earned income: for example, if someone earned $30 000 a year, a 10 per cent tax credit would be worth $3000. If someone earned more than the threshold, they would get nothing at all.

In contrast, Howard's traditional approach of reducing all but the top marginal income tax rate delivered money all the way up the income ladder. Higher-income earners, by definition, got a more generous reduction in dollar terms because they also received the benefit of lower tax rates on their first $75 000 a year of income. This is why 52 per cent of Howard's tax cuts went to the top 20 per cent of taxpayers.

Labor's failure to sell the notion of a targeted tax cut should not discourage either side of politics from pursuing the idea in the future. Fairness and efficiency have always been mutually exclusive concepts in tax policy—if they weren't, someone would have discovered the perfect tax by now. One option that should be looked at is using a tax credit in conjunction with a minor adjustment to the pre-GST tax scales to bring down the top marginal income tax rate. Cutting the 47 cents rate may seem a strange way to get higher-income earners to pay more tax, but the American experience shows that the rich pay more when faced with a lower tax rate that is not worth side-stepping.

Australia's income tax problems are made worse by Howard's plan—despite the appeal of a new 30 cent rate applying to those earning less than $50 000 a year—because the gap between the 47 cents rate and the related goal of a 30 cent company tax rate will encourage more, not less, of the nation's higher-income earners to hide their wealth. The gap between the top rate and the rest does not need to be closed: it just needs to be made small enough to remove the incentive for people to call themselves companies, or to use and abuse trusts. It would be a cheaper and more realistic sweetener for high-income earners than Howard's approach. The tax credit could thus be used in this context to deliver a bigger tax cut to people on low and middle incomes.

Beazley's tax cuts would have cost $7.22 billion by 2001–2, roughly half Howard's $13.52 billion extravagance. The tax credit component of Beazley's policy was worth just $5.8 billion. Imagine if Beazley had been in Howard's shoes and had $13 billion to play with. Imagine if $10 billion of that war chest was poured into the tax credit, and the remaining $3 billion was used to slash the 47 cent rate, and abolish the pesky 43 cent tax band. A tax credit of that magnitude would be a bonanza for the 50 per cent of taxpayers on less than $31 000 a year, and a boon for the middle class, while the traditional tax cut to the top rate would leave the well-off with less reason to dodge than they have at the moment.

The 1998 election showed how a polarised tax debate can deliver the worst of all worlds. Howard won with the superior indirect tax policy but his income tax cuts were fundamentally flawed. If he had had the cunning to steal Beazley's tax credit, there is no doubt he would have won with a sufficient buffer to make a third term seem a good bet. On the other hand, if Beazley had adopted a GST pitched at, say, 5 per cent, he could have doubled his tax credit and gone just as close to winning, if not falling over the line.

Tax reform is about trade-offs. It is also about courage. The GST was not the most daring or desirable device Howard could have tried. Aside from fairer tax cuts, several other reforms need to be tackled. The most pressing is to end the tax-free status enjoyed by the family home under the capital gains tax. This may be the last thing the cowards in Canberra would want to contemplate following Labor's CGT nightmare in 1998, but it is a feasible option, provided the nation's leaders think beyond their own narrow political experience. The trick is to use the revenue raised by a CGT on the family home, along with some of Howard's GST, to replace the existing tax on housing—namely state stamp duties. This way, the family home would be taxed in the hand of the seller, who can afford to pay, rather than the buyer. Of course, the deep-seated greed in the electorate would have to be addressed by ensuring that only homes bought after the start date would be liable for CGT once they are on-sold. That way the winners, future buyers, would equal the losers—future sellers. The party that introduces such a measure need not fear a voter backlash.

Howard should not be asking himself what people would have thought about him 10 or 20 years ago if he had been able to implement the GST when it was still a relatively fresh concept. He should be questioning whether the GST will be important enough in 10 or 20 years from now to secure him the respectable place in the nation's history he aspires to. Is a new tax as momentous an event as, say, pulling Australian troops out of Vietnam, or introducing sweeping social reforms in health and education at home? Will the opinion polls in 10 or 20 years from now show the GST is as popular as, for example, Medicare? The answer is no. That doesn't mean a GST is a bad policy—it is just a disappointingly small legacy for a politician who has outlived all his enemies, both Labor and Coalition, after almost three decades in public life. When the achievements of the Hawke and Keating Governments are listed, the capital gains tax and the fringe benefits tax—two reforms that have made the income tax system fairer—are the last things to roll off one's lips.

In any case, there is every danger that Howard's GST will be a little out of date by the time it is due to start on 1 July 2000. The Europeans, who have had GST-style taxes for a decade longer than Australians have been thinking about them, are already looking for a new way to tax spending. The reason is they are having fits about the Internet. The boom in electronic commerce is hurting them because GSTs are the first taxes to be avoided when a good or a service is delivered directly into the home via a personal computer.

The GST that Australians will be getting just before the

Sydney 2000 Olympics is not what the world's developed economies have been looking at to tax purchases over the Internet. It is prehistoric when judged in cyber years. It assumes businesses with physical addresses will have an incentive to play by the rules because they will want to claim the refunds on taxes paid on their supplies. But Internet businesses can locate anywhere in the world. They also carry very little input taxes because they do most of their own value adding. The spending taxes of the future will apply directly to consumers, possibly through their credit cards.

One way or another, the Internet will make Howard's GST redundant. Hopefully that will be sooner rather than later because it will force the nation's leaders to look seriously at fixing the remaining eight floors of the nation's tax structure.

9

IS WEALTHFARE A SOCIAL HEALTH RISK?
The side-effects of a rationalist prescription

Mike Steketee

AUSTRALIANS ENTER THE NEW MILLENNIUM professing as strongly as ever that they live in an egalitarian society but showing every sign of moving further away from it. In truth, strong as the ethos of the classless society may be, it has long been driven more by myth than reality. The distribution of resources between free settler and convict in the last century, between landholder and tenant extending into this century, and more recently between blue-collar workers and employees in the new information economy, consistently has been more uneven than that in other developed countries, apart from the US and Britain.

Globalisation and the Australian response to it in the form of economic liberalisation have widened the income gap further since the early 1980s. Government taxation and welfare policies have counteracted this trend for the lowest income earners but have not stopped many in the middle being left behind. The overall thrust of policies in the social as well as economic areas suggests the gap is likely to keep growing. In welfare policy, the emphasis is on greater self-provision, less passive government assistance, more stress on the obligations of the recipient and the privatisation of what for most of the past half-century were considered core government responsibilities, including retirement income and employment services. In future, Australia's flat rate pension system will be replaced progressively by a superannuation scheme that relates future pension payments to present earnings. Private provision is being increasingly encouraged in education and health.

Arguably, the benefits of such trends are a more dynamic, entrepreneurial economy accompanied by faster growth. But they also have the potential to produce a two-tier system: an expensive, high-standard private stream of superannuation and health care, and a basic, residual government system. The question is whether we are prepared as a nation to use some of the faster growth and greater efficiency that economic liberalisation has delivered to help those who have missed out on the benefits. This could be a worthwhile investment in purely economic terms, quite apart from any social obligations we may feel. Research by the OECD, the World Bank and the United Nations Development Program have all pointed to high levels of inequality being associated with slower rates of economic growth.[1] Entrenched unemployment extending over generations leads not just to an underclass, alienated and excluded from the rest of society, but also to a reduction in the available supply of labour and therefore less capacity for growth. Higher unemployment means not just more unhappiness but also higher health costs and higher crime rates.

So comprehensively has the attention of Australians been captured by the magnitude of change in economic policy in recent decades that the revolution in social policy has passed relatively unremarked. Partly that is because the impact of many of the changes is long-term. Yet revolution by stealth is no less significant in terms of its end results.

In welfare policy, reforms are directed at a shift from an entitlement mentality to one of welfare as a last resort—or as Social Security Minister Jocelyn Newman puts it in more politically loaded terms, to welfare as a safety net rather than a hammock. The change in attitude the Howard Government is seeking is no better illustrated than in its campaign against welfare fraud and the introduction of work-for-the-dole for young unemployed. There are few aspects of the administration of social security to which it has directed more public attention. And if it is an emphasis which casts doubts in the public mind about the legitimacy of welfare benefits generally, then many in the Government believe that to be healthy.

During the 1998 election campaign, the Liberal Party ran television advertisements boasting that the Government was saving $46 million a week by cracking down on social security fraud. Annualised, this represents 4.5 per cent of total Commonwealth spending on social security. The vast bulk of the money recovered was overpayments, partly attributable to the complexity of the welfare system and partly balanced by underpayments. Compared to the 570 889 people overpaid in the period between July 1996 and March 1998 and the 7.8 million receiving some kind of welfare benefit, just 4471 were convicted of fraud.

The Government's introduction of work-for-the-dole and the announcement in the last campaign of its expansion satisfies community sentiment that taxpayers' money should not be used to support indolent lifestyles, particularly for the young. But it also borrows from the labour market programs instituted by the Keating Government. These incorporated the principle of mutual obligation for the long-term unemployed, whose benefits could be reduced or withdrawn if they refused to participate in training, work experience or wage subsidy programs.

Only in health did the idea of a government service as a universal entitlement advance with the introduction of Medibank by the Whitlam Government, and its reinstatement through Medicare by the Hawke Government. It was not until the Coalition committed itself in the 1996 election to retain Medicare—and substantially kept this promise—that a universal, government-funded health insurance system won bipartisan support.

Yet even here there are increasing moves towards private sector involvement, including taxation 'carrots and sticks' for taking out private health insurance and the building and operation of hospitals. There are even signs of it in the administration of Medicare, with the appointment of Barry Catchlove as chairman of the Government's Health Insurance

Commission while he remains an executive of Australia's largest private health care group, Health Care of Australia.

These are changes driven by ideology, but also by economic, social and demographic change, and the pressures they create on areas of the Budget. The oft-decried short-term perspective that democratic politics encourages is challenged by decisions such as the Keating Government's introduction of compulsory superannuation and the Howard Government's nursing home levy, both of which address Budget issues which, while they have been building up for some time, threaten to become serious not only in coming years but in coming decades.

The Howard Government allocated $53 billion to social security and welfare in the 1998–99 Budget and another $22 billion to health. They are by far the two largest items in the Budget, dwarfing areas like defence ($11 billion) and education ($9.5 billion)—although the states are responsible for a substantial portion of the funding in health and education. Together, welfare and health spending make up 53.5 per cent of the Commonwealth Budget. They are also the fastest growing areas of expenditure: 25 years ago, welfare was 20 per cent of the Budget; by the end of 1998–99 it will have almost doubled to an estimated 38 per cent. Since the introduction of Medicare in 1984, health spending has increased from 9.5 per cent of Budget spending to almost 16 per cent for 1998–99.

A quarter of a century ago, governments treated welfare predominantly as a right—a common pool to which Australians contributed through taxation and from which they were entitled to draw the aged pension and other forms of income support to tide them over in periods of temporary misfortune. The Whitlam Government came to power in 1972 promising to remove the means test for aged pensions. As Gough Whitlam put it:

> I was opposed to a means test on old age pensions because of the assumption implicit in the test that pensions were handouts for the so-called improvident poor. This concept had no place in a modern and wealthy community . . . Moreover, I

felt that Australians had to acknowledge freely and generously that those who had laid the foundations for national prosperity were entitled to share in that prosperity.[2]

This thinking was in line with that of most Western countries: a universal welfare system was the mark of a civilised society, one reinforced by the fact that all citizens had a stake in it. It was the difference in attitude between welfare as the entitlement of all citizens and its provision as an act of charity. The Whitlam Government's first Budget removed the means test for pensioners aged 75 and over. The succeeding Fraser Government reversed that measure, and did not proceed with the second step announced in the last year of the Whitlam Government in 1975—removing the means test for all those over 69.

The Hawke and Keating governments that followed never returned to the principle of universality, except in health. Despite adherents on the political Left, it came up against competing forces. In the short term, the fashion of small government in the era of Margaret Thatcher and Ronald Reagan and the encroachments of internationalisation on domestic policy-making held sway. In the longer run, there was the increasing cost of a welfare system which was changing in nature. As a result, Australia's social security system, with its tightly-targeted assistance at modest levels to those most in need, ended up as a major departure from the universal, insurance-based schemes operating in Europe and the US. These were also becoming an increasing challenge to fund as demands on withdrawals increased with an ageing population.

In terms of economic management, Australia's failure to introduce a universal welfare system was a blessing. Apart from demographic change, unemployment and other welfare benefits have been transformed from temporary 'tiding-over' payments to semi-permanent benefits for hundreds of thousands of Australians. Twenty years ago, long-term unemployment was defined as being out of work for six weeks or more; today, it means being without a job for at least a year. In September 1998, there were 251 900 people in that category—more than the total out of work a quarter of a century earlier. In 1973,

10 per cent of the population relied on government benefits of some sort as their main source of income; now the figure is around 25 per cent.

There are two ways to look at these figures. On one level, they represent a dead-weight on the economy and society, with high unemployment and an ageing population meaning an ever-shrinking proportion of people in work supports an ever-rising proportion dependent on government for income. One way to tackle this is to adopt a much harsher attitude towards welfare recipients, such as stopping payments after a specified period, as applies in the US and as the Coalition advocated when John Hewson was its leader.

The other perspective is that wholesale economic restructuring in the name of increased productivity and higher national income has paid scant attention to the victims of change, and that the social security system is at least providing them some compensation. Economic liberalisation and globalisation have produced gains but they have been spread unevenly. Australia has a growing income gap, one now wider than in most developed countries apart from the US and Britain. In this context, government benefits financed from the taxation of the winners from economic change can be seen as a means of redistributing some of the gains to the losers.

Benefits increasingly have become a supplement for Australians who are between jobs more frequently and for longer periods, for lower wage earners and for families raising children, who are more likely to be worse off. A breakdown of the Budget figures does not support populist rhetoric that 'bludgers' are responsible for blowing out the welfare budget. In the 10 years to 1998–99, overall Budget outlays, including the component for inflation, increased by 70 per cent (although the economy as a whole grew faster, with Budget spending as a proportion of GDP falling from 25.9 per cent to 24.6 per cent over the period). By comparison, spending on social security and welfare rose by 123 per cent.

Within this, unemployment and sickness payments grew by a well-below-average 79 per cent to an estimated $6.6 billion for 1998–99. Assistance to the aged doubled to $15.7 billion, while help for people with disabilities rose by 146 per cent to $6.7 billion. By far the largest increase was in help for families with children, which went up 259 per cent to $14.8 billion. The largest components of that are family allowances, which for families with one child are paid on incomes up to $66 000, and parenting payments for caring for children under 16 years.

The latter is a particular priority of John Howard: he sees it not as a welfare payment primarily but as an encouragement to one spouse to stay at home in the early child-raising years. This reinforces the point that the social security system has moved a long way beyond providing for those who temporarily have fallen on hard times, let alone supporting the indolent. Nevertheless, there has been increasing focus on the undesirability of so-called passive welfare. The developing income gap is not simply the result of wages rising for those at the top and falling or remaining static at the bottom. New divisions have developed between households where both adults work, with usually at least one on a relatively high income, and those where both adults are unemployed. Australia in 1998 had 350 000 families with no employed parent.

Long-term unemployment is bringing with it increasing evidence of inter-generational unemployment, where children of unemployed parents are less likely to work than those in working households. These are the manifestations of an underclass which, on overseas evidence, particularly in the US, can lead to a marginalised, alienated portion of the population, accompanied by increasing crime and health problems. Some argue that such a phenomenon is unlikely to develop on a significant scale in Australia because of the more ready availability of welfare. But welfare payments are far from generous—single unemployed over 21, for example, receive a maximum of $323.40 a fortnight. While this may encourage people to seek work (which they are compelled to do anyway to continue receiving unemployment benefits), means tests have the opposite effect.

Much recent debate about incentives has concentrated on the marginal tax rates facing higher income earners. This was one justification put forward for the reduction in the top marginal rate from 60 per cent to the current level of 48.5 per cent, including the Medicare levy, under tax reforms introduced by Paul Keating as treasurer in 1985. The much more serious problem is the higher marginal rates facing low-income earners because of the interaction of the tax and social security systems.

The inevitable by-product of a welfare system targeted to those most in need is that benefits have to be withdrawn as incomes rise. For the unemployed, every dollar earned above $60 a fortnight results in the government payment being reduced 50c; for those earning more than $140 a fortnight, the reduction is 70c. Combined with an income tax rate of 20 per cent on incomes above $5401, this can mean very little additional income for those moving from welfare to work, particularly when travel and other costs are taken into account.

Where households receive multiple benefits, including family payments, the effective marginal tax rate can be more than 100 per cent. The tax package the Coalition took to the last election proposed an easing of the income test for family allowances. Combined with lower income tax rates, this will reduce these high rates with, for example, a drop from 85.5 per cent to 61.5 per cent over a range of household income. This is still substantially higher than the top income tax bracket.

The largest step towards privatisation of welfare came with the Keating Government's introduction of compulsory superannuation which, under the Coalition Government's revisions, is due to reach 9 per cent of income by 2002. In few other countries has the private sector been given such a large role in future retirement incomes, although both the US and Britain are looking at options for moving towards private pension schemes. The logic is to boost retirement income in a way that does not impose on taxpayers a major burden, and one which is growing rapidly with the ageing of the population. The trade-off is between the promise of greater returns and efficiency from private entrepreneurship and the increased risks and reduced guarantees about the security of funds.

Superannuation fund assets grew by 13.1 per cent in 1997–98, and increased seven-fold to $359 billion in the seven years to June 1998. This is a relatively small amount beside federal government projections of $1500 billion by 2020. Although a large part of this saving is required by legislation, it continues to attract tax concessions which Treasury has estimated as costing $6 billion a year and which favour higher income earners. On one estimate, an income of $60 000 attracts an annual superannuation tax concession of $1200, compared to $400 on an income of $30 000. Even with the 15 per cent surcharge phased in on incomes above $70 000, the value of tax concessions for $80 000 worth of income is more than twice that on $30 000.[3]

In the long term, the Government saves on pension costs by replacing them with superannuation contributions made by employers on behalf of their employees, supplemented by tax concessions. The burden for this substitution falls most heavily on lower income earners, who will receive a future retirement income—effectively financed by a levy on their income—and which will mostly replace the pension they would have received funded by taxpayers. While they benefit from the tax concessions, they do so to a far smaller extent than higher income earners, many of whom would not in any case have qualified for a full pension under the means test provisions.

Nowhere has the tension between conservative ideology and political pragmatism been greater than in health policy. Against the fierce resistance of the medical profession, private hospitals and the private health funds, the Whitlam Government introduced Medibank as a government-funded national health insurance system to provide free access to public hospitals and to general practitioners who bulk-billed. The Coalition promised to retain Medibank in the 1975 election but emasculated it over eight years by handing insurance back to the private health funds. The Hawke Government reintroduced national health insurance under the name of Medicare in 1984. But it was not until the 1996 election, 21 years after Medibank's introduction and almost half a century after the National Health Service was established in Britain, that the Liberal and National parties committed themselves, in the words of John Howard three days before the 1996 election, to 'fully retain the Medicare system

. . . bulk-billing and community rating' (under which private health funds are required to spread the risk of illness among all fund members by charging them the same premiums). It was a promise made in the context of an election strategy designed to minimise controversy and differences with Labor; above all, it acknowledged the popularity of Medicare. Unlike the Fraser Government after 1975, the Howard Government largely honoured its promise.

Of course, widespread public support for Medicare is based on its provision of largely 'free' services. It also acknowledges that the quality of services provided is generally high, even in public hospitals, which attract complaints because they are the only part of the health sector where costs are controlled directly by a cap on funding, creating waiting times for non-urgent operations. The ultimate test of the success of a health system is the health of the population. The Australian Institute of Health and Welfare, a government-funded but independent research body, concluded last year:

> Australia is one of the healthiest countries in the world and Australians are becoming even healthier. This is shown by declining death rates, increasing life expectancy, a low rate of life-threatening infectious diseases and, for most people, ready access to health care when needed.

Male life expectancy increased from 59.2 years in the 1920s to 75.4 years in 1996, for females from 63.3 years to 81.1 years. The male mortality rate for coronary heart disease fell from 497 per 100 000 population in 1968 to 196 per 100 000 in 1996.[4] Such figures suggest that despite periodic cries of crisis in the health system and examples of individual failings, it is producing impressive outcomes overall.

The Coalition's predisposition towards the private sector, reinforced by the strong lobbies of doctors, private health funds and private hospitals, has seen attempts to dismantle the national health system in the past and contributed to the encouragement the Government is giving the private sector now. But evidence that private medicine means better health is elusive. There is clear evidence it means more expensive health. In the US, with by far the largest private health sector in the world, total health spending rose from 8.5 per cent of GDP in 1976 to 14.2 per cent 20 years later. In Australia, it increased from 7.5 per cent to 8.5 per cent in the same period. This raises questions about the Howard Government's large-scale subsidisation of private health insurance, most recently by promising before the last election a 30 per cent rebate at a cost of around $1.5 billion a year. No other private industry has been the beneficiary of such government largesse. If it works—and previous government incentives have not—it will send more patients to private hospitals and reduce pressure on public hospitals. Yet what is the logic of the community paying more for private health as patients than they save in government funds as taxpayers?

One argument is that a robust private sector supports the public sector through competition, interaction and innovation; that this, for example, is the main reason for the superiority of the Australian health system over the National Health Service in Britain, where the private sector plays an insignificant role. It is not clear, however, what share of the health market the private sector needs for this to apply. At 31 per cent, the private sector in Australia is the second largest after the US. Dr Con Costa of the Doctors' Reform Society argues that Canada, with a national health insurance scheme very similar to Australia's Medicare, provides a standard of health care at least as good with virtually no private sector involvement other than dental and optometrical services.[5]

Despite the decline in private health insurance since the introduction of Medicare, the private sector's share of total health expenditure in Australia has actually increased from 28 per cent in 1984. One factor for this is the shift of private patients from public to private hospitals under incentives provided in Commonwealth–state health agreements. Yet this has done nothing to stem the demands for more help for the private sector. One motivation for such campaigns is that private medicine is much more lucrative for the medical profession. Specialists working in public hospitals typically receive a sessional payment based on a period of work. The same doctors treating private patients, whether in public or private hospitals, are free to charge what they like. The difference can be dramatic. Research based on 1993 figures showed that for a 3½-hour session in a NSW public hospital, an ophthalmologist was paid $474.25 for treating public patients. With laser technology, such a specialist may be able to perform as many as four cataract operations during this period. For private patients, the scheduled fees for the two procedures involved in the cataract operation totalled $855. But there is no compulsion to hold charges to this level and many charged $900 or more for the operation. This meant that, for three private patients treated in a public hospital, the specialist would earn not $474.25 but $2700 or more.[6]

Private health insurance is an area which, in theory, can benefit from competition compared to the single government insurer. In practice, health funds are highly regulated, which means competition and cost efficiencies are limited. Administrative costs for health funds represent 12.7 per cent of the benefits they pay out, compared to 3.8 per cent for Medicare. Neither this nor the much higher cost of private health has stopped the Howard Government directing increasing resources to private health insurance. The proportion of Australians holding private insurance fell from 50 per cent in 1984 to 30.6 per cent in June 1998. An important factor was average premium increases of an average 9.8 per cent per annum between 1989–90 and 1995–96, compared to inflation of 2.9 per cent a year. As the Industry Commission pointed out in a 1997 report, private insurance is in an ambiguous position, both replacing public funding and insuring for services not covered under Medicare.[7]

The decline of private health insurance also is a product of the success of Medicare: more people prefer to rely on the public system, particularly if they are young and relatively healthy. The most effective remedy is one the Government has not been prepared to tackle—abolishing community rating, under which the funds cannot charge different rates according to risk. Cheaper premiums for younger and healthier patients would help attract them back to private insurance. It also would mean higher rates for older patients who draw the most benefits. The Government would want to protect existing members by introducing such a system only for new subscribers. In the long run it would help the funds compete on their merits.

The Government has been trying to address another disincentive to people keeping private insurance—the extra bills they face when treated as private patients. While some agreements have been reached between doctors, funds and private hospitals to limit additional charges and tell patients what these will be beforehand, the Government failed before the election to conclude negotiations on a scheme under which it would raise the Medicare rebate from 75 per cent to 100 per cent of the scheduled fee for private patients, and private health funds would cover an additional 25 per cent on average.

Despite the best intentions of economists, nothing approaching a competitive market operates anywhere in health. Demand does not necessarily respond to price. And unlike consumers buying products in a supermarket, patients lack information on which to base choices between treatments and often between doctors. The evidence is that the demand for medical services is driven more by the number of doctors than by the absence of upfront charges.

In the 12 years to 1996–97, the number of GPs increased by 61 per cent in metropolitan areas (as measured by full-time equivalents). After discounting for population growth, the increase was 37 per cent.[8] In 1996, the Australian Medical Workforce Advisory Committee estimated there was an oversupply of 2500 GPs in capital cities but a shortage of 500 in rural areas. The Finance Department has estimated that every additional doctor adds between $176 000 and $220 000 to the cost of the health system, suggesting that the net surplus nationally is adding about $400 million to health costs.

The ability of doctors to generate their own income follows logically from charging on a fee-for-service basis, creating an incentive to over-service. Patients do not exercise effective choice because they generally feel compelled to do what their doctors tell them. According to an OECD review of the Australian health care system, 'The driving force behind growth in health expenditure in Australia is volume growth in the fee-for-service sectors . . . [and] considerable scope remains to narrow the ambit of such payment arrangements'.[9] Thus, while Australia has had more success than the US in controlling health costs, the structure of health charging means government funding of large parts of the system is open-ended. In the 21 years to 1996–97, total spending on health services more than doubled after taking inflation into account. The AIHW has calculated that 32 per cent of the growth was attributable to population increase and another 22 per cent to the ageing population.

The slowest growth has been in public hospitals, the one area in which governments can cap spending. In the 11 years to 1995–96, real spending on public hospitals increased by 40 per cent, compared to 131 per cent for private hospitals. The other fastest growing areas of government spending have been where the Commonwealth Government reimburses for medical and pharmaceutical benefits provided or prescribed by doctors. The cost of medical benefits rose by a real 81 per cent over the 11-year period and of pharmaceutical benefits by 120 per cent.

One response advocated periodically is to impose a charge or so-called co-payment for going to the doctor so as to reduce the demand. But a co-payment already applies to pharmaceuticals, and it has not stopped their use growing faster than 'free' medical services. The experience here and overseas has been that while co-payments have an initial effect in reducing demand, it soon resumes its previous growth path. This is further evidence of growth being driven more strongly by supply than demand. The OECD concluded that the 'concentration of health-care expenditures in a small number of high cost episodes suggests that co-payments would be unlikely to make a significant difference to the growth in total expenditures'.[10]

The Howard Government has claimed some success in reducing the growth in its spending on health from the average of a real 5.5 per cent over the past 10 years to below 3 per cent. It has limited the number of medical graduates, provoking serious protests from the profession. But this is a legitimate response to the rising costs it must meet. It has restricted the growth in high volume areas such as pathology and radiology, and slowed rises in doctors' rebates under Medicare. Permanent solutions, however, may require more fundamental decisions.

Australia is one of the few countries in which doctors charge on an unfettered fee-for-service basis. Given the fierce opposition of the AMA to any notion that doctors should not be able to charge what they like, the Government has been prepared to move only very gingerly on initiatives such as coordinated care for the chronically ill, paying doctors according to agreed outcomes and evidence-based medicine, which involves a more rigorous approach to using the best treatments. While too many GPs have increased the cost of Medicare, too few specialists have done the same. Specialist colleges have controlled their numbers so tightly that they can charge virtually 'at will' rates above the scheduled fee. The Australian Competition and Consumer Commission has started an investigation.

In health, as in welfare, the challenge for governments is to control costs while maintaining equity in areas where an ageing population and a society battered by economic change are making large demands.

NOTES

1 Quoted in *The Independent*, London, 28 July 1996
2 Gough Whitlam, *The Whitlam Government*, Viking 1985, pp. 358-9
3 Australian Council of Social Service, *Agenda for Tax Reform*, June 1998
4 Australian Institute of Health and Welfare, *Australia's Health 1998*
5 Quoted in Mike Steketee, 'Failing health', *The Weekend Australian*, 29 August 1998
6 Mike Steketee, 'Doctors—what they really earn', *Sydney Morning Herald*, 5 July 1993
7 Industry Commission, 'Private Health Insurance', Report No. 57, 1997
8 AIHW, op. cit., p. 181
9 OECD Economic Surveys—Australia 1995
10 OECD, op. cit., p. 107

10

THE FOURTH R: RUINATION
In the Clever Country, education is withering

Catherine Armitage

GREEK CYNIC DIOGENES was plainly a clever fellow. 'The foundation of every state is the education of its youth,' he said around 300 BC. That's pre-information age, pre-global economy. It's even pre-millennium.

Australia now has a universal education system in which the divisions are becoming more apparent. The old-fashioned ideal of a general liberal education is caving in to the demands of work. Schools and universities previously controlled from the centre are splintering into self-managing autonomous units. Co-operation is faltering under the pressure of competition. Funding disparities perpetuate greater choice for the wealthy. Australia spends around $30 billion a year on education. More than five million students are spread across nearly 11 000 institutions. Education employs nearly 8 per cent of the workforce. Yet as a federal political issue, it's a dead duck.

In contrast to his counterparts in the US and Britain, who have placed education centre-stage in their vote-winning strategies, John Howard didn't even mention it during the 1996 campaign launch speech. He was scarcely more vocal on the subject in the 1998 campaign. Surprisingly for a country which once aspired to be known as 'clever', issues of learning and knowledge scarcely registered a blip on the national consciousness. The nation has no education policy. It has, in effect, a mess of nine separate systems (state and federal) pursuing discrete and sometimes conflicting agendas across three sectors: schools, universities and vocational education and training (VET, which includes TAFE).

Successive national governments have failed to bring the disparate elements together. They have failed to articulate a vision for an educated citizenry. What passed as 'education policies' during the latest campaign were simply show-bags of competitive spending promises: $1.5 billion from Labor, $650 million from the Coalition. Labor and the teachers' unions got some mileage from a scare campaign over the impact of a GST on education. Education lobby groups took out paid advertisements as insurance against journalistic indifference. The crusty AVCC used pictures of babies in nappies. In one, a toddler stretches for a mortarboard out of her reach on a book stack. The text whines: 'Mr Howard and Mr Beazley, why won't Sarah go to university?'

Australian education nears the twenty-first century in a state of growing anxiety. Public education systems are being asked to do more than ever with less. Parents are worried that the system is overloaded and standards are slipping. The best students are siphoned off into selective schools. Families are paying more, rekindling fears that two education systems are in the making: a good one for those who can afford it, a residual one for those who can't. More people are fearful that a decent school education will elude their kids, let alone a university one.

The Coalition took government on a platform of no basic change to education policies. But the supposed $8 billion Budget deficit (the 'Beazley black hole') quickly became a pretext for substantial reductions in spending. The 1996 Budget cut spending on universities by up to 15 per cent in real terms. Basic tuition charges through HECS increased sharply (35–125 per cent, depending on the course), and the income at which compulsory repayment of HECS began was cut substantially to $20 700. As education analyst Simon Marginson wrote: 'The Australian higher education system had been free of tuition charges until 1987. Now it was becoming one of the most expensive in the world.'[1]

Meanwhile the Coalition lifted restrictions on private school growth, making it much easier to start a private school at public expense. Private school growth would be funded by direct reductions in grants to the states for public schools. The system was already reeling from two decades of unprecedented change. In 1960, Australia had 2.3 million students, just over one-fifth of the population; in 1995 there were 5.4 million, just under one-third the population.

In post-compulsory education, participation has doubled in the past 25 years. The retention rate—the proportion of students who stay on at school after Year 10—has rocketed from 30 per cent to 72 per cent since 1980. Between 1987 and 1996, the number of university students rose 60 per cent to more than 670 000, while the number of VET students grew by 35 per cent to 1.3 million.[2] It's not that Australians have dismounted the sheep's back to discover, miraculously, the life of the mind. Young people are staying at school not because they're fond of books but because the alternatives have narrowed.

Full-time work for young people has collapsed. In 1970, some 575 000 teenagers were in full-time work; by 1987 it was 394 000, and by 1997 just over 200 000—a 47 per cent decline in 10 years. Full-time jobs as a proportion of total teenage jobs fell from 60 per cent in 1987 to 35 per cent a decade later.[3] In the jobs race, youthful enthusiasm and even family contacts now run a distant second to educational qualifications. And where once the kids who stayed on may have looked enviously to their motor mechanic or messenger boy mates on the other side of the school fence, envious glances are now more appropriately cast in the other direction.

Since 1970, the youth unemployment rate (15- to 24-year-olds) has escalated from around 3 per cent to 17 per cent. Those most at risk are those with least education. People who don't complete Year 12 are three times more likely to be unemployed than those with degrees. And early school-leavers are likely to stay unemployed for longer than their mates who stayed on, and to earn less. Not often today are teachers stumped by that perennial question from the bored student: 'But how is this going to help me when I get out of here?' The aims of schools and universities are increasingly indistinguishable from those of TAFE.

Work is not just harder to get, it is harder. The low-skilled manual labourer is less in demand than ever. The biggest job losses of the past decade have been in sectors such people once dominated: agriculture, forestry, fishing, manufacturing and mining. In the 10 years to 1996, jobs for professionals grew by 35 per cent, for salespeople and personal service workers by 42.5 per cent; for labourers and related workers jobs increased by 10 per cent; for plant and machine operators and drivers by just 0.8 per cent.[4]

If schooling in the three Rs alone was ever enough, it certainly is not now. Consider the employers' wish-list for workers' minimum skills which now form the basis of the curriculum in schools and the VET sector: collecting, analysing and organising information; communicating ideas and information; planning and organising activities; working with others and in teams; using mathematics; solving problems and using technology. It is estimated that the twenty-first century worker will have not one but six or seven careers in a lifetime, and that 75 per cent of the job categories of the year 2020 do not yet exist. The pressure is on education systems to be flexible, adaptive, responsive and accessible. They are expected to deliver learning which is lifelong, learner-driven, just-in-time, customised and 'transformative'.[5] Education systems are also called upon to socialise individuals and create citizens. As society has become more complex, so have the systems' tasks.

School curriculums have expanded to include sex education, stranger danger, personal development, and children's legal rights. The 1998 report of the Senate Inquiry into the Status of the Teaching Profession observed that teaching in the 1990s was 'a profoundly more complex and professionally demanding activity than it was 20 years ago'. Teachers, it said, were 'increasingly a first point of call for parents or young people seeking advice and guidance about a range of personal, domestic and welfare-related matters'.[6]

In the growing movement towards 'full-service schools', the local community school becomes a 'one-stop shop' for the provision of government services to at-risk students. Launceston College in Tasmania, for example, is the workplace of youth workers, social workers, health workers and other welfare agency representatives who provide co-ordinated case management for students in need. But just when the demands for education provision are greater than ever, the public purse strings are tightening. As a proportion of GDP, government education spending has fallen since 1975 by around 1 per cent to 4.9 per cent, from just above the OECD average to just below it.[7] Public spending on education is growing, but costs are growing faster. Cutbacks have been most dramatic in Victoria, where an aggressive reform program undertaken by the Kennett Government closed 352 government schools between 1992 and 1997, compared with 67 closures in the rest of Australia. The retreat of government has partly been compensated for by private spending, which has been increasing at twice the rate of public spending since the early 1990s.[8]

The drive to reduce public outlays has coincided with the ascendancy of free market ideology in advanced Western nations. The public good argument for education—that a well-educated populace serves the interests of the whole society, which should therefore pay for it—has given way to the idea that it is the educated person getting the most benefit from their education who should pay. At a conference in 1996, the Coalition's then education minister Amanda Vanstone was reported to have remarked: 'Education has had it too good for too long. Why should the taxpayer on $400 a week pay for somebody to go to university to get a higher paying job?'[9]

The first significant shift to user-pays in public education was the introduction of tuition fees for universities in 1989 through HECS, at an initial flat rate of $1800 a full-time student. When learning is governed by the market, education becomes a product, teachers and employers are stakeholders, students and their families customers. They force improvements in the product by exercising choice. Federal Education Minister Dr David Kemp spelled this out in a speech in 1996: 'When parents actively choose a school they make a demand on a school in terms of outcomes . . . Teachers are held accountable by parents for their teaching.'[10]

Under the rubric of user choice, both Labor and Coalition governments have presided over an expansion of the private school sector. The states are responsible for the lion's share of school funding; Commonwealth schools funding is split 70:30 between the public and private sectors. But Commonwealth funding for non-government schools increased by 190 per cent between 1983 and 1996, compared with 28.3 per cent for government schools. Budget papers project funding growth of more than 19 per cent to 2002 for non-government schools, compared with 6 per cent for government schools.[11]

The Coalition in 1996 introduced a mechanism for a direct transfer of federal funding from the public to the private system. Under the Enrolment Benchmark Adjustment, the Commonwealth shifts funding from public to private schools at a rate of about $1600 a student when the proportion of students at private schools increases. The federal Department of Education predicts a 7.24 per cent increase in enrolments for private schools by 2000, and a 1.56 per cent increase for government schools. This means public schools will lose at least $130 million by 2001, even while enrolments grow.[12] Meanwhile, the abolition of Commonwealth registration procedures for private schools in 1996 has contributed to their proliferation.

Far from championing the public education systems for which they are responsible, Coalition ministers have led the attack: Kemp over literacy and numeracy, Vanstone over employment outcomes (which she claimed were ten times worse for students of the public system than the private system). Opponents of so-called 'garage schools' ask whether it is right that any ideologue can gather the children of like-minded parents together, call it a school and attract government funding. In Victoria particularly, victims of school closures are outraged that a private primary school can be funded with as few as 20 students while a public school needs 175 students to be considered viable. New private schools have been springing up on old public school sites. Yet public education has proven resilient. Its share of enrolments fell less than 5 per cent, from 75.6 per cent to 71 per cent, between 1983 and 1995.[13]

The diminution of government funding has also placed pressure on fund-raising activities at government schools, where it is estimated that fund-raising now accounts for up to a quarter of non-salary school budgets. It's not so long ago that the annual school fete or 'patty cake day' was adjudged a rousing success if everyone had a good time and there was enough money in the ice-cream tin to buy some books for the library or even a PA system for the school hall. But schools nowadays have a dizzying schedule of tin-rattling, from trivia nights and art shows to the hiring out of school facilities and the recruitment of fee-paying overseas students. Schools are also encouraged to attract sponsors, who provide funds or goods and services in return for publicity and lifelong brand recognition by students who see their name on the school sign every day. No one talks about free education any more. The Brotherhood of St Laurence recently ascertained that the cost of 'voluntary' fees and levies in public schools was around $500 a year for a primary student, $800 for a secondary student. A 1997 survey by the Smith Family discovered that 34 per cent of families experienced discrimination or pressure from schools because of difficulties in paying fees.[14]

Universities now raise about 40 per cent of their funds from private sources, four times the level of 15 years ago. And overseas fee-paying students are a significant source of outside income. Aggressive recruitment campaigns, especially in Asia, saw their numbers grow by 40 per cent annually between 1989 and 1996. They comprise 10 per cent of students. Education is now Australia's fifth-largest export earner, generating an estimated $3.2 billion in 1996.[15] Winning contracts for commercial research or other service provision is increasingly valued as an academic achievement on a par with excellent teaching or groundbreaking research. James Cook University in tropical North Queensland sells stinger nets and treatments for dengue fever. Universities are developing private hospitals (University of Sydney) and retirement villages (Murdoch University). Sponsorships are ubiquitous: there are brand-name students on brand-name scholarships sitting in brand-name lecture theatres listening to brand-name professors.[16]

Universities are now permitted to charge full fees not just to overseas students but to local students as well, limited to no more than 25 per cent of enrolments in each course. Although the Government optimistically predicted revenues of more than $1 billion a year from this measure by the turn of the century, the uptake of fee-paying places has been very low. TAFE, too, has been dragged into the market. Its monopoly position has been under assault, and it now competes for public funding with a booming private sector of more than 3000 training providers. While private providers receive only a tiny fraction of the $3 billion public funds spent on VET annually, their share is growing rapidly. A 1998 report endorsed a proposal that TAFE should have to compete with private providers for access to its own physical facilities, estimated to be worth $6–7 billion.[17]

Successive policy reports in recent years have argued for a much more radical step to place education on a competitive footing: a voucher funding system. This would mean giving potential students a credit voucher for publicly-funded education which they redeem at the institution of their choice. Institutions that failed to attract students would fail to attract funding. Although this proposal has been most frequently raised for universities, it could logically be extended to the entire education system. The West review of higher education financing and policy (1998) recommended it. In a 1996 blueprint for the future, the Victorian Secondary School Principals Association assumed it was inevitable. But it would require co-operation between the states and the Commonwealth on funding, which is elusive. (The 1996 Audit Commission proposal that the Commonwealth take over TAFE funding from the states, which would have sole responsibility for schools, has gone nowhere.)[18] And the benefits of a market model are assumed rather than proven. A survey of overseas experiments with choice-based schooling concluded there was no direct evidence of improvements in school quality arising from increased competition.[19]

There are fears that the application of competition policy to schools will exacerbate their inequalities. In a scathing 1998 report on Victorian state schools, for example, the Melbourne Anglican Synod compared the $2.3 million raised by Melbourne High School in 1996 with $2300 raised by a small country primary school. Student–teacher ratios are already higher in government secondary schools than independent schools while spending per student is about one-third lower ($5876 a year compared with $7580).[20]

The transition to computer-based classroom learning will widen the gap between the two sectors, with public schools already lagging severely despite big-spending programs by state governments. The resilience of public education may merely reflect the fact that in the market system, true freedom of choice is restricted to those who can afford it. A poll published in *The Age* in 1994 found that 'if money was no object', almost 60 per cent of respondents would prefer to see their children in a private secondary school. Nearly 50 per cent thought private schools were better at preparing young people for a job.[21] Greater autonomy for institutions has been accompanied by closer scrutiny of performance.

Education Minister Kemp, brandishing a survey which suggested about one-third of students in Years 3 and 5 cannot read and write properly, has won agreement from the states for national testing of literacy and numeracy at school. But teachers' unions especially have mounted strong resistance to such tests on the grounds that the results could lead to unfair comparisons between schools. Lyndsay Connors, a senior bureaucrat in the NSW Department of Education and Training, warned recently against

> an undue reliance, as a basis for policy, on computer analyses of outcomes based on selective and slender data, and undertaken in isolation from any real knowledge of the context, including the real level of the resources that went into producing them.[22]

Draft national goals on schooling have drawn harsh criticism for their overemphasis on traditional literacy and numeracy, and neglect of visual, communication and media skills. Literacy panics are perennial in the education debate. So is anxiety about falling standards. In schools, that anxiety has been compounded by the escalation of jobs-oriented learning. For some, the fact that 75 000 students now do work training in schools—and that you can work in McDonald's and have it credited towards your Year 12 assessments—is clear evidence of 'dumbing down'.

An undisputed concern is that teachers are declining in both quality and number. University entrance scores for teachers are among the lowest of all courses, and continue to decline, both reflecting and reinforcing the low status of the profession. A shortage of 7000 teachers is predicted by 2003. It doesn't help that teachers' pay has declined by 25 per cent in real terms in the past two decades. The Senate report into teachers' status said the profession was 'infected' by a sense of crisis so profound that many would not confess to their occupation in social situations. The average age of teachers is now 46.[23]

The perception of declining standards is strongest for the elite of educational institutions: universities. What are we to make of the fact that the country's oldest university and one of its most prestigious, the University of Sydney, has recently set up the Herbal Medicine Research and Education Centre? Or that the University of Wollongong recently held an 'academic celebrity debate' on the topic 'Academic charlatanism should be identified and eliminated', complete with a professor arguing in the negative? A fall in undergraduate pass rates from 83.2 per cent in 1993 to 81.7 per cent three years later was widely interpreted as indicating duller students rather than harder courses.[24] In a 1996 Monash University survey of 400 academics at three universities, just under half disagreed with the proposition that the quality of final-year students had improved.[25]

Yet after 30 years of observing the system from the inside, Don Aitkin, the vice-chancellor of the University of Canberra, believes standards have increased: 'The PhDs that are getting up are as good or better than in the past.' He attributes academics' belief that students are not as well prepared for university as in the past to greater variability in the candidature because 'schools have (more) capacity to decide what they will teach'.[26]

The bald fact is that universities are not as elite as they once were. The so-called Dawkins reforms of 1989 removed the divide between universities and former colleges of advanced education, increasing the number of universities from 19 to 35. Since 1983 the number of students at university in Australia has almost doubled. While once university students were drawn from the top 10 or 20 per cent of school leavers, universities now draw from at least the top 40 per cent, and some scoop much lower. Professor Lauchlan Chipman, vice-chancellor of Central Queensland University, confessed in a 1997 interview that his university had 'a lot of people of ambiguous ability' so that staff 'really have a very difficult task'.

Traditionalists are galled to think that you can now major in seemingly anything at university, from real estate and horse management to acupuncture and jewellery design. This disquiet became front page news in 1997 when the head of the federal Government's review into higher education, classicist and former private school headmaster Roderick West, reflected out loud to the effect that universities should be places to nurture the imaginative life of the mind, while vocational education should be confined to technical colleges.[27]

To the discomfort of nostalgists, universities and TAFE colleges are converging in practice as well as in purpose. The Victorian Minister for Tertiary Education and Training, Phil Honeywood, described a 1998 merger between a university and a TAFE college as 'a partnership of equals'.[28] It is common for students to commence their studies at TAFE, where fees are cheaper, then transfer to universities to get a degree. (However, many more university graduates subsequently do a TAFE course than vice-versa, suggesting universities are not yet as far down the vocational path as nostalgists fear.)

It is difficult to evaluate whether the nation's educative effort is meeting its goals because no one has bothered to articulate them. If we accept that the future lies in creating a learning culture, a minimum goal for education would reasonably be to educate 100 per cent of Australians at least to the end of senior school, and preferably beyond. There is still some way to go. Australia has the best-educated workforce in its history. On the other hand, only 61 per cent of the workforce holds post-compulsory qualifications, below the OECD average of 68 per cent.[29] Up to 15 per cent of 16-year-olds are not in full-time education despite the documented risks to their long-term employment prospects. Retention rates have been falling since 1992, with the greatest falls among those from low socio-economic groups, rural areas and government schools.[30] Universities are still populated overwhelmingly by the well-off middle classes.

The Australian Education Union claims that the public school system is underfunded by $2 billion, a claim difficult to evaluate without the kind of comprehensive national inquiry for which support is growing.[31] But there is mounting evidence for impoverishment of the system. In schools, where spending relative to GDP fell by 0.6 per cent between 1984 and 1994, infrastructure is flagging and class sizes are on the up. 'Temporary' demountable classrooms are showing the effects of 30 years' use. The West review of higher education warned that universities would fall behind international competitors in new technologies and infrastructure without 'urgent action . . . to strengthen [their] ability to mobilise resources'. (That review refrained, however, from calling for more public funding, arguing for the development of other funding sources such as capital borrowings and private equity investment.)[32]

No one doubts that tomorrow's education institutions will be vastly different from today's. One American futurist, Lewis Perelman, argues that the classroom of contemporary public education should be done away with because it has 'as much utility in today's modern economy . . . as the Conestoga wagon or the blacksmith shop'. Under a system Perelman has dubbed 'hyperlearning', electronic card-account technology would allow families or students to choose specific learning products and services which allow them to 'learn anything, anywhere, anytime'—by computer.[33] Extreme as this may sound, Victorian secondary school principals imagined something similar in their blueprint for the year 2010. Their prototype student Venus (aged 11) attends a Learning Centre for one and a half days a week for team projects, group support and music lessons. The rest of the time she studies at home on her Portable

Technological Work Station. As Sydney sociologist Bob Connell reflects:

> We are now, for the first time in Australian history, invited to contemplate a school system operating without any concept of the public interest. All schools are selective, but only some can make use of that fact . . . Those schools which 'fail' become sink schools, with a high proportion of poor families, troubled children and ethnic minorities.[34]

The time cannot be too far off when visions for home-based techno-learning like Perelman's are co-opted as the rationale for cutbacks in public spending on education. No major party says it wants to wind back access to good quality education, yet the evidence is convincing that this has been the effect of policy. Australia needs to ask itself whether we have abandoned the ideal of a free, comprehensive and universal system offering education opportunities for all in favour of two unequal systems: a rich and varied one for those who can afford it, a poor one for the rest.

We approach the new century not as a learning culture but as a spurning culture. We spurn knowledge, spurn opportunity, spurn learning, all because we don't want to pay for it. Leading thinkers, the potential engine-drivers of progress, are belittled and marginalised as threats to taxpayer prosperity. So are the advocates of public education. We spurn debate. Yet it is merely assumed, not tested, that citizens don't place a high priority on education in the spending of their tax dollars, or that they're not prepared to pay more tax to learn more.

We need a national bipartisan commitment to build a confident, outward-looking, lifelong-learning culture in which all men and women are entitled to publicly-funded post-school education. The system should be diversified, flexible and inclusive. It should aim for excellence in everything it does, wherever we encounter it: at school, on campus, at home or at work.

We should take for granted the goal of increasing the school retention rate to 100 per cent, just as we take for granted the goal of reducing unemployment. We need to enhance the professional status of teachers, to improve their training, their career structures and their pay. We need to celebrate achievement as well address failings. It will require vision, leadership and confidence. If we don't pay now, we'll certainly pay later. And that price will be way too high.

NOTES

1 Simon Marginson, *Educating Australia, Government, Economy and Citizen since 1960*, Cambridge University Press, 1997
2 Australian Bureau of Statistics, 'Education and Training in Australia', 1996
3 OECD, 'The Transition from Initial Education to Working Life, Country Note, Australia', OECD, 1997
4 National Centre for Vocational Education and Research, 'The Outlook for Training in Australia's Industries', NCVER, 1998
5 Preferred Futures, 'Education 2010: A Preferred Future for Victorian Education', Victorian Association of State Secondary Principals, Melbourne, 1996
6 Senate Employment, Education and Training References Committee, 'A Class Act: Inquiry into the Status of the Teaching Profession', Commonwealth of Australia, 1998
7 ABS, 'Expenditure on Education', ABS, 1998; OECD, 'Education at a Glance', OECD, 1996
8 ibid.
9 Catherine Armitage, 'Vanstone Lectures Don't Impress VCs' *The Weekend Australian*, 25–26 May 1996, p. 2
10 David Kemp, 'Schools and the Democratic Challenge', Bert Kelly Lecture, 21 October 1996, quoted in Anglican Diocese of Melbourne, 'The State of Our State Schools: The Report of the Synod Schools Task Group on Victoria's Public Education System', Anglican Diocese of Melbourne, 1998
11 ibid.
12 Department of Employment Education Training and Youth Affairs, 'States Grants Bill Tables 2 and 3, updated July 1998', Employment Education Training and Youth Affairs Senate Legislation Committee, Questions on Notice 1998–99 Budget Estimates Hearing, Hansard, 1998
13 Marginson, *Educating Australia*, op. cit.

14 Anglican Diocese of Melbourne, 'State of Our State Schools' op. cit.
15 Committee of Review of Higher Education Financing and Policy, 'Learning for Life, Final Report', Commonwealth of Australia, 1998
16 Catherine Armitage, 'The Corporate Campus', *The Australian*, 5 June 1997
17 House of Representatives Standing Committee on Employment Education and Training, 'Today's training, Tomorrow's Skills', Commonwealth of Australia, 1998
18 Bob Lingard, 'Federalism in Schooling Since the Karmel Report', paper for the ACER National Conference Schools in Australia, October 1998
19 Louise Watson, 'Choice Before Quality', *Australian Quarterly*, vol. 69, no. 1
20 Anglican Diocese of Melbourne, 'State of Our State Schools' op. cit.
21 Quoted in Marginson, *Educating Australia*, op. cit.
22 Lyndsay Connors, 'Response to Peter Hill', paper for the ACER National Conference Schools in Australia, October 1998
23 Senate Committee, 'A Class Act', op. cit.
24 Dorothy Illing, 'Standards Slip at Crowded Unis', *The Australian*, 28 October 1998, p. 1
25 Catherine Armitage, 'Academics See Dark Days for Unis', *The Australian*, 31 January 1997, p. 1
26 Interview with author, October 1998
27 Catherine Armitage, 'The Great Dilemma', *The Weekend Australian*, January 18–19 1997
28 ibid.
29 OECD, *The Transition from Education to Working Life*, op. cit.
30 *VicUni News*, July 1998, vol. 8
31 Australian Education Union, 'Liberal Education Promises Fail to Make the Grade', press release, September 1998
32 Committee of Review, 'Learning for Life', op. cit.
33 Lewis J. Perelman, 'Hyperlearning: Would you send your kid to a Soviet collective?', *Wired* 1994, 1.1
34 R.W. Connell, 'Equality in Education: The issue of social justice and the practice of equity programs from "Schools in Australia" to the present', paper to ACER National Conference on Schools in Australia, October 1998

11

BACK TO THE FUTURE IS PASSÉ
Families, women and childcare

Michelle Gunn

JOHN HOWARD IS FOND OF portraying families as the 'heart of our society'.[1] And he likes to describe a united, functioning family as 'the most efficient and effective welfare system any society has devised'.[2] The Prime Minister is right—families *are* the building blocks of community, and the relationships within them are among the strongest and most formative in our lives. But family life in the late 1990s is not what it was 50 or even 30 years ago. How could it be? A raft of social and economic changes have transformed both the structure of family units and the ways family members go about their daily lives.

Men and women are marrying later and having fewer children; more people are getting divorced or living together without marrying; mothers are combining work with family responsibilities; geographic mobility is diluting the influence of the extended family; and the number of sole parent families is on the rise. Then there are the broader but equally important trends—longer working hours, increased job insecurity, rising school and university retention rates, the outsourcing of domestic labour . . . The result is a degree of complexity and diversity that belies traditional or simple policy prescriptions.

A certain nostalgia and revisionism is probably an understandable response to the pressures of unrelenting change, but now is not the time for governments to retreat behind outdated notions of the sexual division of labour. Australian families need bold and creative policies that move beyond the rhetoric of 'choice' into actively helping the nation's mothers and fathers manage their work and family responsibilities. The subtitle of this chapter is 'Families, women and childcare', which suggests women will be more central to the discussion than men. It is a deliberate emphasis, not only because women usually make the decisions about childcare: it is the changes in women's lives that have effected the greatest modifications to family life over the past few decades. The most obvious of these is the increasing number of married women in paid work.

In 1954, married women made up 7 per cent of all people in the workforce; by 1998 that figure was 26.3 per cent. The significance for family formation becomes even clearer when we consider that more than 67 per cent of women aged 25–34 and 71 per cent of those aged 35–44 are now in the workforce, compared to 41.3 per cent and 43.4 per cent in 1970. This trend has been accompanied by a sharp rise in the number of women going on to further education. The results have been a deferral of marriage and parenting (while women pursue higher education and establish careers) and a decline in overall fertility. In 1974, the median age at first marriage was 23.3 years for men and 20.9 years for women. Today, it is 27.6 for men, 25.7 for women. Similarly, the median age of women at first nuptial birth has changed from 23 years in 1966 to 28.7 in 1997, while the overall fertility rate has fallen to 1.8 children per woman from a peak of 3.55 in 1961.

Three key questions arise from these statistics: How do women arrange their lives when they finally have children? What does this mean for families? And has public policy kept pace with social change? In 1997, 56.3 per cent of all couples with dependent children were both in the workforce. Even if we look only at married couples with children aged 0–4, we find 46 per cent of mothers were employed. If nothing else, such figures signal an end to the dominance of the male breadwinner model.

Of course the traditional family, a husband working full-time and supporting a wife and children, is far from extinct—it exists across the social and economic spectrum, from high-income families, where a woman's decision to be a stay-at-home mum often has little impact on living standards, to middle-income families, where the trade-offs are far more acute, to low-income families, where it is often not in a family's best financial interest for the mother to return to work. This is because of the steep rate at which family payments are withdrawn once family income exceeds a specific level. Intriguingly, women on low incomes with a poor level of education most strongly identify themselves as mothers, and have the most marginal attachment to the labour market. Often dependent on the low wages of their husbands, many are critical of government-subsidised childcare and scathing of the notion of 'quality time' used by working women to describe their interaction with their children.

It is not surprising perhaps that women whose working lives may have been tedious or unfulfilling would much prefer to stay at home and raise their children. But the political and social policy implications of this are significant. Politically, it means that a significant number of battling families from Labor heartlands will identify with Howard's conservative agenda on families, and send their votes his way. The social policy issue is one of a polarisation of women's experiences and views by socio-economic status—a situation that did not exist during the 1950s and 1960s when female roles were much the same in all households. Victorian academic Belinda Probert warns that the sexual division of labour in many low-income households is not the product of 'choice' so much as a lack of opportunity.[3] This in turn contributes to rising levels of income inequality.

And what of other family types, where both parents work full-time and the mother has minimal time off after the birth of her children? Or the middle-of-the-road family, where one parent (usually the mother) works part-time while the children are young in an attempt to balance work and family responsibilities? If statistical trends are any guide, these are archetypes of the future. Yet a peephole investigation of these suburban homes reveals that the reality isn't always rosy. Take the world of the alternately celebrated and denigrated 'supermum', a woman whose career is as important as that of her husband's, who enjoys her work and doesn't want, or feels she cannot afford, to take extended career breaks. Tellingly, there is usually no shift in the amount of domestic duties performed by the father. In fact these households use their high incomes to pay non-family members to keep the domestic sphere functioning—the nanny or childcare centre to care for the children and/or run the household, gourmet cuisine couriers for dinner, a gardener for the pool and shrubs, a neighbourhood boy to wash the car and walk the dog. Research also indicates that detachment by both parents from the day-to-day functions of family life causes considerable strain and added pressure.

The solution for many families, in particular the mothers of small children, is part-time work. Latest figures from the Australian Bureau of Statistics estimate that 42.9 per cent of women work part-time (compared to 11.7 per cent of men). Of the 46 per cent of married mothers with children aged 0–4 in the workforce, about 30 per cent work part-time, and 16 per cent full-time. As a trend, it is likely to continue. When Ilene Wolcott and Helen Glezer from the AIFS surveyed women with young children and from all walks of life about their preferred working arrangements if given a choice, 60 per cent of full-time workers, 72 per cent of part-timers and 52 per cent of those not in paid work nominated part-time work as their ideal.[4] The reasons are obvious: it allows time with the children but also permits them to retain work skills and some financial independence, very important given the high rates of divorce and a government insistence that people aim to support themselves in retirement.

The casual/part-time option has its downsides, however, with an associated reduction in job security and benefits. A comparison of the employment conditions of women who want children in the future with women with a child under five, conducted by Edith Gray from the ANU, is revealing: 85.8 per cent of childless women (against 56.9 per cent of those with young children) have access to sick leave, 85.2 (57.7) per cent have holiday leave, 49.3 (29.9) per cent have access to paid maternity leave, and 59.6 (38.8) per cent to family or carer's leave.[5] The decline in conditions that appears to accompany more flexible working arrangements is a serious concern because it is when women have young families that these conditions are most valuable.

The final point to be made about women and part-time work is that men once again show little sign of increasing their domestic responsibilities or taking the opportunity to share more in parenting by working part-time themselves. This can be attributed to stubborn cultural expectations about men's roles but also to financial realities: men very often have higher salaries than women, a situation which perversely is likely to continue so long as women are the only ones taking extended career breaks to care for children.

Such brief descriptions of the ways families juggle the work/family dilemma are meant to illustrate the complex array of situations, preferences and decisions confronting parents, and the ideological minefield facing policy-makers in attempting to cater for them. In many ways, of course, Australian families have never had it so good. We are better educated, have higher living standards and enjoy better health than previous generations. We live at a time when the likelihood of global warfare has retreated further than at any stage this century, and when technological advances are made so rapidly that we feel almost anything is possible.

At the same time, surveys reveal an almost unprecedented level of pessimism and fear. Professor Michael Pusey from the University of NSW is completing a three-year study on middle Australia involving interviews with 400 families in Brisbane, Sydney, Adelaide, Melbourne and Canberra. His preliminary findings show that families are experiencing economic change as social strain, and that women are bearing the brunt of it. More than 90 per cent of Pusey's families, for example, say family life is changing 'a lot' or 'quite a lot' compared to just 8.9 per cent who describe it as 'much the same as it has always been'. When asked whether it is the negative or positive aspects of change that stand out, 65 per cent nominate the negative. Pusey stresses that the source of this negativity is not family life itself but the external forces impacting on family life:

It's not strife between men and women or with kids that worries people—it is a feeling of being on 'the back foot' as they cope with the white noise of changing cultural expectations without adequate support.[6]

Women in particular, he says, are negotiating changing roles and demands without the benefit of road maps from previous generations. Middle-aged women feel particularly pressured—their employer expects longer and longer hours, their husbands are trying to build up their retirement income, their children are in senior high school and need more attention, and their own parents suddenly need help with basic things like going to the doctor or picking up groceries. Many people have a pervasive sense that the world is changing too fast, and that life is somehow getting worse. And how is this insecurity manifesting itself? Says Pusey:

> You can't predict how a population will respond to a sense of intractable ethical and psychological uncertainty. For people who are unreflective it brings 'blame the victim' scapegoating, the Pauline Hanson phenomenon. But for people who are reflective it leads to some sort of intuitive recovery of one's sense of not being alone in this, of the uncertainties being shared. New social movements are formed out of just these sorts of strains.[7]

By this, he means calls for the re-regulation of the labour market, support for government provision of social services, of people turning outwards in an intuitive recognition of the importance of social capital. But social researcher Hugh Mackay has identified a less attractive way in which people respond to uncertainty and change. In a recent *Mind and Mood* report, he describes us as turning inward and developing

> a kind of siege mentality which reinforces the conviction that 'we've got to look after our own'. It is not that Australians believe Australia is seriously on the skids, nor that they themselves are threatened with any kind of ruin. But there is a growing sense of a kind of downward spiral in which it is becoming increasingly important to 'look after Number One' and to seek psychological and emotional solace in a narrowed focus.[8]

This leads to the contentious area of how governments and policy-makers have been responding to these changes and fears. It is contentious because the last change of federal government saw a significant shift in policies concerning women and families. Under previous Labor governments, women's workforce participation was strongly supported through various measures, including affirmative action legislation and a dramatic expansion of government-subsidised childcare.

It was a feminist-driven policy agenda comprehensively rejected by the Howard Government, which in its first term announced a review of affirmative action legislation, cut the staff and budget of the Office for the Status of Women, made enormous cuts to projected childcare expenditure and introduced policies aimed directly at single-income families. This about-face was made to correct a perceived imbalance in government support and recognition for one family type over another. The Government's Women's Policy released before the 1998 federal election makes this explicit:

> Labor neglected women and mothers who chose not to be a part of the paid workforce . . . Unlike Labor, the Coalition's policies are not about promoting particular roles as a stereotype for all women.[9]

The mantra adopted by the Howard Government in relation to this area of social policy has been its desire to provide women with a real choice about whether to stay at home or go to work. It is a laudable objective, but in the absence of paying women something approaching a full-time wage, it is unlikely to be achieved. It is virtually impossible for a government to be value-neutral in this area, and the shuffling of resources from one target group to another tends to create as many new problems as it seeks to solve.

With the exception of the bungled nursing home reforms, the social policy area to give the Government most grief during its first term was childcare. One of the fastest growing areas of public expenditure, childcare was high on the razor gang's hit list, with projected spending reduced by more than $800 million in the first two Budgets and further savings made in the third

Budget as a result of a fall-off in demand. The cuts were made in several ways, some more defendable than others: benefits to high-income families were reduced; restrictions were placed on the number of hours of work and non-work related care the Government was willing to subsidise; direct subsidies to community-based (parent-run) centres were abolished; and the maximum level of childcare assistance was frozen at $115 a week, or $2.30 an hour.

The last two measures were particularly damaging, resulting in a dramatic rise in the cost of formal care, especially for low- and middle-income families. Surveys conducted by community childcare organisations show that the gap between the cost of care and the government subsidy increased to such an extent that many parents found they could no longer afford it. They subsequently either withdrew from the workforce, reduced their hours of work or went in search of cheaper childcare from unregistered and unregulated providers, raising fears of a return to substandard backyard care. Childcare centres across the nation are in considerable difficulty, with many being sold and others struggling with 60 per cent occupancy or less. Working women, already angry at the attack on childcare funding, were further enraged by simultaneous government efforts to reward stay-at-home mums through part B of its family tax initiative. Cuts to childcare, had they been introduced on their own, could have been viewed as heavy-handed cost cutting, but an assessment of the two policies left many women with no doubt that Howard's rhetoric about choice concealed something more sinister—social engineering designed to keep women behind the 1950s white picket fence.

It is a perception reinforced by the release of the Government's tax reform agenda, which extended the principle of rewarding stay-at-home parents by allowing single-income families with a child under five to double their tax-free threshold to $13 000 (regardless of income). This was to be accompanied by a $7.50 increase in the maximum level of childcare assistance, a concession to even-handedness judged by the childcare sector as too little, too late.

The Government has repeatedly denied suggestions that

women are withdrawing from the workforce because of its childcare policies; it quotes ABS statistics that show little change in women's workforce participation over the past three years. The problem with these figures is that they apply to all women with children under 15, a sample too large to reveal changes among the smaller sub-group of working women with children in formal care. In the absence of official statistics, we are left with qualitative research by groups such as the Brotherhood of St Laurence and surveys conducted by childcare providers: all suggest there is significant cause for concern.

Let's turn now to a closer examination of the recent family tax proposals, in particular the one designed to 'recognise the financial sacrifices made by families with young children which opt to have one parent at home'. The inclusion of this policy, which effectively doubles the tax-free threshold for single-income families with children under five, should have come as no surprise to spectators of the political scene. Howard and other members of the Coalition (especially those in the conservative Lyons Forum) have long been in favour of a change in taxation laws to address the perceived inequity of a single-income family paying more in tax than a double-income family earning the same amount. But as Sydney academic Professor Patricia Apps points out:

> Single and dual income families with the same income do not enjoy the same standard of living because the single income family benefits from the additional untaxed home production of the home carer. The dual income family must buy substitutes for this home production—such as childcare—from taxed earnings.[10]

Furthermore, women very often find that total family income goes backwards if they increase their hours of work because various government subsidies and payments are withdrawn as the family income rises. A 1997 study by Gillian Beer from the National Centre for Social and Economic Modelling found, for example, that in a family of three children in which the father earns $560 a week, the family would be better off if the mother stayed at home than if she were to work between

1 and 19 hours a week at $8.60 an hour. In families where the husband is earning a reasonably low wage this can create poverty traps.[11] Both the Labor Party and the Coalition recognised this problem before the last election and made changes to family payment cut-offs and withdrawal rates in an effort to address it. The irony is that the combination of the Government's tax bonuses directed to single-income families and its cuts to childcare may be simply reproducing this work disincentive in a different form.

An individual's attitude to these policy changes will be determined by circumstances. Many full-time mothers view the tax proposal as long-overdue recognition of their contribution to society. Others say the measures do not go nearly far enough because the rebate is simply not enough to encourage reluctant dual-income households to change. Both sides of the debate have also noted that the proposal applies only to families with children under five. This decision was probably made because to extend the plan would have proved cost-prohibitive—nevertheless, it sends the message that full-time parenting should be encouraged only while children are very young.

The downside is that women who have been encouraged by government policy to take five to eight years off work to care for children can find it extremely difficult to re-enter the workforce. This leads to the broader philosophical shift in family policy occurring at the federal level, first under Labor but to a much greater degree under the Coalition. Informed by the desire to reduce social services expenditure, it is a policy direction that stresses the importance of self-reliance and the need for families to take responsibility for their own affairs. Influenced both by conservative and neo-liberal philosophy, it assumes that most families can purchase the social services they need on the open market or alternatively provide the services themselves. This is dangerous, not only because it presupposes that women will be inclined and able to take on such responsibilities but also because it threatens the structural pillars supporting many gains made in the past 20 years.

If women are full-time carers for a significant period of time, they reduce their capacity to provide for their own retirement, potentially reduce their career prospects and if subsequently divorced make life especially difficult for themselves. It is becoming clear that while the sexual division of labour may appear acceptable while a marriage holds together, it can be disastrous when it breaks down. By 1996, almost 20 per cent of families with dependent children were sole parent households, up from 14.6 per cent in 1986. The overwhelming majority of these are headed by women and many of them, in the absence of contributions from the child's father, live in poverty.

In a recent study, the Centre for Population and Urban Research at Monash University found that almost half (47 per cent) of female sole parents receiving the sole parent's pension in 1997 were paid no maintenance. This was because a surprisingly large number of non-custodial fathers were on pensions and benefits, or on extremely low incomes, and were exempt from liability.[12] Child support and its administration are contentious areas because of the hostility that can accompany separation. The Government recently announced more mediation and counselling programs designed to try to save a greater number of marriages. While such measures are to be applauded, governments cannot afford to be naive. Single-parent families are here to stay, and policies impacting on women in the workforce must take this into account.

Governments do not make policy in a vacuum: the nature of the political process ensures their responsiveness to community attitudes. Logic would tell us then that the Coalition must have been confident of tapping into a vein of conservative sentiment in the electorate over the past three years. A large-scale survey conducted by the AIFS confirms this. Based on three national surveys of 8845 people, it found that Australians hold very traditional views on issues such as working mothers, cohabitation before marriage, ex-nuptial births and homosexuality. Most of us believe that a family suffers if a mother works full time, that divorce is too easy to get, that it is not desirable for a single parent to bring up a child, and that men should be the primary breadwinners.

However, when the values of the respondents were broken down by age, a different picture emerged, with women in their

20s (the mothers of the next decade) holding less traditional values than anyone else, including males their own age.[13] One could argue that people become more traditional as they age, and that the views of these young women will change. But it is also possible that the conservatism of older generations reflects the times in which they were raised. If that is so, we can expect the baby boomers, an increasingly powerful voting bloc over the next few decades, to be far more liberal than their parents, and to form with their children and their children's children a set of values very different from those holding sway today.

So where does this leave Australian mothers, fathers and children as they approach the new millennium? Confused and bewildered. And searching for a way forward, for a path through the uncertainty change has brought to their lives. The solutions for them, and for the governments they elect, are neither simple nor easy but there are signposts.

One of these comes in the form of a question often posed by Wolcott and Glezer about how we 'define and achieve an equitable balance between public and private responsibility and between men and women sharing the dual roles of income earning and family caring'. The answers lie in public policies that better enable men and women to move between the worlds of work and family as they travel through the life cycle. The days when most families conformed to the 'male-breadwinner model' are gone, and no amount of tinkering with the tax and social security systems will bring them back. They are gone because feminism has won for women the right to financial independence, a good education and career success. Together with their partners, women also want to be good parents and to raise their children in happy, healthy, functioning families. Governments wanting to support these aspirations should not try to encourage women back into the home or to relegate the care of children and older people to the status of 'private responsibility'. Such approaches marginalise children and family instead of more constructively placing them at the centre of public policy.

As we make our way though the first decade of next century, we need to invest in properly funded, good quality childcare and promote family-friendly practices in the nation's workplaces. Finally, if as a society we are to achieve harmony and balance in our family lives, we must also begin to value fathers and their role as involved parents.

NOTES

1. John Howard, statement 'Our Families, Our Strength, Our Future' 14 September 1998
2. John Howard, speech delivered at the Coalition's Family Policy launch, Wesley Mission, Sydney, 14 September 1998
3. Belinda Probert and Fiona McDonald, 'The Work Generation: Work and Identity in the Nineties', Brotherhood of St Laurence, 1996, p. 6
4. Ilene Wolcott and Helen Glezer, 'Work and family Life: Achieving Integration', AIFS, 1995, Melbourne
5. Edith Gray, 'Childrearing—an analysis of its impact on labour force experience and household work for men and women', paper to Australian Population Association Ninth National Conference, Brisbane, 1998
6. Michael Pusey, quoted in 'Women caught in the middle of a pressured society', *The Australian*, 3 December 1997
7. ibid.
8. Hugh Mackay, The Mackay Report, Mind & Mood, June 1998, p. 9
9. 'Opportunity and Choice', Coalition statement on status of women, p. 2
10. Patricia Apps, 'Tax Reform: A Comment on the Coalition's Tax Plan'
11. Gillian Beer, 'Is it Worth Working? The Financial Impact of Increased Hours of Work by Married Mothers with Young Children', paper to 26th Annual Conference of Economists, University of Tasmania, 1997
12. Bob Birrell and Virginia Rapson, 'A Not So Perfect Match', Centre for Population and Urban Research, Monash University, p. 52
13. David de Vaus, AIFS, quoted in 'Family values maintain hold on social mores', *The Australian*, 15 December 1997, p. 5

12

A NOTION FOR A NATION
Exploring the republic of ideas

Mike Steketee

AUSTRALIANS THIS YEAR FACE THEIR FUTURE in a way they have done only once before, a century ago. Then they agreed by a vote in each of the colonies 'to unite in one indissoluble Federal Commonwealth under the Crown of the United Kingdom of Great Britain and Ireland', as the preamble to the Constitution puts it. It is hard to imagine now that they could have made any other decision.

In time, the arrival of the Australian republic may be seen in the same light: a logical step in the nation's progress. In many ways it is a smaller step, given that Federation created a new nation and a new tier of government. A move to a republic of the kind being proposed in the referendum the Howard Government has promised by the end of 1999 would be powerful symbolism, breaking our last constitutional link with Britain. But if you believe its proponents, it would be more evolutionary than revolutionary in practical terms.

The vice-regal office has changed markedly from the one in the early part of the century reserved for visiting Englishmen representing the British Government as well as the Queen. The appointment in 1931 of the first Australian governor-general, Sir Isaac Isaacs, was a step towards nationalising the office. Recent governors-general, in particular the incumbent,

Sir William Deane, and his predecessor Bill Hayden, have been more inclined to use their position to contribute to the national debate—a further move towards a more independent, assertive role rather than one deferring always to the Queen. Changing the Constitution to replace the monarch with a president seems a logical development.

Yet if the path to Federation is a guide, this will be no smooth rite of passage. The process that culminated in Australia's first national government was a long, sometimes hesitant one, with many slips between aspiration and achievement. Moves were under way as early as the 1840s to unite the colonies, but it was not until some 50 years later that there was the right conjunction of public mood and political momentum to carry the issue forward. A conference in Melbourne in 1890 led to a convention in 1891 which produced the first constitutional draft. It was written by a convention committee whose members—Edmund Barton, subsequently Australia's first prime minister, Sir Samuel Griffith, subsequently chief justice in the first High Court, and Charles Kingston, a future premier of South Australia—focused their minds on nation-building on a three-day cruise on the Hawkesbury River on the Queensland Government's SS *Lucinda*. One explanation for the absence of a bill of rights from the Constitution is that its chief proponent, Tasmania's Andrew Inglis Clark, caught the flu and missed the cruise.[1] Of such stuff is history made.

Despite this strong start, the task of federation-making almost foundered. Governments changed hands in the colonies, most notably that in NSW headed by Henry Parkes, who had first moved for federation at the Melbourne conference. The draft constitution failed to win approval from the colonial parliaments. It took a popular movement through the federation leagues to put the issue back on track with elected constitutional conventions followed by referendums. Even then, it needed two referendums in 1898 and 1899 to win sufficient support, and it took another year for Western Australia to vote in favour. To Alfred Deakin, who was prominent in framing the Constitution and became Australia's second prime minister, Federation 'must always appear to have been secured by a series of miracles'.[2] The same may one day be said of Australia's becoming a republic.

It is one thing for republicans to regard it as self-evident that Australians want an Australian as their head of state. The force of the argument is conceded by many monarchists, who suggest we already have one in the governor-general. The Queen begs to differ: she describes herself as head of state of Australia, among other countries.[3] However, it is quite another matter to jump all the hurdles involved in becoming a republic.

Since Federation, Australian voters have approved just eight of the 42 proposals put to them in referendums to change the Constitution. Never has a change been adopted without bipartisan political support. That includes issues which win almost universal public approval when first proposed but which a major party decides to oppose, often from political expedience. An example is enshrining freedom of religion in the Constitution, one of four propositions overwhelmingly defeated in a 1988 referendum with the help of a Coalition fear campaign. When in doubt, Australians prefer to leave their Constitution as it is. That is why the most successful strategy in a referendum campaign has been to raise concerns, legitimate or otherwise, and it is why this will be the linchpin of the monarchists' efforts this year.

Under the Constitution's so-called double majority provision, a majority of voters in a majority of states have to vote 'Yes' in a referendum, as well as a national majority. That means opponents of change can concentrate their resources in just three states, whereas proponents need to win four states and a majority Australia-wide. The proposal for a 'minimalist republic' adopted by the Constitutional Convention in February 1998 has the support of Labor, including premiers Bob Carr in NSW, Peter Beattie in Queensland and Jim Bacon in Tasmania. It has the backing of many Liberals, including premiers Jeff Kennett in Victoria and John Olsen in South Australia. It does not have the support of Prime Minister John Howard. And there will be no official federal government stand on the referendum.

It is a unique attitude for a major party to adopt in a referendum on an important constitutional change. Howard has made a virtue out of the reality of a divided party by allowing Liberal MPs a free vote in the referendum. Deputy Prime Minister and National Party leader Tim Fischer also described the issue after the election as 'a conscience vote', although official party policy as enunciated by its federal council is to oppose change. Members are not formally bound by this decision and there are republicans in the Nationals' ranks, although most have yet to come out of the closet. While Fischer and the party seem likely to oppose the republic in the referendum campaign, senior party members were uncertain at the end of 1998 just how strongly they would campaign. But with Pauline Hanson's One Nation also opposed, it increases the chances of a 'No' vote in Queensland, where both parties are at their strongest.

According to Opposition Leader Kim Beazley during the convention, 'the only way there'll be a republic in this country is if a prime minister who believes in it argues the case'.[4] If that is so, the 1999 referendum, and with it hopes for a republic by the centenary of Federation on 1 January 2001, are doomed following the re-election of the Howard Government. The Prime Minister said after the election that he would 'stay aloof from the day-to-day campaigning but people will know what my view is.'[5] But in an interview with *The Australian* in the week before the election, he was taking out some insurance against being left to look irrelevant and out-of-date if the referendum is carried.

> I haven't altered my own view just to make myself more fashionable, but equally I haven't carried on as though I will be the last man standing defending the status quo. If it gets up, I will not in any way be a reluctant facilitator of it.[6]

In short, it seems clear that whatever other monarchists do, Howard himself will not be playing a wrecking role. His position is that republicans have not established the case for the superiority of the model adopted by the convention over the present system. Monarchists believe he doubts that this year's referendum will be carried. A hint about his future view came at his swearing in after the 1996 election. He pledged allegiance to the Queen but omitted the phrase which normally follows, '[and] her heirs and successors'. That suggests he can see the strength of national sentiment in favour of ending the one remaining formal tie with Britain, but believes the most appropriate time to do so would be at the end of Queen Elizabeth's reign rather than at the symbolic but artificial time of the centenary of Federation.

After the election, Howard made it plain monarchists could not expect his support on their more strident arguments, including that the move to a republic would divide the nation and mean the end of a democratic Australia as we know it.

> I am of the view that whatever the outcome of that referendum . . . the fabric of the Australian community is not going to be any way damaged or hurt by the process. The constitutional convention demonstrated that, and I'm absolutely confident that whatever the outcome is, we will move forward in a very positive, united way to commemorate the foundation of the Australian nation 100 years ago on first January in the year 2001.[7]

Such comments give republicans hope that despite Beazley's view about the prime ministerial role, they can achieve a 'Yes' vote in a referendum. Indeed, they have come further than many thought possible under a monarchist prime minister. The recent impetus for a republic came, after all, from Paul Keating, who commissioned the 1993 report from the Republican Advisory Committee headed by Malcolm Turnbull, and proceeded to announce the then Government's preferred 'minimalist' model for a president with the same powers as the present governor-general, elected by a two-thirds majority of a joint sitting of both houses of Parliament.

Rhetorically and in some cases in practice, the Howard Government was quick to abandon Keating policies and approaches after its landslide win in the 1996 election. The republic issue was different. Howard could have walked away from his promise to hold a half-elected, half-appointed constitutional convention to discuss the republic without incurring great wrath from the mass of voters, who mostly saw it as a second-order issue, if that. But the reality he had to acknowledge was that Keating had stirred republican sentiments in Liberal as well as Labor breasts. A significant proportion of Liberal Party members and more than half of Liberal MPs in federal and state parliaments favour a republic. Keating was exploiting the issue to divide his opponents. The Coalition, first under Alexander Downer and then under Howard, used the convention as a vehicle for a united Opposition response.

And despite much scepticism, once the Government announced it was going ahead with the convention, it had a stake in its success—perhaps a greater one than it realised itself at the time. Its commitment was guarded: if the convention achieved a consensus on a republican model, that would be put to a referendum; in the absence of consensus, there would be a national plebiscite to test support for several options versus the status quo. The Government kept its options open, avoiding a definition of 'consensus' beyond suggesting it would have to be more than a narrow majority.

The Government's bona fides came under further question with the decision to make voting in the election for delegates to the convention voluntary and by postal ballot. That immediately distinguished the vote from that held in normal national elections, downgrading its status to more like that of the postal ballot for trade union elections. Yet for all the insistence by monarchists that Australians simply were not interested in the republic issue, just under 47 per cent of eligible Australians voted—about the same proportion as in elections for the US president. Republicans fared best, with Australian Republican Movement candidates and those on more radical platforms—especially popular election of the president—comprising 46 of the 76 elected delegates.

Against a background of low expectations, the convention turned into a substantial success. The idea of an elected convention had been advanced initially by those concerned at the lack of popular interest or involvement in government and the Constitution of the kind which the elected conventions of the 1890s had nurtured. If change is rejected this year, it at least is preferable that it is done from some basis of knowledge, rather than purely instinctively.

The Downer/Howard model was a compromise, based on

the unstated view that too much democracy can be bad in terms of producing an outcome politicians regard as acceptable and practical. The appointed half of the delegates ensured the convention benefited in turn from the expertise provided by constitutional lawyers, from the politicians who would be responsible for enacting any change and from broader community representation than could be expected from direct election. The venue of the former House of Representatives chamber in the old Parliament House lent an air of history and importance to the occasion. At the same time, it looked and sounded different from a standard parliamentary sitting. There were more women, more young people, more ethnic and indigenous delegates than in any of the federal or state parliaments. Moreover, it functioned more like parliament originally was intended to, before the formation of party blocs made debates and votes predictable. This was a forum in which logic and reason could influence the outcome, and did, because of the number of delegates, mainly those appointed, without fixed positions.

The high point for republicans came on the last day when, to applause from the public galleries, the convention voted by 89 to 52, with 11 abstentions, 'that this Convention supports in principle Australia becoming a republic'. It was in moving beyond the principle that the republicans' problems became apparent at the convention, as they will do in the referendum campaign. The ARM's Malcolm Turnbull argued that republicans who wanted more than a minimalist republic in the end would side with him because the only alternative was supporting the monarchists. But some, like former Brisbane mayor Clem Jones, who led a team of three Queensland delegates, were elected specifically on an elected-president platform that they were determined to uphold. They and others, such as former Independent MP Ted Mack, took the view that the cause of a 'real' republic would be better advanced by opposing any 'Mickey Mouse' change that might become entrenched in the Constitution and instead waiting for a more opportune time. As a result, they abstained on the modified Turnbull model or voted against it.

Thus it was that the convention reached the point that it needed a monarchist prime minister to help republicans over the line. Howard came to regard the option of a plebiscite as dangerous: if it resulted in majority support for an elected president, which opinion polls strongly suggested probable, he would be obliged to put that to a referendum against the status quo. The likelihood is that with the Coalition parties and possibly the Labor Party campaigning against it, it would have been defeated. But it is a risk Howard did not want to take. A popularly-elected president presaged a quite different system of government, with a head of state carrying a competing popular mandate to that of the prime minister. In theory this need not happen, as the example of Ireland demonstrates: there, an elected president with few powers can be a unifying influence.

But in Australia there is another factor—a Senate with the power to block a government's Budget. If most of the extensive powers of the governor-general are taken from an elected president, including the power to dismiss a PM, how is a parliamentary deadlock such as in 1975 to be resolved? By the political process, some argue, with one or other major party forced to back down. Yet even if this had been the case in the absence of Sir John Kerr's sacking of Gough Whitlam, it will not automatically be so in future.

At the convention, the minimalist republicans offered another route to resolution of this issue: taking away the Senate's powers to block supply, while at the same time removing most of the president's powers. But the Senate's powers have remained controversial ever since 1975, and a resolution to remove its right to block supply was defeated at the convention. For the minimalists, that emphasised the point that whatever the popular sentiment for direct election of the president, the complications would ensure a referendum defeat.

By the start of the convention, Howard had redefined the 'consensus' required for a referendum to a 'clear view'. On the final day, the minimalist republican model fell four short of a majority. Nevertheless, Howard accepted the vote of 73 to 57, with 22 abstentions, as a sufficiently clear expression of the convention's will to proceed to a referendum. Such flexibility was the product of a decision to avoid at all costs a plebiscite in which the direct election option would be put to the people.

The republican proposal to go to a referendum is based on that advanced at the convention by the ARM, with important modifications. The president would have the same extensive powers that the Constitution now vests in the governor-general, including command of the armed forces, calling and dissolving Parliament and appointing and dismissing ministers. Apart from very rare occasions, these are exercised only on the advice of the government. The convention recommended that Parliament consider spelling out these powers 'as far as practicable'. It also suggested Parliament state that the reserve powers would continue to exist. These are the powers that give the governor-general discretion, and generally are taken to include the appointment and dismissal of a prime minister and the dissolution of Parliament. The term of office of a president would be five years and he or she would be chosen by a two-thirds majority of a joint sitting of federal Parliament. The advantage over the present procedure of prime ministerial recommendation to the Queen would be that it ensured a bipartisan appointment. The convention added to the ARM model a public nomination procedure aimed at winning support from advocates of direct election, with details left to Parliament to spell out in the referendum bill.

It was on the method of dismissal that the ARM compromised to meet the objections of conservative delegates at the convention. Whereas the Turnbull model had proposed dismissal by the same means as appointment, delegates such as former Victorian governor Richard McGarvie pointed out that this could result in a deadlock if, say, a president behaved in a partisan fashion and one side of politics refused to agree to his dismissal. The convention opted for dismissal by the prime minister, who would be required to seek ratification by the House of Representatives within 30 days. The argument of critics, who include figures of the stature of former chief justice Sir Anthony Mason and prominent republicans such as Professor George Winterton, is that the dismissal procedure has gone from being too difficult to too easy.

Turnbull among others argues that the real political constraints on a prime minister would prevent this being a problem in practice, but it is an issue that monarchists will exploit in the referendum campaign. Republicans argue that this and other wrinkles should be resolved by reconvening a brief session of the convention or by Parliament. But the attitude of Special Minister of State Nick Minchin, who had carriage of the republic issue before the election, was unequivocal: the purpose of the convention had been to determine such issues and the Government would not depart from them. After the election, Attorney-General Daryl Williams, who has responsibility for the referendum bill in Parliament, suggested the Government would be more flexible with parliamentary amendments. While the Senate, where the Government lacks the numbers, can amend the bill, it cannot press those amendments on an unwilling government because the Constitution does not give the Upper House power to stop the referendum going ahead.

Even if the referendum succeeds, each state will have to decide individually whether to become a republic, requiring separate referendums in at least some states. The convention also decided on a new preamble to the Constitution acknowledging, among other things, the original ownership and custodianship of Australia by Aborigines and Torres Strait Islanders, representative democracy and responsible government, the rule of law and Australia's cultural diversity. Winterton argues that the preamble should be put to the people in a separate question on the referendum ballot paper: 'Even if we remain a monarchy, we might want to adopt some of these changes, while there are other people who are perfectly happy to have a republic but don't want a preamble.'

Australians this year get an opportunity to take their own collective step in the march of the nation. It will be a tussle between instinctive scepticism about change being advocated by politicians, and pride in a still-developing nation.

Notes

1 Michael Coper, 'Lucinda's Legacy' *The Australian*, 29 March 1996
2 Quoted in Helen Irving, 'An Historic Compromise' *The Australian*, 29 March 1996

3 'Commonwealth realms', in the royal family's home page, www.royal.gov.uk
4 Transcript of doorstop, 3 February 1998
5 Transcript of radio interview with Jeremy Cordeaux, Radio 5DN, 19 October 1998
6 Unpublished transcript of interview by Paul Kelly and Dennis Shanahan with John Howard, 30 September 1998
7 Transcript of news conference, 14 October 1998

13

SILENCING THE IMMIGRANT SONG
Closed doors or open minds?

Richard McGregor

ON HIS OWN TERMS, John Howard made significant achievements on immigration policy in his first term of government. He cut the numbers sharply, skewed the intake to favour skilled migrants, removed the right of tens of thousands of foreigners to go on welfare and almost single-handedly wiped the word multiculturalism from the mainstream political lexicon. Just as significant, though, was the fact that the Labor Party went along with him. Surface noise aside, Labor has bowed to the new consensus for lower, more targeted immigration in such a decisive way that it would be difficult for them to ratchet the program back up on returning to government.

There is no small irony in Howard presiding over a new, if soft bipartisan consensus on immigration. After all, he came to office intent on destroying a cosy compact he thought excluded the public. That he has fractured what he regarded as the false consensus stifling debate over immigration meets an important goal he set for his prime ministership. That he has done so by staring down and calling the bluff of new-class interest groups, from old-style ethnic lobbies to Asia-boosting foreign policy advocates, in favour of his beloved 'mainstream' is also something of which he would be proud.

It's been a hollow victory. The uneasy new compact, which

conceals deep differences within the formal party groupings, masks a vacuum of public policy on immigration—that is, the inability of the major parties, or indeed the political process, to sustain a debate about building a new rationale for a robust immigration program. Rather than leading on immigration, politicians are responding to what they believe is entrenched community antagonism to a greater inflow of foreigners, and the multicultural ethos that comes with it.

Advocates of the alternate view have also let themselves down. They have failed to confront honestly the implication of their policies—a less equal society, with greater potential for division. There is some evidence, in fact, that the public does not want a large immigration program, but not nearly as much as self-styled community advocates would have us believe. Academic Ian McAllister from the ANU, for instance, says in a recent study that 'the greater weight that is accorded to public opinion, the more likely it is that immigration will be reduced'.[1] Another study by Katherine Betts of the Swinburne University of Technology says that nearly two-thirds of Australians thought in 1996 that the intake was too high.[2]

A more definitive study of polling and immigration by Sydney University's Murray Goot pulls apart the headlines created by surveys depicting overwhelming public opposition to immigration, especially from Asia. He illustrates that the wildly different results recorded by pollsters, both for and against, are a product of the different sets of questions they ask. 'Public opinion on the rate of immigration is not only "soft", it is created in the very attempt to measure it,' he says. In other words, public opinion can be led, both by pollsters seeking responses and by politicians following the pollsters. Under such circumstances, says Goot, claims about 'what the majority thinks' are largely meaningless.[3]

Still, common sense tells us that at a time of high jobless rates, of insecure employment and of dysfunctional families, immigration, especially from Asia, is not going to be instantly popular. There is nothing surprising about this. The 30 years that have lapsed since Canberra abandoned the White Australia Policy is barely a generation. Societies do not easily abandon views on race, repugnant now but which only a short time ago represented an unremarkable orthodoxy, passed from government to government and family to family. While the official line has certainly changed rapidly in Australia in favour of non-discrimination, it doesn't follow that the latent racial views of ordinary people have been speedily transformed along the way. Liberal MP Ross Cameron is typical of a new breed of conservatives who feel that the pendulum has swung too far for ordinary people to keep up. He represents Parramatta, in the heart of Sydney's west, and more than one-third of his constituents were born overseas. The bulk of the English-speaking population accepts diversity percolating through their communities, he says, but not

> capital M, state-sponsored Multiculturalism. In the wealthy North Shore and Eastern Suburbs of Sydney, multiculturalism means which restaurant will I go to tonight or which country will I visit next. The force-fed, state-sponsored capital M Multiculturalism has sat undigested in the electorate for about a decade. What Queensland (election) represented is a vomiting up of that meal.

By crude extension, you might expect the major parties to exploit the race issue. After all, their internal polling picked up on Asian immigration long ago as an issue. But they don't, because immigration and race are risky battlegrounds on which to engage opponents, other than in code. The gains are speculative, the downside steep in terms of losing elite support and creating media frenzies. Immigration and race are not what party professionals call vote-changers, except among city-based Hanson supporters. Rather, they show up in polling as national issues in high-pitched, short-lived spikes, often when the issues are being debated publicly, and then fade away again.

Howard had good practical, even cynical, reasons for putting immigration back in a box. Not the least of these is that battling over an issue as volatile as immigration drowns out the Government's message on other topics. Like many other pundits, the Prime Minister misjudged the Pauline Hanson phenomenon. Initially flirting with her to ensure he did not alienate her supporters, he soon found he had as much to lose as he stood to gain within the Liberals' own broad church. The Queensland state election proved that whatever could be won in regional areas doing deals with One Nation was lost in the cities. Another good reason for leaving immigration on the shelf is that the issue contains the potential for deep divisions within all main political parties. Howard's scepticism about the economic benefits of immigration and his instinctive antagonism to multiculturalism, for example, find no support with senior Liberals such as Alexander Downer, Peter Costello and Jeff Kennett, who are comfortable with both concepts. Nor do his views thrill leading conservatives in the business community, like Western Mining's Hugh Morgan, who support increased immigration.

Similar divisions between internationalists and localists, if you like, splinter Labor. Kim Beazley is a big immigration man, largely because of his bleak, often apocalyptic view on Australia and the vulnerability that comes with its large land and small population. Martin Ferguson, Labor's spokesman in the first term, has a traditionally restrictive union view at odds with Beazley's but one that suited Labor's low-profile agenda in the first Howard term. Like Howard in many ways, Ferguson regards migrants as competitors for scarce Australian jobs.

Influential figures in both camps, such as Labor's NSW Premier Bob Carr and Liberal minister Nick Minchin, lean towards the newly-fashionable 'populate-and-perish' school, which contends that Australia's fragile ecology cannot sustain more people. The most extreme advocates of this position assert that Australia's sustainable population is 8 million, about the same as tiny Hong Kong will have by the turn of the century.

The Greens deride supporters of immigration as either pawns of property developers (the housing industry supports immigration for obvious commercial reasons), or naive and/or self-serving Asia-boosters. The Australian Democrats support the Greens' view, which, uncomfortably for them, means they have about the same immigration targets as One Nation.

Amid all this, Howard has shown himself as pre-eminently sensitive to community disquiet over immigration and, in recent years, politically adept at reflecting it. It has left him stubbornly running against an agenda rather than creating one of his own. As with other institutions and policies puffed up by what he would regard as 'elite' views, Howard in his first term campaigned against Paul Keating's legacy on race, immigration, multiculturalism and Asia, as much as he has promoted ideas of his own.

Political consultant Malcolm McGregor captured this phenomenon by re-tooling a joke American comedian Mort Sahl told about Ronald Reagan's landslide presidential defeat of Jimmy Carter: 'John Howard only won in a landslide because he was running against Paul Keating. If he had run unopposed, he would have lost.'

If you want an analogy for the style of Howard's first term, one that can be applied to immigration and multiculturalism among other policies, think of the bruising, blokey contact sport of rugby league. On any team, the PM would make an invaluable defender, someone who can absorb punishment tirelessly in preventing opponents crossing his team's line. In attack, the picture looks different. With no one to beat and the line wide open, Howard often gives the impression of not knowing what to do.

He also brought dreadful baggage to immigration in government, most spectacularly his considered 1988 comments about the need to slow Asian immigration. He apologised for these comments before the 1996 election, and his supporters insist he was simply reflecting community concern at the time. In so doing, he ignobly made himself the only Australian political leader since the mid-1960s to support using race as a basis for selecting migrants. He lost his leadership partly because of the outcry following his comments. And in some respects, he has never lived them down, despite numerous efforts to disown them. Although he has never revisited the issue in explicit racial terms, suspicions linger. His critics charge that the Coalition used coded, American Republican Party-style racial messages in its 1996 election slogan, 'For All of Us', urged by the party's sharp pollster Mark Textor. They also flay Howard for initially hedging his bets on Hanson.

The PM did, however, show a degree of finesse in one area

of immigration—his choice of minister, NSW moderate Philip Ruddock. He has both a lengthy and distinguished record on ethnic issues and is a skilled administrator and policy-maker. His clear-eyed stance on race had also bought him into direct conflict with Howard in the past. In 1988, Ruddock crossed the floor to vote with Labor on a motion condemning Howard's Asian immigration comments. He also negotiated with Bob Hawke on behalf of the Liberals a compact on multiculturalism in 1989 in response to Stephen Fitzgerald's scathing report on community attitudes to this ethnic sacred cow. This document survives as the basic policy guide for multiculturalism.

Ruddock and Howard have known each other for decades. They met in their late teens in the NSW Young Liberals, and this foundation has served them well. Despite Ruddock's floor-crossing and his status as a leading 'wet', his relationship with Howard has survived and, in the course of government, prospered. His administrative and policy skills have made him a successful immigration minister, so much so that he has been rated highly not just by Howard but also by the bureaucracy and Labor.

A thornier question is whether he has been a success on his own terms, or simply implemented a program dictated by Howard. Just as difficult to judge is the impact of his wooden style and glacial manner. Ruddock is no salesman: he cannot deliver a media-wise message via television, a handicap in ensuring he generates enthusiasm about the immigration program rather than merely defending it.

Howard's fingerprints were certainly stamped all over the portfolio in the first year. He overruled Ruddock in Cabinet to ensure that the intake for 1996–97 was substantially lowered from Labor's last year in office. And judging by the questions Ruddock was asked by his own colleagues in Parliament—always a good gauge of the issues ministers want to highlight, as they arrange these questions themselves—the picture for immigration is bleak. For they detail not a flourishing melting pot enriched by waves of immigration but the Government's tightening of border controls, expulsions of undesirables, crackdowns on sham marriages and withdrawal of welfare benefits. Said one colleague at the time: 'In some respects, Ruddock was almost choking to death putting in place an immigration program primarily dictated by the Prime Minister.'

Even as prime minister, with the office's manifold responsibilities, Howard jumped on seemingly trivial issues where foreigners were supposedly threatening our borders. Take his stridency over the Australian visit of Lorenzo Ervin, a pardoned former plane hijacker correctly described by one newspaper as a 'clapped-out Black Panther'. Howard recalled Ruddock home from a state visit to Belgrade to sort out a kerfuffle over Erwin's low-key speaking tour, which apparently made him a menace to national security.

Ruddock was also extremely uncomfortable about Howard's intervention when Hanson claimed credit for lowering the migration intake. The Prime Minister was prompted to say that he—and not the Queenslander—has been first to support lower immigration while unemployment was high. He was correct to point to his consistency, but the clumsy alacrity of his intervention gave the impression that the Government was jumping to Hanson's tune. In truth, she affected the atmospherics of the immigration debate but did not influence the substantive policies. In part, that was because Howard had anticipated many of her worries, or had like-minded concerns, and in part it was because the Coalition refused to countenance racial targeting of migration numbers.

It is possible to make too much of the differences between Howard and Ruddock. On core issues, re-skewing the intake away from family reunion towards skilled migration and cutting the cost of the program by reducing welfare benefits paid to migrants, the pair is as one—and has been for years. The controversial policy of the two-year waiting period for welfare benefits was not dreamt up by a flinty Howard but proposed first in 1993 by Ruddock. The Coalition's rationale was simple—they cut the program in areas where they could save money, a government priority in its first Budget. They also argued that the cuts had the positive effect of allaying community concerns that the program was being run at the expense of ordinary workers.

This re-skewing has been backed by a dominant new strain of influence of government policy-making, led by Monash University's Bob Birrell. He noted with approval in a recent paper with Virginia Rapson that Australia's tightened family reunion policies were

> now more in accord with the restrictive patterns evident in Western European nations than with those of Canada and the USA, the 'settler' societies which Australia's migration program used to parallel.[4]

It should come as no surprise that, even after nearly 50 years of a nation-building immigration program, Australian policy can be remoulded to resemble an increasingly xenophobic Europe more than the US and Canada. After all, Australia has received both migrants and refugees for decades, but its practical generosity has never been idealised in the way immigration was in America. The open-door policy for Vietnamese migrants, pushed through by the Fraser Government with little enthusiasm from Labor, is perhaps an exception. Generally, the welcoming, idealistic images of Ellis Island and the Statue of Liberty, which ushered newcomers into the US, have no equivalent here. 'Populate-or-perish', in one form or another, has been the rationale for Australia's program. It was a defensive rather than a positive ethos, and remains so today.

By next year, family reunion will have fallen from 70 per cent to about 45 per cent of the program. English-language requirements and skills tests have been strengthened. The Government has also capped the aged parents category and tightened requirements for approving spouses and finances. Another change emphasised by Ruddock favours refugees over people in the Special Assistance Category—in other words, foreigners with relatives in Australia who are allowed in as special cases. The upshot of the Coalition's changes is that if you are over 45 and don't have a bundle of money and extraordinary talents, you have scant hope of getting into Australia these days.

Nothing Labor offers will substantially change this. Beazley attempted to carve out a niche for himself by advocating a population policy to get around the annual haggling over the size of the intake. But his speeches on this were as much philosophical exercises as policy proposals. No detailed numbers were offered. Otherwise, Labor has given very public support to the Government on issues like anti-racism campaigns, and run dead on issues like the two-year welfare ban before finally adopting such policies as their own. The only significant area where Labor refused to back the Government, tacitly or otherwise, was Ruddock's determination to reduce the power of tribunals and courts to challenge departmental and ministerial decisions. (Ruddock was running the departmental line here as much as his own. The Department's overriding concern is to control the program and ensure that its rules aren't broken, rather than to involve itself in the more political debate about the size or composition of the intake.)

Labor did take a principled stand against Hanson's views on race long before Howard. It was not without risk. Even though Hanson's support came off Howard's 1996 base, Labor could not have been sure its own traditional supporters would not flock to Hanson at its expense. Ultimately, it was only marginally successful. Certainly Labor's stance threw the Coalition into a spiral after the Queensland election but in the end the ALP lured few Hansonites back to the fold. Behind the scenes, senior Labor figures tried to use the issue to undermine the Liberals, offering informal advice to the anti-Hanson and anti-Coalition party, Unity, in the 1998 election. Unity had little impact on the poll but it did indicate one thing—the end of an era for traditional ethnic politics. The Federation of Ethnic Community Councils failed to adapt to life under Howard, and has not found a clear voice to position its view with the Government. Not that Howard would care—old ethnic politics for him represent the kind of special interest politics he wanted to marginalise.

Labor has been placed on the back foot on immigration for several reasons—mostly the need to rebuild its own blue-collar base which felt neglected during Keating's final years at the expense of other agendas, like multiculturalism and Asia. The ALP has also had to counter accusations that immigration had been co-opted as just another cog in its political machine. There were allegations the Special Assistance Program had been rigged to favour people from Sri Lanka and Lebanon, for example. Labor was also criticised for using Migrant Resources Centres as recruitment grounds. Numerous cases of branch-stacking would seem to bear this out, although such tales say more about Labor Party culture than they do about immigration. Branch-stacking did not start with migrants—they are simply the latest, and most fertile, low-income recruitment pool, just as Irish Catholics or other disadvantaged groups were decades ago.

Building support around ethnic clusters is a deadly course for the ALP, nonetheless. The only votes ethnic warlords can deliver are in pre-selections—they cannot do much to sway the results of the elections themselves. And in allowing faction leaders to turn pre-selections into ethnic bidding wars, Labor is breeding a culture that will alienate ordinary voters from the party even further, and provide a disincentive to outsiders to join the party and climb the ranks. The quality of Labor candidates was a particular problem in the last election.

Chasing the so-called ethnic vote also has little going for it. Various ethnic groups have supported different parties at different times for different reasons. Jewish people, for example, were initially enthused about Labor because of Doc Evatt's support for Israel. Migrants from the Baltic States supported the Coalition because of the clarity of their anti-communist stand. The Chinese, natural Coalition supporters because of their small business bent and aversion to collectivist politics, may have drifted towards Labor because of concern over Howard's stance on Hanson. Over time, though, the voting of migrants and their children reflects community trends.

Labor is not guilty of all the sins it has been accused of—criticisms of the family reunion program as a giant ALP rort are largely misplaced. Ultimately, the blow-out in the program was fuelled for the most part not by some Tammany Hall politics, allocating country quotas like political gifts, but by Bob Hawke's single decision to allow tens of thousands of Chinese students to stay here permanently after the 1989 Beijing crackdown. It is easy to criticise the decision with hindsight, but Hawke did only what the US, France and other countries with

Chinese students did in the emotional aftermath of the Beijing killings. The real problem was not that we had lots of Chinese students but that so many were not students at all, and had used the pretext of study to come here for work and to procure a passport. The then immigration minister, Robert Ray, used to joke that ELICOS stood not for English Language Intensive Courses for Overseas Students but English Learners Intending Change of Status. Successive Labor immigration ministers tried to stop these bogus student rackets but were defeated by more powerful forces in government pushing the sale of education services and closer ties with China.

The number of Chinese coming here to join their families has swelled in recent years as a knock-on effect from the Hawke decision. The Howard Government's crackdown on sham marriages and the capping of the parents category has hit the Chinese especially hard. The Prime Minister wanted growth in these two areas curtailed, prompting many to mutter darkly about his aim of cutting migrants from mainland China. These conspiracy theories are not borne out by the facts. In coming years, it is not the Chinese who will be buffeted by government policies but refugees from the war in the former Yugoslavia. That's because they have recorded the greatest growth in intake recently, and will naturally want to bring their families to join them, as the Chinese have. But as with the Chinese, they will face formidable barriers to qualify.

The broader issue is whether family reunion programs and the high proportion of elderly people who go on welfare tell the whole story about balance in the immigration program. Most modern studies attempt to calculate the cost to the Budget of migrant welfare. Birrell and Rapson, for example, say that after two years of residence, 57 to 58 per cent of pensionable men and women from countries with which Australia doesn't have social security agreements were receiving welfare. There is ample anecdotal evidence of a small industry in Chinese nursing homes. Not so easy to calculate, though, is the value to the community, let alone the savings to the Budget, of the care and stability provided by close family members for their relatives. It is a different kind of social benefit, one out of fashion with economists and their models.

So what stands in the way of a big immigration program? The great failing of those who want to revive a larger intake is that they have not dealt honestly with the implications of their arguments. Nor have they won the argument in the community in the first place. A renewed big migration push cannot be imposed by bi-partisan stealth. An enlarged program, first of all, requires a new and positive rationale, with the ballast of community support. In an era of systemic high unemployment, people must be convinced that migrants are adding to the country's wealth and not draining scarce resources and jobs. Minchin put the issue with a cold definitiveness when confronted by the latest big business push for more migration at an ACCI dinner in Canberra in November 1998. 'There is absolutely no political constituency in this country for higher immigration,' he said. The scary corollary for any politician who dares to push for more migration is that there is a large constituency which can now be marshalled against them.

The present emphasis on skilled migration is essentially demand-driven: the Government only just manages to fill the places it now sets aside for skilled migrants. In other words, expanding the program would mean lowering, or changing, the entry standards. That in turn has profound implications for the kind of society that Australians want to have. Just which qualifications that the Government uses to screen migrants should be dropped to expand the program. Functional English? Capital? Skills? And which professions would be willing to open their ranks to foreigners, or indeed, should be forced to? The bitter battles waged by foreign doctors to get their qualifications recognised here is a microcosm of the difficulties in this area.

A bigger program, and more unskilled migrants, inevitably entails significant decisions about reforms in other sectors, notably further deregulation of the labour market and lower wages. That's because the plentiful blue-collar jobs available in Australia's first wave of immigration are no longer there. The good, new jobs are mainly in the service sector, and are highly skilled. Bringing in more unskilled migrants almost certainly means depressing wages in other sectors, with the potential to entrench an emerging migrant underclass that many commentators say is already developing. Australians will say no to more migrants if they believe it means an increasingly stratified society.

The bipartisan political compact which transcended community opinion on immigration has to be replaced by a new consensus with the community at its heart. Otherwise there are more than enough politicians, some with genuine concerns, others with more malevolent intent, to ensure the program remains static and moribund, instead of the vigorous and enriching process that it can be—and has been for Australia in the post-war years.

NOTES

1 Ian McAllister, *The Politics of Australian Immigration*, eds. James Jupp, Mave Kabala, 1993, pp. 161–78
2 Katherine Betts, 'People and Place', Centre for Population and Urban Research, Monash University, vol. 4, no. 3
3 Murray Goot, *International Journal of Public Opinion Research*, vol. 3, no. 3
4 Bob Birrell and Virginia Rapson, 'People and Place', vol. 6, no. 2, vol. 6, no. 3

14

THE BLACK MARK ON OUR SOUL
Reconciling reconciliation

Stuart Rintoul

MAY 1997: RECONCILIATION CONVENTION, Melbourne. John Howard is lecturing an audience thirsty for an apology to the stolen generations on why they will not receive one, but why there will be a Ten Point Plan to stop an imaginary legal pendulum that has swung too far towards Aboriginal rights. He shouts and pounds on the lectern. One-quarter of the 2000 delegates to the convention stand and turn their backs on him in silent protest. No prime minister has been subjected to such a direct and personal affront by Australia's indigenous people.

> Personally, I feel deep sorrow for those of my fellow Australians who suffered injustices under the practices of past generations towards indigenous people. Equally, I am sorry for the hurt and trauma many here today may continue to feel as a consequence of those practices. [But] Australians of this generation should not be required to accept guilt or blame for past actions and policies over which they had no control.[1]

Alex Boraine, South Africa's deputy chair of its Truth and Reconciliation Commission, will later say: 'Your Prime Minister's got balls but he hasn't got a hell of a lot of heart.' Sitting on the stage, just a few metres from Howard, the chairman of the Council for Aboriginal Reconciliation, Patrick Dodson, felt his optimism draining away. Six months later he had bowed out.

Although no other black leader in the nation was perceived as possessing Dodson's qualities of statesmanship, despite his desire to continue in the job, he had lost confidence in the willingness of the Government to achieve a meaningful, just outcome. The indigenous crusade that began with the High Court's Mabo ruling on 3 June 1992 was breaking apart.

One of the great challenges for Australia in the rush towards the new millennium has been to come to terms with its history, in particular the darkest aspects and consequences of Aboriginal dispossession. The historian Henry Reynolds describes it as 'a nagging disquiet' in the national psyche, a whispering in our hearts.[2] Twenty years earlier, Xavier Herbert had written:

> Until we give back to the black man just a bit of the land that was his and give it back without provisos, without strings to snatch it back, without anything but complete generosity of spirit in concession for the evil that we have done to him—until we do that—we shall remain what we have always been so far, a people without integrity, not a nation but a community of thieves.[3]

The Prime Minister, whose job it is to position the nation at the turn of the millennium, had rarely, prior to Mabo and the push for reconciliation, turned his mind to Aboriginal issues. At the end of the millennium, he has found it hard to be prime minister and not turn his mind to reconciliation as an issue of national identity. Yet in many respects he seems peculiarly ill-equipped to deal with the emotional, as well as political and legal complexities of the issue. Howard is widely perceived as a man hankering for the certainties of the 1950s. At the time of his first election, he said he wanted a country that was 'comfortable and relaxed'. Redressing the wrongs of the past and affording Aboriginal people an honourable place in the life of the nation will not be comfortable and relaxed. It is a challenge of historic dimensions. In many parts of Australia, white and black tensions are acute. Exceptional indigenous people, athletes and artists, are welcomed to the table, but most ordinary Aboriginal people are not. Most Aboriginal people live in abject poverty.

By personality as well as politics, Howard belongs to that

part of mainstream Australia for whom Aboriginality is extrinsic. In 24 years in Parliament, he has made just two journeys into Aboriginal Australia. The first, in 1988, was a scarring encounter; the second, a decade later as prime minister, he described as one of the most moving experiences of his life.

Howard has several times suggested that in his second term, which includes the 2000 Olympics when international attention will be focused on Australia, he will be a different prime minister and that social issues, including Aboriginal reconciliation, will 'bulk large on the political horizon' as the nation gathers 'millennium momentum'. But the gap between government and Aboriginal expectation of the basis for reconciliation is immense. Howard told the Reconciliation Convention that reconciliation

> will not work if it puts a higher value on symbolic gestures and overblown promises rather than the practical needs of Aboriginal and Torres Strait Islander people in areas like health, housing, education and employment.

In the lead-up to the election, he supported a 'document of understanding': not a treaty, with its implication of separateness, which he found repugnant, but a recognition of prior occupation by the indigenous people and of their unique characteristics. He also said that in the event of the nation voting to become a republic, which he opposed, a new constitution should contain a preamble recognising the indigenous people. He said he had 'thought for a long time that some kind of sensible document which recognises the past, but more, is aspirational about the united future would be a good thing'.

Two weeks later, after Howard exhorted Aboriginal people to see themselves 'as part and parcel of a harmonious Australian community', the director of the Kimberley Land Council, Peter Yu, wrote in *The Australian*:

> In his election night victory speech, John Howard pledged his new Government to the reconciliation process. Yet, only two weeks later, the Prime Minister has again showed himself to be part of that awful Australian ignorance that has so marred the path to reconciliation in the past few years.[4]

Yu outlined several principles he said were essential to any document of reconciliation. They were:

- constitutional recognition and protection of indigenous rights;
- recognition of traditional customary law within the Australian legal system;
- development of an agreed document on Australian history;
- symbolic protocols recognising the special status of indigenous people within the Australian nation;
- establishment of a substantial long-term capital fund that compensates indigenous people for past dispossession and provides for economic security;
- formulation of regional indigenous governance arrangements as a key mechanism in a new political relationship between indigenous people and Australian governments;
- the creation of a national funding formula that will deliver community infrastructure and services on an equitable basis.

Pat Dodson endorsed each of these points as matters that had to be the subject of 'genuine negotiation if Howard is serious'.

Two explosive issues have dominated Howard's black horizon: native title and stolen children. On 3 June 1992, the High Court in *Mabo and Others v Queensland* reversed 200 years of legal presumption and struck out the concept that the nation was *terra nullius*, an empty land, at the time of colonisation. The decision, technically concerned with the remote island of Mer, fundamentally elevated the nature of Aboriginal rights. In December 1993, the Native Title Act was passed by Paul Keating's Labor Government despite the Coalition's opposition. Effective from 1 January 1994, the Act provided for the recognition and protection of native title, a National Native Title Tribunal to adjudicate on claims, the validation of past government acts that extinguished native title, and an Indigenous Land Fund that would allow the 95 per cent of dispossessed Aborigines who could never establish a native title claim to purchase land.

But Mabo and Keating's legislation were shot through with

unresolved issues, the most significant being whether native title was restricted to vacant crown land or could co-exist with pastoral leases, covering about 42 per cent of the nation, and to what extent Aboriginal people had a right to negotiate with mining companies operating on pastoral lease land. Amendments to Keating's legislation by the West Australian Greens in the Senate lowered the threshold test for making claims to the NNTT, with the result that there was a flood of ambit and conflicting applications.

A key assumption of Keating's Native Title Act was that pastoral leases would extinguish native title, but on 23 December 1996 the High Court ruled 4–3 in *Wik Peoples v Queensland* that they could co-exist. Three members of the majority referred to the instructions of Earl Grey, Secretary of State for the Colonies, to Governor Charles FitzRoy (1847–48), which noted:

> It should be generally understood that Leases granted for this purpose give the grantees only an exclusive right of pasturage for their cattle, and of cultivating such Land as they may require within the large limits thus assigned to them, but that these Leases are not intended to deprive the Natives of their former right to hunt over these Districts, or to wander over them in search of subsistence, in the manner to which they have been heretofore accustomed, from the spontaneous produce of the soil except over land actually cultivated or fenced in for that purpose.[5]

Wik woman Gladys Tybingoompa danced for joy outside the High Court. 'Out of here we go, no one being a loser,' she said. I had met Tybingoompa five years earlier at Aurukun, on the west coast of Cape York Peninsula, where the missionary Bill MacKenzie once ruled with a Bible in one hand and a set of chains in the other. It was a place where alcoholic violence had laid siege to a culture of incandescent beauty. In Wik–Mungkan culture, *pul-uchan* are two young boy spirits who walk hand in hand. They are good spirits and do not hurt people. They live under the rocks and near the Watson River. They created the season *Onchan Min* (when there is no more rain and bush food is very plentiful) for those without parents, and *Onchan Wayath* (a short season following the real wet season when the countryside is still wet but the rain has virtually stopped) for those who have parents. There are eight seasons in Wik–Mungkan knowledge.[6]

But where Mabo had ushered in a new era for Aboriginal land rights, the Wik ruling strained it to breaking point. 'That's the end of reconciliation,' NFF president Donald McGauchie declared. Five months after the Wik decision, the federation launched an advertising campaign that threatened to ignite the politics of race. The first showed two young children, one Aboriginal and one blond and freckly, playing a grim game of Twister on a black and white board, with a voice asking 'Can black and white Australians live in harmony when the High Court's Wik decision on native title has created uncertainty, especially for farmers? Whose land is it? Who can use it? Farmers want their rights restored and control of their future. The Wik decision—it's not a game.' A second advertisement showed a farmer, his hands work-scarred, his eyes blindfolded, unable to put a post into his parched red earth as his family looked on helplessly.

In reality, both Mabo and Wik were limited opportunities for Aboriginal people to reclaim sections of their ancestral land. They were remnant rights. Mabo opened up vacant crown land for claim only where claimants could prove uninterrupted traditional occupation—no easy matter given the extent of dispossession and acquisition that had occurred—while Wik made it clear in its interpretation of coexistence that where native title and pastoralists' interests conflicted, native title would yield, although the concept of common law rights yielding to prevailing rights under a state title appeared to invite a challenge of discrimination.

While Howard said he had reached the view that the Mabo decision was 'completely unexceptional . . . based on a great deal of logic and fairness and proper principle', he believed the shift in certainty towards Aboriginal interests in Keating's Native Title Act and Wik had 'pushed the pendulum too far in the Aboriginal direction'.

A protracted dispute over CRA's 1990 Century Zinc discovery in Queensland, forecast as the world's largest zinc mine, reinforced the perception. The project quickly became subject of claim and counter-claim. Called in by the Borbidge Government to negotiate, in March 1997 former governor-general Bill Hayden published an explosive letter referring to the right to negotiate as coming 'perilously close at times to being extortion'. Agreement was finally reached in May 1997, but the delays had been costly for the company and soured conservative attitude further.

Howard was under enormous pressure to extinguish native title from within his Liberal Party, the National Party and the conservative governments of Richard Court in Western Australia—where there were large tracts of vacant crown land and where more than 70 per cent of mineral production occurred on pastoral lease land—and Rob Borbidge in Queensland, where the sheep and cattle of 1500 pastoralists roam over half the state. But Howard was constrained by the Racial Discrimination Act (RDA). Instead, early in May 1997, he announced a 'Ten Point Plan', the centrepiece and crunch issue of which was the removal of the right to negotiate, portrayed by the mining industry as a 'de facto veto'.

Howard then went to Longreach in Queensland, steeped in dust and history, to face pastoralists who were demanding a 'one point plan'—blanket extinguishment. For the first time, he alluded to the prospect of a double-dissolution race election. On the eve of Howard's address at the Stockman's Hall of Fame, his Coalition partner, Deputy Prime Minister Tim Fischer, told ABC radio that each of the ten points, formulated by industry before the election, represented a 'winding back from an extremist, unpractical decision of the High Court . . . There are bucketfuls of extinguishment in the Ten Point Plan, on a fair basis.'[7]

Howard, who declared he had a covenant with the mining and pastoral industries to not back down on native title, had to negotiate his legislation with the independent Senator from Tasmania, Brian Harradine, who held the balance of power in the Senate. A staunch Catholic, Harradine prayed for an 'honourable compromise'. There were four sticking points: the Government's intention to toughen the threshold test for native title registration and base it on physical and not just spiritual connection to land; the imposition of a six-year sunset clause on claims; the right to negotiate; and the application of the RDA. At the end of March 1998, Tybingoompa danced with Harradine barefoot outside Parliament. Harradine said: 'I sensed a feeling of freedom, a feeling of participating in ancient customs . . . I was experiencing something genuinely Australian.'[8]

Early in July, increasingly fearful of the consequences of a race-based double dissolution election that could propel Pauline Hanson's One Nation into the Senate, Harradine blinked and struck a deal. After an 18-month stalemate, he agreed to the Government's physical connection test for registration but provided for the stolen generation and Aborigines locked out of their land by pastoralists, the Government abandoned the sunset clause, the Bill was made subject to the RDA, and a state-based administrative system was introduced to determine the right to negotiate. Under the Howard–Harradine compromise, the right to negotiate would remain in place until a state took it away. After the longest debate since Federation, Howard's Ten Point Plan was introduced with 314 amendments. Native title, Galarrwuy Yunupingu said, had been 'permanently allocated to the bottom of the heap'.[9]

The same month, the Howard Government began lobbying for the United Nations to drop the term 'self-determination' from its draft declaration on the rights of indigenous peoples and replace it with 'self-management', or 'self-empowerment', phrases consistent with Howard's philosophy and devoid of legal meaning. In June, Hanson had described the UN draft declaration as a 'treacherous sellout of the Australian people' that would 'tear the heart out of our country and deliver that heart to one of our very smallest minority groups'.[10] In July, Foreign Minister Alexander Downer was reported as saying:

> In the case of Australia, we don't want to see a separate country created for indigenous Australians. We will . . . be arguing . . . that it might be better to use the term 'self-management' rather than leaving an impression that we are prepared to have a separate indigenous state.[11]

The Government's opposition to self-determination for

indigenous people—government policy since 1972 and pivotal to the reconciliation process—was a frontal attack on the central pillar of the Aboriginal struggle. Bob Hawke established the Council for Aboriginal Reconciliation in 1991 with a ten-year charter to produce a document of reconciliation. It was a compromise position. In the Bicentennial year, 1988, Hawke had rashly promised a treaty within two years. Keating then set the scene, after the Mabo decision, with his Redfern Park, Sydney, speech on 10 December 1992, penned by Labor historian Don Watson.

> We simply cannot sweep injustice aside . . . It was we who did the dispossessing. We took the traditional lands and smashed the traditional way of life; we brought the diseases, the alcohol; we committed the murders; we took the children from their mothers; we practised discrimination and exclusion. It was our ignorance and our prejudice, and our failure to imagine these things being done to us. With some noble exceptions, we failed to make the most basic human response and enter into their hearts and minds. We failed to ask: 'How would I feel if this were done to me?'[12]

The election of the Howard Government in March 1996 reversed the political dynamic. Howard, who in 1988 had promised that he would rip up any treaty struck with Aboriginal people, had derided Keating's embrace of the issue as a political distraction. He was contemptuous of what he saw as a pernicious 'black armband' view of Australian history that subverted the nation-building story to which he subscribed. While he told senior ministers privately that something had to be done about the profound social and economic disadvantage of Aboriginal people, which continued to attract international condemnation, his first press conference on coming to office—the very first—was to announce an inquiry into the spending practices of ATSIC, which was responsible for allocating large amounts of government money to indigenous communities. He boosted Aboriginal health spending, but stripped ATSIC of $470 million.

Throughout 1992–96, Aboriginal leaders negotiated in Canberra in an atmosphere of harried optimism. They received the election of the Howard Government with a despondency that grew into bitterness when the Prime Minister appeared on national television on 4 September 1997 with a map in hand falsely warning that further development of 78 per cent of Australia's land mass, not covered by exclusive tenure, could potentially be subjected to Aboriginal veto. At the end of October 1997, relations between Government and indigenous leaders bottomed. Aboriginal lawyer Noel Pearson, who had formed the view that Howard was motivated by the politics of the wedge, described his Government as 'racist scum'. At almost exactly the same time Pearson was speaking, Pat Dodson told Aboriginal Affairs Minister John Herron that he had lost confidence the Government would deal fairly with Aborigines.

As Howard wound back the native title pendulum, pressure was building for a national government apology to the stolen generations, the most evil chapter of Australia's dealings with indigenous people: the forcible separation of 'light-skinned' Aboriginal children from their parents in order to absorb them into white society as servants and labourers. In April 1997, 'Bringing them home', the excoriating report of the inquiry into the separation of Aboriginal and Torres Strait Islander children from their families, concluded that in the period 1910–70, between one in three and one in ten indigenous children were forcibly removed from their families and communities.

> In that time not one indigenous family has escaped the effects of forcible removal . . . Most families have been affected, in one or more generations, by the forcible removal of one or more children.[13]

The president of HREOC, Sir Ronald Wilson, described it as a form of genocide. By the end of 1997, apologies had flowed from across the Australian community. State parliaments and churches had apologised, thousands of people had signed sorry books. There had been a national Sorry Day. It was the greatest outpouring of support for Aboriginal people since the 1967 referendum that ended constitutional discrimination against them.

Howard refused to apologise: it was a decision based on speculation about the extent of compensation for which the

Commonwealth would be liable, a view in Cabinet that the removal of children from their parents was essentially a state and church issue that was being used politically against the Prime Minister, and Howard's own view of history. He believed that an apology would serve no purpose, that history could not be rewritten, that the removal of children from their parents was seen at the time as in their best interests. He was caught in the cleft stick of his conservatism, satisfying neither soft liberal opinion in the inner suburbs of Melbourne and Sydney nor the hard-edged country conservatives who hurled Hanson across the political horizon. The combination of his refusal to apologise to the stolen generations and apparent indecisiveness on Wik contributed immensely to the popular perception that he was a weak prime minister.

Howard's first trip into black Australia was in 1988 when as the federal Opposition leader he visited Ernabella in Pitjantjatjara land in South Australia. It was a political debacle. At a meeting with Aboriginal elders, Yami Lester, the blind chairman of the Anangu Pitjantjatjara, criticised the Coalition's 'one people, one nation' policy and said that in the way of the Pitjantjatjara, Howard was like a young boy. 'We are willing to talk to you, we are happy to teach you,' he told Howard, who did not enter another Aboriginal community until February 1998 when he went to Elcho Island and Yirrkala with ATSIC chairman Gatjil Djerrkura. It was a very different experience. Howard was accorded the respect of a national elder and was allowed to witness secret ceremonies. He described it as one of the most moving experiences of his life. 'I have always respected Aboriginal culture, but until today I don't think I had understood the depth of feeling the indigenous people have in relation to their culture.'[14]

While some of those who were with Howard thought they detected a shift in attitude, he said that it had not changed his view on native title. It was not, he told television presenter Ray Martin later, a step towards Damascus.

October 3 1998: John Howard's re-election victory speech, Sydney:

> I want to commit myself very genuinely to the cause of true reconciliation with the Aboriginal people of Australia. We may differ and debate about the best way of achieving reconciliation, but I think all Australians are united in a determination to achieve it.[15]

Most Aboriginal leaders were sceptical, some openly scathing. In the French city of Lyon, where he was attending a human rights conference, the former Aboriginal and Torres Strait Islander Social Justice Commissioner and co-author of the stolen children report, Mick Dodson, spoke unambiguously when he told me:

> I simply don't trust him. How can you have reconciliation with someone like him, who spent most of his time in his first term constantly on the attack on Aboriginal people. His has been a government of utter black bashing.[16]

Howard's biggest problem was that few Aboriginal people trusted him. The well of trust had been poisoned by his position on the two issues upon which reconciliation would ultimately be determined: native title and the stolen generations. The question now is not whether he can achieve reconciliation, but whether he can revive it. By his own assessment—leaving aside the Aboriginal quest for constitutional change or their embittered belief that the federal and state governments are engaged in the final act of dispossession—Howard will need to provide the basis for significant improvements in Aboriginal health, housing, education and employment, something that even the best intentioned governments have failed to do. And the reason that so many governments have failed to alleviate the social and economic crisis that plagues Aboriginal communities is that they have failed to address the primary cause of the crisis, the loss of land and law.

Seeking to improve the living conditions of Aboriginal people will not in itself be enough to bridge the gulf that exists between indigenous and non-Aboriginal Australians, or to turn a history of dispossession towards a future in which the original nations have their share of wealth and dignity. Reconciliation will not succeed without fundamental change, the essence of which is recognition of the unique status of the indigenous peoples. We must replace the language of *terra nullius* and extinguishment with a commitment to the principles of decolonisation, self-determination and coordinate rights and an acknowledgement that the first nations have survived a hurricane of dispossession with enforceable legal rights. We must recognise those rights and give them constitutional force.

The foundation stone for reconciliation should be a national government apology, with compensation for policies that resulted in children being taken from the arms of their parents simply because of the colour of their skin.

The last decade of the millennium has been tumultuous for black Australia. Aboriginal rights have been unearthed and cannot be reburied. As NNTT president Robert French noted:

> If there is one absolutely pointless activity, it is to imagine that native title can be swept away by some legislative magic. Such a belief belongs in the company of beliefs about the flat earth and the tooth fairy. Native title is a property right recognised in common law. It is here to stay.[17]

At the time of Howard's re-election, there were 709 active native title claims with the NNTT. Another 54 had been sent to the Federal Court for resolution, a further 19 had been rejected by the tribunal, 89 others had been withdrawn by the applicants. There had been only three consent determinations of native title. The Dunghutti people negotiated title over 12.5 ha of land at Crescent Head in NSW in a deal that allowed for those rights to be immediately acquired by the NSW Government to create a national park; 13 Aboriginal clans and 10 government and private industry interests negotiated agreement over 110 000 ha in the Aboriginal community of Hopevale in North Queensland; and the Western Yalanji people secured co-existence access rights to a 25 000 ha property in North Queensland on land they were driven from more than 100 years ago. The agreement guaranteed the Western Yalanji recognition and access to the land for camping, hunting and fishing, collection of bush medicine, the use of resources such as ochre for ceremonies, timber for spears and berries for dye, access to plants for seed collection and the taking of bush tucker. In exchange, the pastoralists at the Karma Waters property, Alan and Karen Pederson, were able to upgrade their title from an occupational to a perpetual lease.

Of enduring benefit will be the Indigenous Land Fund, which was established with bi-partisan support. By June 2004, it will reach $1.289 billion, permitting annual payments of $45 million that can be used by Aboriginal people to purchase and manage land. There has also been an outpouring of profoundly moving apologies for the great wrongs that have been done to Aboriginal people. And yet, as he approaches the millennium, Noel Pearson says he has never known a time when Aboriginal people have been so dispirited. They have been taken to the mountaintop and shown a land of extinguishment.

NOTES

1 *The Australian* 31 May 1997
2 Interview with the author, October 1998, and H. Reynolds, *This Whispering in Our Hearts*, Allen & Unwin, Sydney, 1998
3 I first saw this passage by Xavier Herbert on a board outside Oyster Cove, where the 'last Tasmanians' were taken to die. At the time, there was a small wooden shack in the cove and in the shack there was a shrunken severed head of a Tasmanian Aboriginal man that had just been returned from England, a macabre reminder of the 'scientific' attempts that were made to prove the racial superiority of the white man.
4 *The Australian*, 15 October 1998
5 The Wik decision, High Court, discussed in F. Brennan, *The Wik Debate* UNSW Press, Sydney, 1998, p. 44
6 Wik–Mungkan
7 Tim Fischer, ABC radio, discussed in F. Brennan, *The Wik Debate*, op. cit., p. 57
8 *Sydney Morning Herald*, 1 April 1998
9 *The Australian*, 8 July 1998
10 Hansard, 2 June 1998
11 *The Age*, 21–22 August 1998, discussed in M. Dodson and

S. Pritchard, 'The Debate about Self-Determination and Indigenous Peoples', *Indigenous Law Bulletin*, October 1998
12 Keating extract in Stuart Rintoul, *The Wailing*, William Heinemann Australia, Melbourne, 1983, p. 12
13 National Inquiry into the Separation of Aboriginal and Torres Strait Islander Children from their Families, 1997, p. 37
14 *The Weekend Australian*, 28 February 1998
15 *The Australian*, 5 October 1998
16 *The Australian*, 16 October 1998
17 Address to Western Australian Pastoralists and Graziers Association, 11 September 1998

15

BUSHWHACKED BY THE MARKET
Why rural Australia is bleeding

Asa Wahlquist

NEVER HAS THE GREAT DIVIDING RANGE seemed more aptly named. This ragged spine of low mountains running down the eastern seaboard of Australia has on one side the ocean, fringed with rapidly growing coastal towns and dominated by the cities of Brisbane, Sydney and Melbourne and, on the other, the great tablelands, the 'vision splendid of the sunlit plains extended', the Murray–Darling Basin, the food bowl of the nation. They are now countries apart. Although the bush may loom large as part of the national self-image, Australia is the second most urbanised country in the world. On 1996 census figures, 12.6 million Australians—70 per cent—live in metropolitan areas. And many of these have no links with the bush, or with its people.

The distance between city and bush has been growing as country areas depopulate and migrants overwhelmingly settle in the city. On the mainland, only Queensland has a significant population outside the capital city, living in the regions and the provincial cities. Rural Australians, once secure about their place in Australian society, believe they have been abandoned by the decision-makers in the cities. As the executive director of the NFF, Dr Wendy Craik, notes: 'There's a feeling that they have contributed significantly to the development of the country and that contribution is no longer valued.'

And it is true that agriculture no longer makes the contribution it once did: it has been overtaken by tourism, with education and information technologies becoming increasingly important. While city lifestyles have changed under the pressure of less job security, skyrocketing housing costs and information overload, stereotypes of the bush tend to be stuck with the whingeing cocky, and Hanrahan who complained 'we'll all be rooned'. Yet city people do feel sympathy for the bush, as evidenced in the donations of more than $12 million to drought-stricken farmers in 1994. And the farm sector receives a higher rate of assistance than any other industry.

Nevertheless, in the period prior to the last federal election, farmers felt besieged on three fronts: the environment, native title, and the waterfront. The conservation movement has been focusing on 'brown issues' like the massive degradation of the Murray–Darling Basin and the fight to return water to the once mighty Snowy River. Craik says farmers have no doubt their farm practices are being criticised as being environmentally unacceptable, that they are bearing the brunt in the native title debate and are 'perceived by the urban sector as being intolerant and unreasonable'.

The NFF's pivotal role in the confrontation over waterfront work practices by backing the rebel P&C stevedores led to a backlash from some in the city, with threats there would be no donations to drought-affected farmers next time. Craik says country people also feel 'they are the last ones on the line when things are handed out like health services or communication services or post offices or banks. And they are the first areas where things are closed down'.

It is more than a feeling that country people are disadvantaged: an investigation by *The Australian* prior to the election found it to be fact. At the time of the 1998 campaign, non-metropolitan Australia accounted for 35 per cent of the workforce but was home to 42 per cent of the unemployed. And although unemployment in the cities had eased during the period of the first Howard Government, in many rural areas it worsened as government services continued to be cut, and banks and other rural businesses closed their doors.

Rural Australians have higher death rates from preventable causes, get less medical attention, experience lower levels of education and frequently receive inadequate telecommunications services. And they are overwhelmingly poorer: at the last election, of the 40 poorest electorates, 36 were rural or provincial; of the 40 wealthiest electorates, only two were rural—Kalgoorlie in Western Australia and Macarthur in the southern Highlands of NSW.

The past two decades have seen first massive deregulation, and then the introduction of competition policy. When Labor won government in 1983, statutory authorities imposed orderly marketing on a wide range of products. Banks were highly regulated, the dollar was fixed. In 1989, however, the guaranteed minimum price for wheat ended; the next year prices fell to the lowest on record. The wool reserve price scheme collapsed in 1991; the next year wool prices halved to the lowest level on record. Most woolgrowers have not made a profit since. Interest rates soared in the late 1980s. Farm debt increased by 18 per cent in the decade between 1985 and 1995, reaching a record $17.9 billion. In 1995, beef prices sank to a 20-year low. Drought struck, and at its peak in 1994/95 reduced production by $1.95 billion.

While country towns were dealing with the severe downturn in money coming in from agriculture, government positions and services were also being withdrawn. In the decade before the election of the Howard Government, more than 19 500 state government jobs were lost in country NSW alone. All up, in those years regional NSW lost more than 30 000 jobs—and the $1 billion in salaries they brought in. In South Australia, in the provincial cities of Port Pirie, Port Augusta, Whyalla, Port Lincoln, Murray Bridge and Mt Gambier, one in every 12 workers lost their job. The deputy director of the SA Centre for Economic Studies, Michael O'Neil, says that while there were job losses in Adelaide as well, 'they tend to be magnified in provincial cities and associated with bank losses, losses from

Telstra and other utilities. And if your population starts declining, some firms, like butchers, disappear.'

In the 1996 federal election, Labor won 30 of the 54 seats inside the Sydney–Canberra–Melbourne triangle. Outside that triangle, the party was overwhelmingly rejected, capturing just 18 of the 94 seats. The Howard–Fischer Coalition boasted more regional than city seats, and expectations were high, very high, that the new Government's debt to country Australia would be repaid. But the job losses and erosion of services continued. Together with key policy decisions on guns and native title, a series of hotly-argued decisions on the restructuring of agricultural bodies and changes in the allocation of irrigation water, it added up to a sense that rural voices were not being heard by policy-makers in capital cities.

After the election of the Howard Government, closures nationally included 14 regional tax offices, 125 CES offices, 48 corporate Australia Post Offices and 95 bank branches. About 600 bush communities no longer have access to a financial institution. The ramifications are huge: when a bank closes, it costs the community an estimated $350 a person a month as people transfer their shopping to their banking town. More than 2200 rural Telstra jobs were lost and the privatisation of Australian National Railways led to the loss of around 1000 jobs in the southern states. Abattoirs, clothing factories, timber mills, coal mines and gold mines shut down, while agriculture continued to lose workers.

Nevertheless, in the run-up to last year's election and faced with a plethora of issues, Craik nominated as the most serious problem facing country Australia 'the deplorable reduction in education and in health services—hospitals, specialists, doctors, nurses, even pharmacies'. Country people suffer higher levels of death from coronary heart disease, injury, asthma, road accidents and diabetes. There is a shortfall of 1000 GPs in regional Australia: on a per capita basis, rural Australians receive $226 million less in benefits from General Practice items than urban Australians do. Worst of all is the high suicide rate of young men: rates in remote areas are more than twice those of the city.

As Associate Professor of Social Work at Charles Sturt University in Wagga Wagga, Margaret Alston, has noted, 'Suicide is always the biggest issue for a small town. There is a huge sense of grief and loss, about loss of community and loss of hope and choice'. And the Howard Government, she said before the last election,

> has been particularly harsh in its lack of attention to social justice and health in rural areas. I think that's why there is such a backlash in public opinion. It really came in on a promise to facilitate change, rural people thought they may have a chance of resisting what has been happening, but this Government has accelerated what's going on in rural Australia. They have lost a great deal of sympathy among rural people.

Most city businesses can access 64 kilobytes per second of phone lines, and most city residents have access to at least 28.8 kbit/s, which Telstra says is 'preferable for the operation of sophisticated Internet applications'. It is a level provided to only 30 per cent of rural dwellers. Many farms get just 2.4 kbit/s, so low as to make it difficult to run a fax. Human Rights Commissioner Chris Sidoti, who since early 1988 has been conducting a series of hearings into human rights in regional, rural and remote Australia, notes that:

> The reduction in services to rural Australia also seriously affects the competitiveness and ultimate survival of rural businesses. Whether these are large beef or crop farms or the local post office, many businesses are affected by the changes facing rural communities. Yet the support of, and investment in, small business and industry in rural Australia are necessary to address the downward spiral of rural life. During our consultations, people have spoken repeatedly about their concerns for telephone, postal and banking services . . . For months people have been telling me about the poor quality of, and inadequate access to, telecommunications services in the bush.

One key problem facing country people is that there is no one lobby group, no one voice, speaking for them. The NFF has taken up the challenge in health and telecommunications services, but its brief is to farmers, and its funding is limited by the rural downturn. The Country Party, which emerged in the

1920s and was later re-badged as the National Party, was formed to represent the bush. The links between farm organisations and the Country Party were once so strong that joining a farm organisation meant automatic membership of the party. The growing opposition of farm groups to protection (a policy supported by the National Party) tried, then essentially severed the relationship. Formed in 1979, the NFF, as the peak farmer representative body, was the first lobby group to embrace the free market philosophy, and it opposed National Party policy on a range of issues. In fact, former NFF office holders and elected officials who have later engaged in politics—including Ian McLachlan, Andrew Robb, David Trebeck, Winston Crane and Senator Jeannie Ferris—have overwhelmingly favoured the Liberal Party. In the first Howard Government, there were more rural regional Liberals than there were Nationals.

The National Party's Deputy Leader and Primary Industries Minister, John Anderson, has come under sustained attack from the bush. He oversaw and bitterly argued restructuring of the red meat and wheat industries. There were demands for more drought money, for tariffs for the pork industry (which were opposed by the cattle and sugar industries), and Anderson was humiliatingly rolled when Cabinet voted, too late to actually bring it into effect before the election, to freeze the wool stockpile. The National Party has also been criticised for being too close to the Liberal Party, to have sided with, rather than against, Howard on the guns issue and Wik (although farm organisations did support the Prime Minister's gun stance).

In December 1996, when the High Court announced its decision that native title could co-exist with pastoral leases, the president of the NFF, Donald McGauchie, retorted that 'this has just about ended Aboriginal reconciliation, certainly with the pastoral industry'. The decision had the potential to affect around 6900 leases, held by less than 3500 lessees, some 100 of which are Aboriginal land trusts. (Those figures include 4250 pastoral leases in NSW, currently subject to a Commonwealth government-funded test case.) The NFF launched an aggressive campaign for total extinguishment of native title on pastoral leases. It was a battle they could never win: the Government would not countenance the huge compensation bill that would result from total extinguishment.

Their action was in direct contrast to the miners, who directed their efforts at making the Native Title Act work. McGauchie said the Wik debate resulted in an 'enormous amount of ill-feeling in the bush' towards the city people he described as sitting very safely on freehold title and wanting to salve their consciences by handing over some of the pastoralists' rights. The NFF arguably shifted the ground in the debate to the right: native title rights over pastoral leasehold remained, but the rights of native title holders were wound back under Howard's Ten Point Plan, which, after threats of a race-based double dissolution if it failed, was passed by the Senate in July 1998.

Pauline Hanson and her One Nation Party gave those disenchanted with the major parties an option. After her election as an MP in 1996, she did the rounds of the Queensland rural shows. She was there when they set up. She was still there, listening to people, when the show packed up. She might lack analytical skill but she knew how to hear what people were saying, and repeat it in her catchcries. Many in the bush and towns who believed themselves forgotten by the main parties felt Hanson had given them a voice.

One Nation reached its zenith in the Queensland state election, winning 11 seats. Former ALP minister and now executive director of Cotton Australia, Gary Punch, says its vote in that election was related to local wealth: 'West of the ranges, where there has been a significant economic driver, whether it be cotton or mining, One Nation didn't do nearly as well.'

One Nation did, however, force rural Australia onto the agenda of the federal election. The Coalition, hearing the cry from the bush, offered rural apprenticeships, rural transaction centres, incentives for rural doctors, rural health centres, an upgrade of the universal telephone service obligation to 64 Kbps, internet services, a resolution of the analogue phone phase-out, an extension of the untimed local call areas, money for roads, and more.

One scapegoat for the gutting of rural Australia was

competition policy. During the election campaign, Fischer announced an Industry Commission Inquiry, 'Impact of competition policy on rural and regional Australia', saying there must be a human dimension to the policy. The chairman of the Centre for Agricultural and Regional Economics, Dr Roy Powell, argues that rural regions have borne much of the brunt of the structural adjustment of the Australian economy. Not only has the recent economic recovery passed many rural regions by, he says, but there is also an expectation that the level of inequality among regions will increase:

> Competition by its nature destroys jobs. You have to create new businesses just to stand still. The opportunities in small rural communities is pretty limited in terms of the opportunities and the number of entrepreneurs.

Powell believes Sydney's share of NSW's economy has been increasing 'for quite a while'. The underlying economic theory suggests, he says, that the more you deregulate the economy and allow market forces to determine where business locates, the more likely those businesses are to concentrate in larger centres. 'That's what we've seen over the last 20 years or so as we move to a market economy.'

A population analyst from KPMG, Bernard Salt, has identified three distinct population movements in rural Australia. The first is the clamour for the coast—13.12 million people lived along the east coast alone in 1996, with a net growth rate over the previous 20 years of 34 per cent. The second trend is the growth of sponge cities, regional centres like Wagga Wagga in NSW, Horsham in Victoria and Narrogin in WA, which have grown at the expense of their local communities. The third is the erosion in communities along the wheat belt: 205 rural municipalities lost population in the 21 years to 1997, with 79 municipalities losing a devastating 20 per cent of their population. But there have also been stunning success stories in regional Australia. Says Punch: 'What is happening in rural and regional Australia is a rapid polarisation. It is either booming with crops like cotton, or dying a death of a thousand cuts.'

The two big agricultural money-spinners over the past

decade have been in irrigated agriculture, cotton and wine grapes. A third irrigated industry, the dairy industry (which has gone through extensive readjustment) is also producing good returns. All three create regional jobs in processing and, in the case of wine and milk productions, manufacturing. Punch maintains there are plenty of similar irrigation opportunities:

> Those sorts of multipliers are sitting there like caged horses waiting to burst out and drag whole rural communities along. Our national priorities seem terribly confused. We do irrigation probably better than anybody else in the world, yet most of the irrigation industries will tell you they spend most of their lives feeling like a pariah.

Irrigation, however, is one of *the* environmental pressure points in rural Australia. The past decade has seen a series of crises in the Murray–Darling Basin: in 1991, there was a 1000 km blue-green algal bloom in the Darling River; more than 10 000 km of the rivers in the system have rising salinity levels; the area affected by dryland salinity is expected to rise to 10 000 sq km of the Basin by 2010; by 1997, all intensively irrigated areas in the southern parts of the Basin had high water tables; and more than half the wetlands have been lost, and six of the 36 fish species are threatened.

Under natural conditions, the mouth of the Murray was in severe drought one year in 20; had development proceeded at the planned rate, that would have risen to three years in four. In 1995, the Council of Australian Governments agreed to cap the amount of water taken from the river; all the governments committed themselves to managing water in an economically viable and ecologically sustainable manner. Doing that has been a highly contentious, often politically charged process. In the bush, water means money. Factoring the needs of the environment into river management has meant irrigators giving up some of their allocation. As Punch notes:

> The communication gap between policy regulators and the bush has never been greater. People who make decisions every day of the week about the life and death of rural commodities have very limited ideas of exactly what is going on and what the effects are.

Water, once subsidised, is now sold at market prices, and is increasingly freely traded, subject to environmental considerations. Irrigation, though, has invigorated a chain of river communities such as the South Australian Riverland, a former rural basket case where bulldozers are busy ploughing paddocks for the planting of wine grapes, almonds, vegetables, olives and specialty fruits. Between 1990 and 1997, the value of the Riverland's irrigated agriculture grew by 40 per cent.

The practice of European-style agriculture in Australia has been devastating. Since European settlement, nearly 70 per cent of all native vegetation has been removed or significantly modified, with an estimated 20 billion trees cleared. Nearly half the agricultural land is in need of some rehabilitation, with more than 1 million hectares seriously affected by dryland salinity (due largely to tree clearing). The cost of degradation is calculated to be $1 billion in lost production. And that does not include the cost of remedial action and non-agricultural impacts.

Farmer attitudes to land management, however, have changed dramatically under the Decade of Landcare, which began in 1989 and has been funded more recently by the Natural Heritage Trust from the one-third privatisation of Telstra. By 1997, Landcare groups numbered just under 4300, while 34 per cent of broadacre and dairy farms had a representative who was a Landcare member. Landcare has led to four far-reaching changes in rural Australia. The first is the instillation of the Landcare custodian ethic; the second is the growing number of women who, through their activities in Landcare, publicly identify as farmers; the third is the extension of the sense of responsibility beyond the farm gate to seeing the property as part of a community, perhaps a catchment, with a set of wide-ranging responsibilities; and the fourth is growing adoption of best farm management practices.

It all sounds to the good, but questions are being raised. Patrick Morrisey from Southern Cross University and Professor Geoffrey Lawrence from Central Queensland University have observed that 'one of the main activities of Landcare groups in regions throughout Australia is to lobby for substantial increases in public funding to be allocated for remedial on-ground works on private land'. Rick Farley, as executive director of the NFF, was instrumental in working with the Australian Conservation Foundation to set up Landcare. Now working as a native title negotiator, he believes the strong community links established through Landcare would provide an excellent basis for setting up regional native title agreements.

According to the Industry Commission, assistance for agriculture is higher than for any other industry, as a percentage of added value. In 1994/95, the Commonwealth spent $1.3 billion and the states $682 million on assistance to the sector. Punch believes that

> We can develop regions of Australia and add jobs, but it needs state and federal government co-ordination—you need to have industry and the Greens included in that process. The bush represents the best chance to resolve the development versus the environment conflict.

Powell says the vision put by the National Party to the electorate at the last election was 'fairly limited' in that:

> It was a perspective pretty much based on agriculture; it didn't come to grips with the question of how regions maximise the wealth of their natural resource base. Agriculture is a bit like mining—the real value comes from what you do with it.

He, along with many others, would like to see value-adding in regional Australia and 'government has to have a role in it. I don't believe markets can deliver regional development, markets are inherently centralising.' He argues that governments must provide first-class telecommunications and transport infrastructure. 'Governments are going to have to provide support to develop infrastructure and carry some subsidies through under-utilisation for a while, until you build up the economic capacities of the regions.'

And he says there needs to be an overall plan for health and educational services, plans that acknowledge that while small country towns cannot have high quality specialist health services, they can be placed in a clear hierarchy of service provision, linked to regional centres, then the main cities.

Howard appears to have realised there is more to the country than agriculture, that rural communities do matter, by setting up Anderson as 'Minister for the Bush'. His task will be to upgrade rural and regional development services, and improve the quality and standards of life in rural and regional Australia. Howard has also committed himself to a more 'people-oriented' government. As one person told the Human Rights Commission: 'Governments must acknowledge that *people live* in rural communities and need to be recognised as being a part of society rather than part of an economy.'

Upgrading services will be a welcome start, but the profound structural problems facing rural and regional Australia will need much, much more than that. Country people have been calling for regional development programs, incentives for locating businesses in rural locations and subsidies for new rural industrial developments, as well as well-planned health and education services and good, low-cost telecommunications and transport systems.

The first Howard Government failed to understand the pain being endured by rural Australians. It only began to respond to their anger as the election neared. The second Howard Government has made a step towards improving rural service, but there are few signs yet that it is prepared to tackle the far-reaching changes needed to resuscitate rural Australia. The ramifications of not doing so could be a bitter harvest.

16

STEALTH MISSILE FOR THE STATES

The rise and rise of Federalism

Alan Wood

AUSTRALIANS, SO FAR AS ONE CAN TELL, value their federal system of government. Since Federation, 38 proposals to amend the Constitution have been put in referenda. Of these, 30 involved a proposal to increase Commonwealth powers. Only two—the power to grant social service pensions and the power to make laws in respect to Aboriginal people—have succeeded. That suggests a conservative attitude to the Constitution and to the extension of the power of central government. While there are periodic suggestions that Australia is over-governed and that the states should be abolished, it is generally agreed that no such proposal would have a hope at a referendum—at least not outside Sydney, which lives under the quaint and parochial delusion that it is Australia.

Australians would therefore presumably be shocked, or at least surprised, to be told their Federation has changed so profoundly from the intentions of its creators that by its centenary in 2001 the de facto abolition of the states will be virtually complete. Yet that is the assertion of a former premier of Queensland, Wayne Goss. In a speech in 1994,[1] he sought to put reinvigoration of the states on the agenda for the centenary of Federation, warning that a real problem was evolving in the constitutional structure:

Public debate talks of a new Australian nation by the year 2001—I suspect the de facto abolition of the states will be complete by then. While some may cheer the demise of the states, the relevant question is whether this is the way to do it. Is it a good policy result to have the states finished off in the sense of having no real power or independent role but with six parliaments and administrations still constitutionally alive and locked into the structure?

Goss then answered his own question:

I believe it would be a poor result because it would leave Australia with a constitutional and administrative structure in conflict with the reality, leading to inefficiency, a lack of accountability and duplication of administration . . . the course we are on leads to de facto abolition of the states with the logical result of the states becoming a dead-weight in the baggage of our constitutional make-up.

As that becomes a reality, the danger was that the states would become a real impediment to an efficient and competitive nation. When the Australian Constitution was drafted, he wrote, the powers of the Commonwealth Government were 'closely circumscribed and all residual power remained with the states. This was to ensure that the states had the "upper hand" in the new Federation.' Since Federation, he suggested, there had been a massive shift of power from the states to the Commonwealth, of which much had been a sensible part of building a nation. 'However, it must also be said that a great deal of this power shifting has occurred in areas and circumstances never envisaged . . . by the authors of the Constitution.'

That same year, the Premier of Western Australia, Richard Court, issued what he called 'an audit and history' of state powers and responsibilities 'usurped by the Commonwealth in the years since Federation'.[2] In its introduction, he offered his view of the original intentions of the framers of the Constitution and their subversion by the increased centralisation of power in the hands of the Commonwealth:

The Constitution was intended to create a federal system of government in Australia. From the text of the Constitution itself and the records of Constitution Convention debates, the founders intended to establish a Commonwealth Government with limited and defined powers while leaving the states with their general plenary powers to regulate, and the responsibility for the majority of social, economic and political concerns of Australia.

This balance of power, what he called 'the essence of the Federation', was seen as critical in ensuring that 'both the national interest as well as the interests of the people living in the regions of Australia were served'. He declared that he had become deeply concerned about the 'weakening' of the federal system of government in Australia 'caused by a growing concentration of both political and financial power in the Commonwealth Government.'

Are the fears of the two premiers, one Labor and one Liberal, reasonable? An objective appraisal suggests so. The central thread has been the Commonwealth's use of its growing financial power to extend its political hegemony. In doing this, it has been greatly assisted by a long run of decisions of the High Court favouring the extension of Commonwealth power. The first to see which way the financial wind would blow was one of the framers of the Constitution and the new nation's second prime minister, Alfred Deakin. His observations on the future of Federation were written for the *London Morning Post* on—some might say appropriately—April Fool's Day 1902.

> As the power of the purse in Great Britain established by degrees the authority of the Commons, it will ultimately establish in Australia the authority of the Commonwealth. The rights of self-government of the states have been fondly supposed to be safeguarded by the Constitution. It left them legally free, but financially bound to the chariot wheels of the Central Government. Their need will be its opportunity.
>
> The less populous will first succumb; those smitten by drought or similar misfortune will follow; and finally even the greatest and most prosperous will, however reluctantly, be brought to heel. Our Constitution may remain unaltered, but a vital change will have taken place in the relations between the states and the Commonwealth. The Commonwealth will have acquired a general control over the states, while every extension of political power will be made by its means and go to increase its relative superiority.

Deakin could not, of course, foresee precisely how this would happen, and in particular the role the High Court would play, but his prescience is remarkable. The Commonwealth began building its financial power early, starting with the Surplus Revenue Act of 1908, which got around a constitutional provision to pay surplus customs revenue—that is, surplus to the Commonwealth's needs—to the states. World War I saw a rapid expansion of Commonwealth control over the economy and the introduction of a Commonwealth income tax in 1915 that operated side by side with state income taxes. But it was World War II and the period immediately after that saw a massive expansion of the Commonwealth's financial power at the expense of the states. In 1942, after unsuccessful negotiations, the Commonwealth seized income tax from the states. Victoria, South Australia, Queensland and Western Australia challenged the legislation as unconstitutional but in the Uniform Tax Case of 1942 the High Court upheld it. Ominously for the states, the court not only held the Commonwealth's income tax legislation valid under the defence power of the Constitution for the duration of the war, but also under the normal powers of the Commonwealth in times of peace.

While the original understanding was that the states would return to the income tax field after the war, it hasn't happened. Post-war challenges to the Commonwealth's monopoly of income taxation by the states were rejected by the High Court. Income tax had comprised about 60 per cent of the states' tax base immediately before the war; with its takeover by the Commonwealth in 1942, the states' share of total taxation revenue fell to 10 per cent. The lost income tax revenue was replaced by a system of general revenue grants to the states that were effectively under the Commonwealth's control, as Premiers' Conference after Premiers' Conference has shown.

The Commonwealth's takeover of the income tax base marked a watershed in Commonwealth–state relations and a massive extension of Commonwealth power. Its financial dominance was extended by a further series of High Court cases that effectively excluded the states from levying taxes on commodities (sales taxes), beginning with a case know as *Mathews v. Chicory*

Marketing Board 1938 and substantially widened by *Parton v. Milk Board 1949* and subsequent cases that followed the line of authority in Parton. The key feature of these was a broad interpretation of what constituted an excise under Section 90 of the Constitution, which gives the Commonwealth exclusive power to levy duties of customs and excise.

The original intention was to ensure individual states could not frustrate the ability of the new Commonwealth government to impose a uniform tariff on imports by levying their own customs and excise duties. The High Court, however, greatly widened the scope of this section in the Commonwealth's favour so that the states were largely excluded from both income tax and sales taxes. There was one important exception on the sales tax side, whereby the High Court accepted the validity of franchise fees levied by the states, beginning with the Dennis Hotels case in 1958.[3] By 1997, the states were raising some $5 billion a year from franchise fees on liquor, tobacco and petrol. In that year, in the Ha & Hammond case,[4] the High Court ruled franchise fees constitutionally invalid by a 4–3 majority. This effectively completed the financial emasculation of the states, leaving them almost entirely dependent on the Commonwealth. The tax bases left to them are, with the exception of payroll tax, narrow and inefficient.

This progressive attack has created an extreme degree of imbalance between the revenue-raising power of the Commonwealth and the states, completely out of line with their spending responsibilities. This is known as Vertical Fiscal Imbalance (VFI), and in Australia is more extreme than in any other federation. Following the Ha case, the Commonwealth now collects 76 per cent of all taxation revenues (80 per cent if local government is excluded) while accounting directly for only 56 per cent of total government expenditures. The states raise 20 per cent of revenue but must fund 40 per cent of outlays. The states' independence has been further undermined by the Commonwealth's use of Specific Purpose payments under Section 96 of the Constitution, which gives it the power to grant financial assistance to any state on such terms and conditions as federal Parliament thinks fit. This has allowed the Commonwealth to impose its policy wishes on the states in a wide range of areas.

It is possible to see this expansion of Commonwealth power as a response to the very different world we live in compared with the founders of the Federation. And there is obvious truth in this. It is plainly unrealistic to expect the Federation to remain frozen in time, or that the role of the central government would not expand beyond its minimalist beginnings. But there is no denying that the extent of fiscal imbalance in Australia offends against a fundamental principle of a constitutional federation. This principle was set out by a founding father of the American republic, which is also a federation. Writing in The Federalist Papers, Alexander Hamilton held that in an ideal federation, 'Individual states should possess an independent and uncontrollable authority to raise their own revenues for the supply of their own wants.'[5]

One of Australia's leading authorities on the Constitution, former chief justice of the High Court, Sir Harry Gibbs, has noted that in practice this ideal is seldom if ever obtained; some degree of fiscal imbalance seems inevitable in any federation. But as he also observed, Australia nowadays offends against this fundamental principle far more than any other federation. This is widely recognised. Speaking ahead of the 1998 federal election, Prime Minister John Howard said he did not believe Australia 'can go on any more with a taxation system where the relations between the Commonwealth and the states are so profoundly out of balance and so screamingly in need of reform and change'.

Before examining his proposal, it is necessary to look at the other paths by which Federation has moved away from the intention of its founders. The Constitution (Section 51) gives the following legislative responsibilities to the Commonwealth:

- defence and external affairs;
- navigation, quarantine and meteorological services;
- immigration, citizenship, matrimonial status;
- international and interstate trade and commerce, together with specific powers such as in respect to patents, companies

and bankruptcies which were intended to allow the Commonwealth to regulate certain areas of business activities;
- currency, non-state banking and insurance;
- conciliation and arbitration for the prevention and settlement of interstate industrial disputes;
- postal and telecommunications services, and conditional powers with respect to railways;
- invalid and old age pensions.

Sole responsibility for everything else was left to the states, including:

- law and order;
- regulation of commerce and industry;
- transport services;
- natural resources, including land;
- essential services such as water supply, sewerage, drainage, electricity and gas;
- local government;
- education, housing and health;
- the environment.

According to Court's audit document, since Federation, Canberra has intruded into 'every one of these sole state responsibilities, in some cases to such an extent that the Commonwealth effectively has usurped the states' role for all practical purposes'. Among a long list of examples, the document cites 15 High Court decisions of general application supporting the trend to centralisation of power between 1908 and 1992. These include:

- the Engineers' Case of 1920, which established that Commonwealth powers should be interpreted broadly, thereby expanding them;
- the Seas and Submerged Lands Case of 1975, which found the territorial boundaries of states ended at the low water mark and not three nautical miles from the coast as previously thought, limiting state powers in areas such as fisheries, minerals and navigation;
- the Koowarta case in 1982, which gave a very wide inter-

pretation to the external affairs power, enabling the Commonwealth to overrule state parliaments and laws via international treaties on human rights;
- the Franklin Dams Case of 1983, which gave a broad interpretation of the corporations power as well as the external affairs power, expanding the Commonwealth's reach in environmental matters;
- the Mabo Case of 1992, which extended the reach of the Commonwealth into land and land title, previously the jurisdiction of state parliaments.

Combined with its takeover of the taxation field, it adds up to a powerful extension of the Commonwealth's role. Another unique element of the Australian Federation has been important in changing its nature and making it unlike any other federation in the world: the Commonwealth Grants Commission. It was set up in 1933 at a time of immense dissatisfaction with the Federation, particularly among the smaller states where threats to secede were rife—Western Australia actually passed a secession referendum that year.

The commission's initial role was to inquire into and report on requests by the states for financial assistance. However, its operations became more important post-war with the Commonwealth's dominance of revenue raising. Its function was to recommend on the allocation of Commonwealth grants to the states so as to ensure all Australians enjoyed a similar standard of government services despite the very different taxable capacity of individual states. In effect, tax revenue raised in NSW and Victoria by the Commonwealth was redistributed to the other states. From time to time NSW and Victoria have objected to this and sought to change the arrangements, the most recent example being NSW Premier Bob Carr's attack on the Grants Commission arrangements in November 1998 in the lead-up to the special Premiers' Conference on revenue sharing under a GST. These attempts have failed, and some form of revenue redistribution is no doubt inevitable, given the very different resource, population and revenue bases of the individual states. In their 1972 volume *Federal Finance*,[6] ANU academics Russell Mathews and Robert Jay comment on its importance:

> The significance of the Grants Commission's procedures is that they introduced, for the first time in a federation, the concept of approximately equal treatment for all citizens irrespective of the state they lived in. In terms both of the obligations for taxation and claims for administrative and social services, the net effect was intended to approximate the situation that would have existed in a country with a unitary government. The concept has thus had far-reaching consequences in extending Commonwealth responsibility *vis-a-vis* state responsibility and independence.

It would be wrong, however, to say that the operation of the Grants Commission has destroyed any possibility of competitive federalism in Australia—that is, the opportunity for different states to follow different policy approaches in areas such as health or taxation. It is still possible for them to make a range of taxation and expenditure choices within commission framework, as is confirmed in the commission's reports. The Grants Commission ensures that each state government has the financial ability to provide a similar standard of services, but they are not compelled to provide a uniform percentage of their budget to specified service areas, or to make a uniform level of tax effort. On a broader level, the commission's activities do contribute to uniformity and a blurring of political responsibility—two important problems of Federation. Professor Wolfgang Kasper, writing in the closely related context of restraining the opportunism of political agents, observes that

> Ensuring the same living conditions throughout the country, irrespective of location, resource endowment and political behaviour cannot be an objective of policy if one wants administrative creativity and power control. This objective is the equivalent of income redistribution: it stifles self-reliance and competition.

The result of the loss of financial independence and the intrusion of the Commonwealth into areas intended by the framers of the Constitution to be the responsibility of the states has been a profound change in the nature of our Federation.

One way to characterise this is to say it has been transformed from a fiscal federation to a managerial or administrative federation. The framers of the Constitution set up a fiscally decentralised federation, with the states retaining substantial revenue-raising powers and wide expenditure responsibilities. This was much closer to the Hamiltonian ideal of federalism, where those spending the money were politically responsible for raising it.

An administrative federation is where the central government raises revenue and then allocates funds to decentralised entities who act as its agents. The central government imposes policy, performance and efficiency requirements on their management of the allocated funds. This latter model is much closer to the current Federation; recognition of this is reflected in periodic complaints from the states that they have become branch offices, or post boxes for cheques from the Commonwealth. However, in moments of frankness the states acknow- ledge they have often been willing parties to the Commonwealth's financial takeover. In a June 1998 speech,[7] Victoria's Treasurer Alan Stockdale acknowledged that the decline of the Federation's finances was not just the Commonwealth's fault: 'For much of the history of our Federation, states have been happy to allow the federal Government to progressively take over revenue-raising responsibilities in return for greater grants from Canberra.'

The reason for this complicity is not hard to work out—the Commonwealth Government bore the opprobrium of raising the revenue, the states gained the political benefits from spending it. But the states have come to realise that there was a long-term cost to this political game. In the 1990s, they have made two attempts to restore a better fiscal balance with the Commonwealth, and their chosen vehicle has been the restoration of state access to the national income tax base. The first was in 1991, when the states and Prime Minister Bob Hawke almost agreed on an arrangement to give the former a limited but significant capacity to piggyback a state income tax onto the Commonwealth income tax base. Paul Keating scuttled this as part of his struggle with Hawke for the prime ministership. The second attempt was made in 1998[8] when the states again sought to have state access to the income tax base agreed to as part of Howard's tax reform package. Stockdale saw this as a last chance:

> If the federal Government fails to address state taxes and Vertical Fiscal Imbalance, then both will effectively be locked in for all time, possibly worsened. Thus the Commonwealth Government now must face up to a threshold question, namely whether they seek to preserve or destroy the spirit of the Australian Federation.

The solution proposed by Howard is a radical one—to introduce a 10 per cent GST and hand over most of the revenue raised to the states. In return, they would abolish a range of inefficient state taxes such as financial institutions duty, the bank account debits tax and some stamp duties, and would cease to receive financial assistance grants from the Commonwealth. Howard has described the new regime as an historic change in relations between the Commonwealth and the states. Treasurer Peter Costello sees it as the best financial deal the states have had since uniform taxation came in as a temporary measure during World War II. It has obvious attractions for the states. Once more the Commonwealth would be collecting the tax and the states spending the proceeds. These proceeds, after a transitional period, would be large and growing. According to Commonwealth estimates, by 2004–05, the states would be more than $1 billion a year better off than under existing arrangements. And that gap will continue to grow because revenue from the GST grows in line with spending and the economy.

But as always in the history of Federation, this gift horse comes at a price. It would increase the already extreme degree of VFI—the cancer eating away at the Federation. As much was admitted by Victoria's Premier and self-declared champion of the states' case for tax reform, Jeff Kennett, at a press conference to promote the Howard Government's tax package:

> What is being offered is certainly better than we have now. We have greater revenue certainty, although it does increase the states' financial dependence on the Commonwealth. In other words, it doesn't address the issue of VFI. In fact it may even make it worse. But having said that, we think the deal is substantially better.

In short, the old story of the states taking the money and turning a blind eye to the decline of the fiscal federation. Under the Government's tax package, the Commonwealth will move to raising more than 80 per cent of taxation revenue. As Deakin foresaw, the states will be constitutional relics bound to Canberra's chariot wheels. Is this something Australians should be concerned about on the eve of the centenary of Federation? Yes, because a vigorous Federation of the sort envisaged by the constitutional authors has many virtues. Some have been listed by Professor Emeritus Geoffrey de Q. Walker.[9]

- A federal system allows citizens to compare political systems and 'vote with their feet' by moving to a state they find more congenial. The right of exit is a recognised political right as important as, but much older than, the right to vote.
- Federalism encourages experimentation in political, social and economic matters. It is more conducive to rational progress because it enables different approaches to be compared more easily.
- The federal division of powers hampers the rise of despotic central government and thus protects liberty.
- Federal decentralisation makes government easier for the people to supervise.
- Federations produce more stable governments than unitary systems, and stability is a cardinal virtue in government.
- Competitive federalism facilitates the discovery of the rules and devices that will enhance the competitive position of Australia in world markets.

There is also the fundamental point that there is no realistic prospect of the states being abolished, so the imperative is to make Federation work as effectively as possible. The need for a national government is not the issue. As Goss said, the Commonwealth Government reflects the common interests of all in national unity.

> For example, economic union and the free movement of people, goods and services within an Australian national market have offered greater prosperity than any regional economy could achieve. Also, an integrated macroeconomic policy

is required to ensure stability in the national economy. The Australian people have consistently sought nationally consistent policies on income distribution, basic living and service standards and on citizenship rights.

That leaves a wide range of responsibilities better discharged by state governments and, most importantly for the health of the Federation, by state governments with greater responsibility for raising the revenue they spend, and greater accountability.

Is it too late? Has the de facto abolition of the states gone too far to be reversed? That will depend on whether the states can rise above the 'bucket of money' mentality that has undermined the foundations of Federation. They may yet do so, because the arrangements being proposed by the Commonwealth, with the GST at their centre, are inherently unstable. Even putting to one side difficulties posed by an unstable Senate system, the history of Federation says future Commonwealth governments will move to change financial arrangements in their favour.

The states should recognise that now, and move to convene a fundamental review of the Federation on the eve of its centenary. Otherwise it will enter its second century as a very different, much weaker institution than envisaged by its founders in 1901.

Notes

1 Wayne Goss, Premier of Queensland, 'Re-inventing the States', 2020 Vision Conference, 19 September 1994
2 Richard Court, Premier of Western Australia, 'Rebuilding The Federation: An audit and history of State powers and responsibilities usurped by the Commonwealth in the years since Federation', February 1994
3 *Dennis Hotels v. Victoria 1958* (liquor licence fees), *Dickenson's Arcade Pty Ltd v. Tasmania 1974* (tobacco franchise fees), *H C Sleigh v. South Australia 1977* (fuel franchise fees)
4 *Ngo Ngo Ha & Anor v. State of New South Wales & Ors* and *Walter Hammond & Associates Pty Ltd v. NSW & Ors 1977*

5 The Federalist Papers, no. XXXII, quoted by Sir Harry Gibbs in his introduction to 'Reshaping Fiscal Federalism in Australia', ed. Neil Warren, Australian Tax Research Foundation, Conference Series no. 20
6 R.L. Mathews and W.R.C. Jay, *Federal Finance*, reprint of 1972 edition by Centre for Strategic Economic Studies, Victoria University, Melbourne 1997
7 Alan Stockdale, Treasurer of Victoria, speech to ATAX conference, 'A State Tax Reform Package', 11 June 1998
8 For a detailed explanation of how this would work, see Government of Western Australia, 'Submission from Western Australia on National Tax Reform and Reform of Commonwealth/State financial relations', May 1998
9 Professor Emeritus Geoffrey de Q. Walker, 'Ten Advantages of a Federal Constitution', address to Samuel Griffith Society Annual Conference, Brisbane, 7–9 August 1998

17

TOO MUCH TRUFFLE OIL
Baby boomers and the generation war

Shelley Gare

ON A SUNNY DAY LAST OCTOBER, I went to an elegant lunch eaten in the fluffy clouds over Sydney in the newly refurbished Summit restaurant high above Australia Square. The glossy magazine *Australian Gourmet Traveller* was holding its annual Restaurant of the Year awards. The guest judge was American restaurant critic Patricia Wells, who loves Australian restaurants, as well she might given that so many now fill our streets—you might be forgiven for thinking that what we do best these days is eat, and eat demandingly of only the finest ingredients from the freshest menus.

Yet Wells had criticisms. Too much truffle oil, she admonished her audience of chefs, restaurant owners, gourmets and journalists. And far too many rocket stems littering salads and garnishes. Breads were offered that didn't make sense and why, oh why, did we open oysters so far in advance? Wells's view of the world is necessarily microscopic but I was struck by its pungency. 'Too much truffle oil' could be the leitmotif of the baby-boomer generation as it metamorphoses from the gorgeous, spoiled darlings of the 1960s and 1970s to the stressed, picky, anxious, hemmed-in greying adolescents of the 1990s. As Wendy Wasserstein declared in *The Independent on Sunday* about the tarnishing of US president Bill Clinton: '[Baby boomers] are members of a narcissistically arrogant generation who once chanted "don't trust anyone over 30" and are now rounding 50."[1]

The term baby boomer—which covers the influential bulge in the population brought about by the soaring post-war birth-rate between 1946 and 1960—had pretty much vanished from view after the 1970s. David Stewart-Hunter, managing director of Customised Research at A.C. Nielsen, says:

> Talking about baby boomers seemed old-hat for a while. The BBs dipped below the horizon as they turned into people getting on with family formation and child-rearing and lurking in the lieutenant's role in companies.

That changed when the first baby boomers turned 50. Now floods of them are facing up to the birthday that marks, in anyone's mind, the dividing point between youth and age. Stewart-Hunter's theory is that while the baby boomer has always been a force because of the numbers involved, consciousness of the generation has gone up and down depending on just where in their lives BBs were. The term is back in usage because of this peak anniversary. Turning 50 means you are past the midway point of the natural life span. Once everything lay before this generation of mine. Now, with much of that in our hands, we worry about it being taken away from us. As one 52-year-old stockbroker confesses: 'I'm an eternal child. I don't think there's much percentage in getting fixated in middle age. You use it or lose it.'

We're spoiled. We want it all. We want it now. And forever. Too much truffle oil.

In the 1960s when the first baby boomers made their presence felt, this generation initiated attitudinal changes that are still having an effect. As John B. Judis pointed out about the generation of 1968 in the American magazine *New Republic*:

> The era left an indelible mark on the decades that followed. It vastly expanded the scope of what citizens expect from their

government—from clean air and water to safe workplaces, reliable products and medical coverage in their old age.[2]

The 1960s also signalled a change in what that generation wanted out of their lives. Instead of 'making a living', the focus shifted to 'quality of life' and 'lifestyle'. The past 20 years of baby-boomer consumption has seen a kind of mass movement on the part of business to art-directing the landscape. Everything is tasteful, from shops to restaurants to franchises to little hideaway hotels in the countryside. The couple togged out in careful co-ordinates will have a family equally stylishly kitted out; their kitchen, bathroom, bedroom and livingroom will also be decorated with the same eye to detail. This is the generation that filled its kitchen cupboards with moulis and Magimixes, pasta and ice-cream makers, rice cookers and expensive, exotic groceries . . . sundried tomatoes, pesto, balsamic vinegar, fresh pasta rather than the dried, quince paste, pink peppercorns. The ubiquitous biscotti, for instance, is the perfect indulgence food for today's baby boomer. It is sweet but allowable because it is also very, very thin. It is satisfyingly snappy to the teeth but palely elegant with its slivered, pale green pistachios. Best of all, who—but the real cognoscenti—had heard of biscotti five years ago? Certainly not a BB's parent.

This concern with the new and the indulgent is also why BBs are classified as the selfish generation. If your focus is on your own quality of life and aspirations, that means less time to worry about anyone else's lifestyle. Close to home, that has shown up in rising divorce statistics with people believing it is better to pursue happiness in a new relationship than stick with the failing one they have. There is less commitment; consequent to that has been the rise in the numbers of children with divorced or separated parents. As social researcher Hugh Mackay points out, almost one million dependent children now live with one parent, which has become another source of stress:

> They [baby boomers] acknowledge that most of their contemporaries would not be prepared to stay together 'for the sake of the children' if their marriages were unsatisfactory, yet those who have been through divorce often wonder whether

they have made guinea pigs of their own children in some vast social experiment.[3]

The pursuit of the perfect life and the perfect career has also made this the stressed generation. And while we may yearn for the quieter times of our parents and for an era when one income was enough to support the nuclear family, we wouldn't dream of giving up all the things we take for granted: the possessions, the holidays, the perks that come to both men and women who have fulfilling jobs, children who study but also have a multitude of extra-curricular activities from rugby to trumpet-playing, our own adult hobbies, toys and pastimes . . . Thus, the stress of juggling all this in a 24-hour day continues.

For better or worse, BBs will continue to be influential. The pre-war birth rate, writes Mackay, was 17 per 1000 of population. Immediately after World War II it rose to 24, 'remained high through the 1950s and only began to fall away in the early 1960s'. There are more than 3.5 million BBs hitting a crucial period. Between 1996 and 2001, this 40-54 age group will increase by 12 per cent. Marketing consultant Carol Davis, who specialises in the 40-plus area, identifies babies born between 1946 and 1956 as being on the leading edge of boomerdom.

John Stirton, associate research director at A.C. Nielsen, has figures that show baby boomers are exhibiting traditional voting patterns by becoming more conservative with age. Their freer-wheeling outlook displays itself elsewhere. It is overwhelmingly the 40-54 age group which supports the republic. A poll taken immediately after the 1998 Constitutional Convention had 61 per cent of that group saying yes to a republic compared with 53 per cent of the 25-39 group. Says Stirton: 'The baby boomers have done well so they're more likely to vote for economic management in a government. But that doesn't mean they've lost their idealism.'

This makes them a tricky proposition for politicians. There is always comfort in numbers and the baby-boomer bulge has not only been a solace to every one of its members, it has provided us with a battering ram. As Stewart-Hunter notes: 'It's a wonderful feeling to be part of a majority, and a very satisfactory feeling for a generation that is selfish and hedonistic.'

People have had to pay attention to us. There was money in it if you dreamt up goods and services that would appeal to baby boomers. There were votes in it. There were just so many of us that you couldn't ignore us, not if you wanted to stay on top yourself. And then, of course, the BBs commandeered the pinnacles of success as well. Stewart-Hunter remembers thinking about the 46-year-old Democrat Clinton taking over the US presidency from the 68-year-old Republican George Bush, who had succeeded the 77-year-old Ronald Reagan. At the time, he was CEO of Saatchi and Saatchi Australia:

> As Bush gave way to Clinton, the same thing started happening in business here. One of our clients was the Commonwealth Bank and I saw the bank's CEO, in his mid-60s, give way to David Murray, who was in his early 40s. I was conscious this was the first sign that the baby boomers were coming back into public focus again.

Many, many BBs are now happily ensconced in the top jobs from those in the CBD to those in media, academe, the public service and politics. As Mark Davis asks bitterly in the introduction to *Ganglands*:

> Is there a backlash against young people and the way they think? Has an older generation of cultural *apparatchiks*, used to being at the centre and having a strong media presence, more or less systematically set out to discredit young people and their ideas, even progressive opinion generally?[4]

Davis's book, he's keen to emphasise, is not an attack on BBs but rather it is about 'those cultural and political elites who have adopted as their own the stereotypical privileges associated with baby boomers. They are used to being at the centre, used to being listened to . . .'

That last sentence pretty much sums us up. But wait, there's a canker in the rose. In this decade, things have finally started to spoil. Since the early 1990s, the catchword has been downsizing. The climate of mergers, takeovers, restructuring and recessions has bitten savagely into the job market. The generations behind the baby boomers—Generation X and Generation Next—are not inclined to be sympathetic. Not only do they want their turn in the sun, they feel that if the BBs have squandered theirs, tough luck. The effect of these pressures on a generation that has always been good at spending and thinking about 'me' but markedly less good at saving—and thinking about the future—is now revealing itself. Says Stewart-Hunter:

> So now these baby boomers, still feeling vital in their 40s and 50s, still walking regularly with brains in good order, are anticipating their futures with some nervous apprehension. If we fall off the merry-go-round—and plenty of people are—we fear we might not be able to get back on again. We were the generation that shouted 'I want it now'. That's the trouble. You could say we're now saying: 'I wanted it now; I had it now; and now I'm worried.'

This is the Age of the Nervous Baby Boomer. One successful BB investment banker is coldly ruthless in comparing the downsizing merits of his 'worn-out' age peers with younger, more flexible, more energetic workers with better computer skills. If you wanted a CEO now, he suggests, 'you would be looking at someone in their 30s, early 40s. The demand on a CEO from investors is so much greater now. And the people who will go will be the baby boomers.'

American author Gail Sheehy says that many of the BB generation, having defined themselves through work, are now asking themselves: what do you do when it stops? 'And the higher the status conferred by one's work, the steeper the slide to anonymity. Most men want to feel before they die that they have made a difference.'[5]

This may be why, says Craig Littler of the School of Management at Queensland University of Technology, that the managerial level is most worried about downsizing and job insecurity even though the other end of the workforce has the most casualties. But there is good news if you look for it. Squeezed out of the big corporations and public sector, BBs will go into small businesses and consultancies. In a new study written with Martin Robinson on where Australians will be in 2010, Ann Harding notes: 'For the overwhelming majority of baby boomers, if they want work, they do have it and that will continue. If you can believe the latest forecasts, a lot of new jobs will be created.'[6] The expected growth in aggregate employment between 1994 and 2010 is 32.2 per cent, and some areas will show even greater growth: wholesale and retail trade, personal, recreational and community services. Says Harding:

> Baby boomers are prepared to pay for all sorts of services and that tendency will become more pronounced as they hit the empty nest syndrome. They've had two incomes most of their married life, the kids have left home and, given they probably benefited from the asset inflation of the 1980s when house prices rose so dramatically, and that they've been stressed trying to juggle all their different roles on the way through, they're happy to pay other people to do everything from rubbish removal to domestic work.[7]

Baby boomers will also help create work for baby boomers. In the report, Harding and Robinson point out that although Generation X will still be important, 'many of the areas of strongest market growth in the next decade will be fuelled by the preferences of the baby boomers and their parents'. Nevertheless, problems apart from employment loom for this generation. Vince Fitzgerald, author of the National Savings: A Report to the Treasurer (1993) and now executive-director of the Allen Consulting Group, says that the generation before the baby boomers already had a sense of entitlement.

> They had their taxes and they felt the pension was due to them and unless you were in the public service, banks or mining, you weren't terribly switched on to providing for yourself in old age. The baby boomers are even more entrenched in that attitude. If you had to pencil a line on a time chart as to when there was a marked change in attitude ... you'd have to put it at the Whitlam period. That's when baby boomers became visible in adult life and it was the apotheosis of the post-war welfare state. There was an impression that you would have good health care and good income in old age.

This has been a spending generation—household savings as a proportion of householders' disposable income reached its lowest level in 1994, at just 2.3 per cent, but figures for the last complete financial year, 1997/98, are still only at 2.7 per cent. Meanwhile, households continue to consume by going into debt, either by adding to mortgages or through credit cards. And while they're now being forced by the Government to put money into superannuation, says Fitzgerald, 'they're taking heaps of it out in housing and credit card debt. And if money is going into super, it is to a fair extent at the expense of other savings.'

Nevertheless, a lot of the money borrowed bought an asset, like a house or other property, which has improved in value and has been a good investment tax-wise. And changes in superannuation, to which since 1988 employers have been obliged to contribute a gradually rising percentage of their employees' income, have meant that aging BBs will probably be able to support themselves better than most people think. Still, children will affect baby-boomer wealth, says Carol Davis:

> Their future depends on how successfully they can launch their kids into life. If your kids are still at home at 26 or 27, that catches you when you should be topping up your own retirement planning. If they're going to help their kids, and that's what they want to do, that'll disadvantage their retirement.

Above all, says Harding, the most crucial area will be health: 'The impact of this generation on social security spending will be a drop in the bucket compared to that.' BBs will demand the best of health care. As Fitzgerald comments, 'they will want yuppie health care that keeps them in working age lifestyle'. They will not be happy to have a quiet retirement. At 50, many are taking up pursuits like white-water rafting and surfing—'now we all have to go bungy-jumping,' wrote one disgruntled 'older' person to *The Australian* recently. This is a group that will want themselves fixed. Future governments will not be able to cut back services. Either there will be an increasing shift to user-pays or taxes must be raised to cover expanding costs. But as Harding notes:

> Higher taxes will affect Generation X and there will be a backlash against that. What we will see is a competing

generations scenario. On our projections, there will be a five-fold increase in government spending on subsidised pharmaceuticals by the year 2020. That's if government doesn't change its policies; the corollary is that government policy will change. But it's a dilemma . . . because the baby boomers are such a powerful and articulate voting group. Meanwhile, there will be higher education costs to the consumer because of government cutbacks. This won't affect the baby boomers so much as Generation X, whose children will still be at school . . . there will be competing generations as one sector pushes for greater health funding and the other for more spending on education.

Fitzgerald believes government should introduce a scheme similar to the one for super to cover health costs in old age—both out of pocket and insurance. This would build up a pool to cover the BB bulge. What is increasingly clear is that politicians will have to juggle their demands against the resentment of the generations following. Meanwhile, the better-heeled baby boomers will continue to throng to cosmetic surgeons. As journalist Kirstie Clements has observed:

> The anti-aging industry is racing ahead, with procedures such as collagen injections, skin resurfacing, botox injections, fat transferral and surgical lifts and implants becoming more and more commonplace—and the results better and better . . . These interventions are no longer seen as indulgences of the rich, but as aesthetic maintenance for an aging population. Fight time, fight gravity. Get it before it gets you.[8]

Sydney cosmetic surgeon Dr George Mayson happily talks of a boom because of 'the pressure of our culture where you never see fat or ugly people in advertising'. There are also, he says, a lot of people in jobs like sales and personal service where

> if you look good, you'll do better than those who don't. And we know that people who are good-looking are considered by their peers to be more socially successful than those who aren't. People aren't afraid to say anymore that they've had cosmetic surgery. It's no longer a sign of vanity.

These days, three out of ten of his clients are males. Figures from the American Academy of Cosmetic Surgery show that the top five male procedures are hair transplants, chemical peels, liposuction, vein treatment and eyelid surgery. The top five procedures for women are chemical peels, vein treatments, liposuction, laser resurfacing and eyelid surgery. Says Mayson valiantly, 'It isn't that the baby boomer is finding it hard to get older, rather that it's no longer necessary to have to accept it'.

There has also been an increase in another surgical procedure, the vasectomy. In the financial year ending June 1996, 14 000 vasectomies were performed around Australia in hospitals and day clinics. Stewart-Hunter, who had a vasectomy in his 40s, notes that it would have been unusual in an earlier generation for a man to have such an operation 'because it's implicit that there's an expectation of a continued sex life, and a sex life for enjoyment but without the worry of pregnancies'.

'Elastic adolescence' is Hugh Mackay's very clever phrase for all of this:

> . . . the Boomers are now heavily into nostalgia. They are reluctant to part with their youth because they associate it with a time when everything looked rosier than it does today. They love to be reminded of the promise of their earlier years.[9]

Volkswagen has revived the Beetle, he reports, because they want to cash in on 1960s nostalgia among middle-aged BBs. Radio stations around Australia play nostalgia rock, with some of them (5AA in Adelaide, 3AW in Melbourne and, most notably, 2WS and 2SM in Sydney) targeting the boomer. Playing 1960s music almost non-stop, 2SM is owned by former INXS manager Chris M. Murphy: 'Baby boomers grew up smoking pot, protesting . . . It's an exciting category. It's the most informed and intriguing sector of our society.' His ambition—let's not forget that being born in 1954 he is a boomer himself—is to make radio sexy again. If he wins a hefty slice of the BB market (and since the strategy was launched, there have been significant rises in the station's share of that audience), he will have a potent lure for advertisers who would normally avoid a station close to the bottom in Sydney rankings.

This hankering for an earlier, happier and more peaceful

time is also evident in the booms for everything from therapy to alternative medicine to the sweet, comforting scents of aromatherapy to books that may contain the vital clue for prolonged happiness. There are practical volumes like Sheehy's *Passages For Men* and Anne and Bill Moir's recently released *Why Men Don't Iron* (HarperCollins), which ties neatly with Allan and Barbara Pease's *Why Men Don't Listen and Women Can't Read Maps* (Pease Training International). And, of course, John Gray's phenomenally successful relationship books, with their endless Mars and Venus theme. And there are other more ethereal, moral works like *Recasting the Stone* by Rosemary Williams (HarperCollins), *The Secrets of the Rainmaker* by Chin-Ning Chu (Stealth, distributed by Tower) and *Doing The Right Thing* by Aaron Hass (Pocket Books).

The stress of the baby-boomer lifestyle, with its conflicting and competing roles, and the insecurities of having lost either a partner or a job can drive people to seek out answers. Take the advertising executive, a BB whose life until the age of 50 was unmarked by anything other than hard work, meteoric success, influence and wealth until his wife left him for another man—the pain still shows in the soft cadence of his speech but the experience, he says, has made him a better person.

In that may lie the clue to the future. Setbacks can make us bitter. Or they can make us better. What will they do to the BBs? In the short term, there seems already to be a souring of the national mood, and that could be put down in part to so many people hitting mid-life crisis at the same time. The joyful optimism of baby-boomer youth has given way to a cynicism and resignation which is playing out in everything from the rancour associated with the celebrated Abbott and Costello versus Random House (aka Bob Ellis) court case of last October and November to the general down-in-the-mouthedness that strikes whenever a group of BBs get together over a barbecue in a backyard. Hansonism has many causes but disillusion and resentment, the belief that life should be better than it is, is also behind it. One cannot but be nervous of the force of this generational pessimism on national and foreign policy if it continues.

Generational friction will also take its toll. Through the decades until now, it has been simply a case of 'old codgers' giving way to 'pushy young things'. What is happening today is far more complex. First, of course, the codgers aren't giving way with anything but extreme reluctance and that is breeding tension, animosity and disrespect on both sides. Second, with limited economic resources, each generation will have to fight for its own good.

As noted above, health funding will be the priority for the over 50s, education funding for the under 50s. Canberra politics will increasingly be shaped by the conflicting demands of the different groups and politicians will have to bear in mind that because of the animosity, there will be little good will or charity between the groups. The divisiveness in this country that was seen with the Hanson phenomenon could become more pronounced with each group self-centredly concentrating on its own needs rather than being mindful of the overall good of the nation. This will take careful handling from the centre.

Nevertheless, as Judis reminded us in his article in the *New Republic*, it was the baby-boomer generation which had utopian dreams and which realised many of them.

> The 1960s unleashed conflicts within these new areas of concern—over affirmative action, abortion, homosexuality, drugs, rock lyrics, air pollution, endangered species, toxic waste dumps and automobile safety.

In their teens and 20s, the BBs took on the establishment and changed us forever, and for the better. If you don't believe that, ask yourself again about the state of women's rights, racism, equal opportunity for all, homophobia, freedom of speech, press freedom and access to legal, medical and welfare help for instance in the 1950s. It was baby-boomer indignation that stopped the Vietnam War. If many of these gains are now on the backslide, there is an argument that this is the fault of succeeding generations—Generation X and Generation Next—who are more interested in the tangible benefits of boomer lifestyle than the idealism which, as Stirton's figures reveal, still ticks away in the baby-boomer heart.

And there is the hope. The generation that achieved so much is unlikely to go out grumbling. It has been said that leaders do not shape us so much as we shape our leaders, that leaders fill a need. If you believe this, then the gap that waits to be filled is the one that exists in the soul of the baby boomer. It is in times of cynicism that we are most ready to look for inspiration. When we are at our gloomiest, we are most susceptible to someone pointing towards the rising sun. Life is cyclical. Today's crestfallen 50-year-old is tomorrow's re-energised and re-born warrior. And today's 40- to 54-year-olds still have the voting clout that Canberra cannot ignore. Writing about generalship, the American historian Barbara Tuchman noted the importance of resolution in her collection *Practising History* (Papermac).

> This is what enables a man to prevail—over circumstances, over subordinates, over allies, and eventually over the enemy. It is the determination to win through . . . whatever the circumstance, to prevail . . . if a man has it, he will also have, or he will summon from somewhere, the courage to support it. But he could be brave as a lion and still fail if he lacks the necessary will.

This succinctness could just as easily apply to the baby-boomer dilemma, and writing this I find myself wondering if the piece of grit at the very centre of all this baby-boomer nervousness is that BBs have not lost their will but their direction. Which brings us back to the leadership vacuum.

No one can predict what will happen or who may or may not fill that void but history shows us that voids do not exist for long. And looking to the more hopeful lessons of history, it is not just idealism on my own baby-boomer part that makes me think that the time is ripe for a leadership that will flourish by playing all the chords so familiar and so welcome to the baby-boomer soul.

NOTES

1 Wendy Wassterstein, *The Independent on Sunday*, 13 September 1998

2 John B. Judis, *New Republic*, 31 August 1998
3 Hugh Mackay, *Generations* Pan Macmillan, Sydney, 1997
4 Mark Davis, *Ganglands* Allen & Unwin, Sydney, 1997
5 Gail Sheehy, *Passages For Men* Simon & Schuster, 1998
6 Ann Harding with Martin Robinson, 'Forecasting the characteristics of consumers in 2010', the National Centre for Social and Economic Modelling, University of Canberra, 1998
7 ibid.
8 Kirstie Clements, *Australian Harpers Bazaar*, October 1998
9 Hugh Mackay, op. cit.

18

Message from the melt-down
What the Asian crisis has taught us

Robert Garran

The economic and political crisis that erupted in East Asia in mid-1997 was a defining force in the history of the region, and of the world. Politically and economically, old Asia was changed radically. Before the financial crash, there had been grand talk about the coming 'Asian century'—its booming economies, said the pundits, would decisively alter the balance of world economic and political power. In the event, Asia did deliver profound shifts in power—but not of the as-expected kind. Only now are we beginning to glimpse the consequences.

The Asian crisis signifies a radical change, not simply in views about Asia but also about how to manage the global capitalist system. It has delivered a more powerful shock to thinking on economics than did the collapse of communism a decade before. It has, however, settled two longstanding issues in the debate about the reasons for East Asia's spectacular growth by demolishing inter-related myths: that of a distinctive Asian model of economic development, and that a superior set of Asian values could guide the region to a more prosperous, stable future. Notwithstanding the successes, we now see there were deep flaws in economic and political institutions and structures in many Asian countries.

One important consideration is whether economic success

arose from efforts to beat the market, to engineer outcomes superior to those that could be delivered by the market, or to conform to market principles. As in any debate where much is at stake, this argument has become highly polarised. Political scientist Francis Fukuyama prematurely declared the controversy concluded in his essay 'The end of history' and subsequent book *The End of History and the Third Man*. He was partly right: evidence favours his preferred 'Market Model' over the interventions favoured by advocates of the 'Japan Model' and its successor, the 'Asian Model'.

The Asian crisis also demonstrates there are limits to the Market Model, although this shouldn't be overstated. To my mind, the strong presumption should remain in favour of market-based solutions, on the well-tested principle that markets generally are the best way to allocate resources. As always, the substantive debate occurs at the margin, and if nothing else the Asian crisis has proved that the promise of unfettered capital markets is a chimera, that capital markets unconstrained can have devastating consequences.

Internationally, the clearest signpost to the change of mood came in an article in *Foreign Affairs* in May/June 1998 by Jagdish Bhagwati:

> Until the Asian crisis sensitized the public to the reality that capital movements could repeatedly generate crises, many assumed that free capital mobility among all nations was exactly like free trade in their goods and services, a mutual-gain phenomenon. Hence unrestricted capital mobility, just like protectionism, was seen to be harmful to economic performance in each country, whether rich or poor.

But because capital flows are characterised by manias and panics, Bhagwati wrote, the cost of unfettered capital flows is considerable, while the benefits 'may be negligible'. From an arch-interventionist, this may have been unexceptionable. From the foremost proponent of free trade, this was striking.

In Australia, there was an equally dramatic indicator of the changing intellectual climate. In October 1998, Reserve Bank Governor Ian Macfarlane, previously a guardian of free-market rectitude, echoed Bhagwati's comments. The point is not that either man had deserted his enthusiasm for markets but that both recognised there were limits to the reliance on markets. Events since the start of the Asian crisis had demonstrated a clear case of market failure justifying some sort of intervention as a remedy. The most difficult question—still unresolved—is how and to what extent it will be possible to manage flows of capital in ways that avoid the pitfalls of the Asian crisis.

Economic Causes of the Crash

At one level, the story of the Asian crisis is simple: it was a classic boom and bust. Investors and speculators had jumped onto the Asian bandwagon, kidding themselves the good times would last forever. This boom was different from others, the story went: Asia really had discovered a recipe for miraculous growth. Inevitably, investors realised they had been promised or expected too much. Asia was subject to the same laws of economic gravity as everywhere else.

Admittedly, it was an unusual boom. One factor obscuring the pitfalls during the glory days was that for many East Asian countries, this was their first economic boom in modern times. They hadn't learned through experience that booms always bust. Insiders and outsiders alike believed Asia really had discovered how to beat the West at its own game. And there were some important differences compared with the West: differences of culture, history and politics, and differences in the shared experiences that define social and political perceptions. They were not so great, however, as to justify the widespread notion of an Asian miracle, a term that suggests performance beyond that explicable by conventional accounts.

The economic explanation for the Asian crisis comes in two versions. The first, favoured by the IMF, is that it emanated from corrupt and incompetent economic management within East Asia. The crisis, said IMF managing director Stanley Fischer, was 'mostly homegrown'. The alternate view, championed by Malaysian Prime Minister Dr Mahathir Mohamad, is that the crisis was the fault of rapacious foreign speculators. The truth, unsurprisingly, lies somewhere between these views. Mahathir's argument may have been self-serving but there was some merit in it: a fundamental shift in perception by investors and speculators had finally tipped the balance against East Asia. Of late, opinion has firmed that he may be right on another point; that the high-tech revolution in the world financial system contributed to the mayhem. It introduced a new element of volatility and instability that has magnified the size and increased frequency of financial booms and busts.

Mahathir overlooked, however, that investors had good reason to become wary of East Asia's prospects. The basic elements are well known. The countries worst hit by the crisis all shared, in varying mixtures, high levels of short-term debt, opaque financial and accounting systems that prevented investors from knowing fully how their money was being used, and investment decisions often heavily influenced by corruption and cronyism. Fixed exchange rates made the crash much more sudden: central banks were forced abruptly to abandon their exchange rates rather than allow them to adjust gradually, as they would have done under a floating currency regime such as Australia's.

All these flaws were ignored whilever investors believed the miracle would continue. When they realised it would not, sentiment shifted rapidly—much more rapidly than anyone expected. The activities of the infamous hedge funds made the change especially swift. These funds were ill-supervised and often had very high borrowings that magnified their potential gains and losses. But the hedge funds were just one manifestation of what US Federal Reserve Board chairman Alan Greenspan calls the 'new high-technology international financial system'. Developments in communications and computer technology mean that vast sums of money can now be sent around the world almost instantaneously, at minimal cost. The pool of capital available for investment has also increased sharply through the growing nest-eggs of ageing baby boomers, which have swelled pension and superannuation funds throughout the West.

The countries that best survived the Asian crisis suffered

least from the flaws of crony capitalism. Countries such as Taiwan, Singapore and the Philippines had some combination of less debt, flexible exchange rates, and more credible, less corrupt economic management.

OTHER REASONS FOR THE BUST

Beyond the immediate economic causes of the Asian crisis lie deeper undercurrents. Many flowed from Japan, which served as both an economic and philosophical model for the rest of Asia. Japan was the original miracle economy, the first to match the West in achieving outstanding economic performance. Its success set the standard for the so-called 'tiger economies' of South Korea, Taiwan, Hong Kong and Singapore, and later for their Southeast Asian neighbours, Indonesia, Thailand, Malaysia and the Philippines. The Japan model was so appealing that it evolved over time into the Asian Model—not a detailed blueprint for economic growth but a style of government, a general belief that governments could beat the market, usually by force-feeding investment in selected manufacturing export industries. The argument over whether the Asian Model did actually represent a superior path to economic success was settled only when the Asian crisis demonstrated the belief was mistaken.

Asian economies succeeded almost entirely because they followed principles espoused by market economics. This does not mean there is no role for government, but that government functions best when it takes a role where markets have failed. The arguments for a distinctive Asian Model are strongest in the earlier stages of economic development, when a country is well behind the technological frontier of the leading nations. There may be some benefit then in directing credit to selected industries, in 'picking winners', although even there evidence is inconclusive. These countries' successes can equally or better be explained by their adherence to pro-market policies, and by accidents of history.

The successful Asian economies emphasised the importance of education and sound macroeconomic policies, and promoted exports. But they were not alone throughout the 1950s and 1960s in advocating industrial policies of one sort or another. Similar philosophies were followed by many Western governments with, at best, mixed success. And Japan had another benefit: living under the security and protection of the US, and receiving large American military orders during the 1950–53 Korean War. Korea and Taiwan, in turn, benefited in the late 1960s and early 1970s from orders to supply American forces in the Vietnam War.

Japan had another significant role in the Asian boom and consequent bust; it was the source of a capital flood into Southeast Asia. Inflows of speculative capital are a critical factor in almost every financial boom, but the deluge of money was magnified in East Asia by the ready availability of Japanese capital, itself a function of Japan's cosseted and protected financial system. Advocates of a superior Japanese model argue that the country's skewed financial system was one reason for its success. Yet its very controls inhibited the efficient allocation of capital, and encouraged risky and careless investment. By the 1990s, its financial system had become a substantial burden.

Japan's over-investment, both at home and abroad, fuelled yet another problem at the heart of the Asian crisis, and contributed to its escalation in 1998 into a global issue. The Asian boom was of such a scale as to cause a worldwide over-capacity in key manufacturing industries from computer chips to ships, and in automobiles and other consumer goods. The boom in investment was exacerbated by the rapidly growing thirst for capital from China, whose market reforms since 1978 further expanded manufacturing capacity in the region. And this over-capacity was prolonged because of a failure to scale back investment. Throughout East Asia, it created a phenomenon not widely seen since the Great Depression: deflation, or falling prices—the opposite of inflation.

In a mild form, deflation need not be damaging. If prolonged, its effects can be highly disruptive. When asset prices are rising, there is some sense in borrowing heavily to maximise capital gain. But when the prices of assets such as shares and real estate begin to fall, those with high levels of borrowing find themselves holding loans backed by property of declining value.

The credit creation process that usually fuels such economic growth becomes a millstone as investors find it increasingly difficult to service debt. Such deflation became entrenched throughout East Asia during 1997 and 1998.

Deflation in the prices of goods and services can have more serious consequences. Given the resistance to cuts in nominal wages (the dollar amount of a pay packet), a fall in prices means that wages in real terms (spending power) are rising. This tends to make hiring labour more expensive, and leads to higher unemployment. In financial markets, symptoms of deflation began to emerge in 1997 and 1998 in the extremely low interest rates paid for long-term government bonds. In Japan in October 1998, the interest rate paid on 10-year government bonds dropped to 1.06 per cent, the lowest on record. But a contrary process was occurring in the market for short-term private debt, where growing risk and uncertainty led to higher interest rates, as lenders grew wary and conservative.

The spread of this contagion to Russia in August 1998 and to the US a month later signalled the escalation of the East Asian crisis into a global financial crisis. In a kind of mass global gloom, investors began to fear diminished economic prospects in all developing markets. Those that had borrowed heavily on expectation of growth withdrew funds when prospects turned sour. They fled East Asia, then Russia. Most worrying for the West, including Australia, banks in the US and Europe began to retreat, their unwillingness to lend causing a credit crunch that will slow growth throughout the world and could lead to a slump worthy of being described as a depression.

The deepening gloom is a crucial reminder of the importance of that intangible factor, confidence. Faith in the credit-creation process of the banking system underpins well-functioning economies. With that confidence now undermined, it may take a long time—several years at least—to recover. One hopes that the mistakes of the 1930s have been learned well, and that restrictive economic policies won't be applied when expansion is needed. But expansionary policies alone will not provide an instant solution, as Japan demonstrated in 1998.

Consequences of the Crash

The impact of the economic crisis in East Asia has been magnified by other changes. The economic turmoil came amid significant political transformations fuelled by the shifting balance of political power—the delayed consequences of the collapse of communism and the end of the Cold War. The crucial questions in the strategic picture for the region arise from the roles of China and the US, and the way they interconnect, along with other key regional players such as Japan and Korea.

China's strength in the near term will depend on its ability to insulate itself from the crisis, a performance that so far has been admirable but is unlikely to be sustained. China faces two possible futures: one involves a growing estrangement with the US and its allies; the other that it becomes an internationally responsible 'normal' country. A further crucial strategic issue is the continuing American engagement in the region. The US is the glue that holds the region together, in security terms, in the absence of strong regional institutions or a regional hegemony. But even though the US is a benign influence, its presence in Southeast Asia is only tolerated, not welcomed. As the circumstances change, that welcome may diminish.

The most fundamental plank of Australian policy will be to keep the US engaged in the region. But we must also consider the possibilities if America should fail to remain as deeply engaged as it is today. Any diminution of the American presence would wholly alter the region's strategic architecture. And there are two reasons why this might occur, the first internal to the US, the second external: the US might well engage in one of its periodic bouts of isolationism and wind back its role in the Asian Pacific, or in spite of contrary intentions, it may be forced to retreat.

The US has been so central to the security balance in Northeast Asia that disengagement would leave a vacuum. Nevertheless, it could be forced into a retreat through the reunification of North and South Korea, and the disappearance of the last vestige of the Cold War. At present, the military risk posed by a hostile North Korea is the strongest and most explicit justification for the presence of American troops in Japan and South Korea. When, as seems likely in the not-too-distant future, the Korean peninsula becomes unified, it will be much more difficult to justify that presence. Korean and Japanese support for the US will also become less certain.

Strategically, the greatest stress points in the region are all in Northeast Asia. Southeast Asia is likely to remain inward-looking for years to come, a process that will be reinforced by the Asian crisis—its nations do not have the wealth or inclination to become leading strategic players. Like Australia, they have been significant beneficiaries of American-imposed peace for the past 50 years. Southeast Asia will not, however, escape stresses and strains, as is seen in the continuing spat between Singapore and Malaysia, or in the displeasure shown by Indonesia and the Philippines over the treatment meted out by Mahathir to his former deputy prime minister, Anwar Ibrahim.

The strains were apparent in the November 1998 meeting of the APEC forum in Kuala Lumpur. The controversy over Anwar's trial generated most of the headlines from the meeting, but there were deeper questions over whether APEC could fulfil its goals of promoting free trade now that economic conditions had turned sour. With Malaysia and Japan on the defensive over trade, the meeting sidestepped proposals to move ahead with 'voluntary' reductions in selected trade barriers, referring them to the WTO. The failure to achieve its preeminent goal left APEC badly wounded, but its deeper purpose, usually unstated, remains vital. APEC does not have the legally binding rules of the WTO or the cultural affinity of the European Union, but is still highly valuable as the only regular forum for the region's leaders to meet, and sometimes cooperate.

The economic crisis has increased pressure on ASEAN countries to make their economic and political systems more open, transparent and democratic. The legitimacy of many Southeast Asian regimes has relied on economic success. Now that that success has been undermined, their legitimacy is threatened. In Thailand and the Philippines, the move towards democratisation has provided another source of legitimacy and made it easier to accept unpalatable remedies to cope with the economic crisis.

In more authoritarian countries, economic failure is seriously undermining regime legitimacy, as Indonesia discovered early in 1998 and Malaysia later in the year.

Northeast Asian countries have begun to develop the capacity to give them military capability similar to those of Western countries, but they had wrongly assumed that accelerated growth would be enough to allow them to meet the challenges of globalisation. As in Southeast Asia, the virtues of globalisation had been sold to the public as a 'one-way train'. Increasing prosperity became synonymous with liberalisation and globalisation. But, says Chung Min Lee, associate professor of international relations at Yonsei University in Seoul:

> The crisis ruptured a major hole in this marketing strategy with the stark realisation that East Asian societies, the governments which ruled them and the values which they espoused are all vulnerable. Not even Japan, the second largest economy in the world, had credible defences against the globalisation onslaught.

This is a challenge, he says, that cannot be overcome through multilateral organisations like the ASEAN Regional Forum or the APEC forum.

> No matter how many layers of multilateral schemes one can think of, they are all missing the point. East Asian countries embraced multilateralism because none of them is willing to pay the political and social costs for wrenching restructuring on the home front . . . multilateralism offers the easy way out.

Most Southeast Asian states still focus their resources on domestic security 'simply because all of them are still in the process of nation-building', argues Joon-Num Mak, the director of research at the Maritime Institute of Malaysia. The drive towards democratisation can easily be overturned if incumbent governments fail to meet the expectations of the people, which means implementing sustainable growth-oriented policies. Electorates in most new democracies have been accustomed to the outcomes-oriented approach of authoritarian rule, and do not value the democratic process in itself, says Mak: 'Giving the populace a stake in the status quo through economic development will still be crucial, even for democratic regimes, otherwise there could be a rollback to authoritarianism.'

With their economies under stress, this will be difficult to achieve. And ASEAN concerns about American enlargement are ironic, he argues, given that ASEAN's economic growth emanated largely from an export-led strategy in which the US was the main market. The dilemma for ASEAN has become how to foster an export-oriented economy without the political underpinnings of a free market. The more authoritarian a state is, the more concerned it is about the potential loss of national sovereignty, and the accompanying inability to direct and control economic development and distribution and politics. The more authoritarian Southeast Asian states, resentful of these pressures, might find they have more in common with China's developmental and social norms than with those of the West.

While globalisation has made Europe and America (and Australia) think in regional and universal terms, 'Southeast Asia is still obsessed with sovereignty and national power,' says Mak. These so different developmental models could lead to an East–West estrangement, with some countries finding the model they share with China more attractive, others preferring the American–European model. More optimistically, ASEAN could accommodate such strains by adopting a neutral approach among its members, in line with its principle of 'non-interference' in each other's affairs.

Australia is likely to hold firmly to the US alliance, but in doing so risks being regarded by some Southeast Asian countries as 'part of the plot' to undermine the sovereignty of Asian states and to disempower them economically. 'Australia cannot take Western norms for granted where Southeast Asia is concerned,' says Mak. It must choose whether it wants to link its future with Asia, the US or Europe—a tri-polar approach is possible, 'but with limited resources, priorities must be made'.

One World or Many?

The debate between Fukuyama and his intellectual opponent, political scientist Samuel Huntington, offers a useful perspective on Asia's future. Neither on their own gives an adequate account of the new post-Cold War world, but they do highlight opposing strands in the argument and indicate possible directions. In blunt terms, Fukuyama in his essay 'The end of history' saw the end of the Cold War and the death of communism as a conclusive victory for liberal democratic principles. It was a victory that would end forever the debate about the broad principles that should guide political behaviour. Huntington, in his 1993 essay 'The clash of civilizations' and then 1996 book *The Clash of Civilizations and the Remaking of the World Order*, took an opposing stance. The end of the Cold War, he suggested, had removed the defining issue of world power politics and replaced it not with the end of history but with uncertainty and instability. World politics would become a battle between civilisations with incompatible values and institutions, each fighting to establish the pre-eminence of its world view and interests.

If a different strain of political economy remains dominant in parts of the region, Australia will face difficult choices in trying to balance its interests. One perplexing choice among many would arise if China and the US became involved in some military tussle, perhaps over Taiwan. Such a development seems unlikely but it does illustrate a type of dilemma we could face: do we ally ourselves with a rising power in the region or back the country that hitherto has been presumed to provide the best insurance of our security? There are many permutations to this kind of question. Where, for example, would other large and powerful countries in the region, such as Japan and Korea, line up in such a dispute? There is no reason to suppose they would automatically back America in any regional contest, especially once North and South Korea become unified.

Into this mix, the Asian crisis has imposed another imperative: a debate about how to manage the world capitalist system, and whether it can be sustained in its present form. The exigency has undermined the legitimacy of authoritarian regimes, most starkly in Indonesia with the departure of former president Suharto, but also in Malaysia where Mahathir undermined his own authority through his treatment of Anwar. In a sense, this illustrates the tension between the Fukuyama and Huntington views of the world, the end of history versus the clash of civilisations.

We don't know how this will evolve, but we must be cognisant of the possibility that Huntington will prove correct. Although democracy and liberalism are powerful ideas, there is nothing inevitable about their victory.

REFERENCES

Francis Fukuyama, *The End of History and the Last Man* Avon Books, New York, 1982

Robert Garran, *Tigers Tamed: the End of the Asian Miracle* Allen & Unwin, Sydney, 1998

Samuel P. Huntington, *The Clash of Civilizations and the Remaking of World Order* Simon & Schuster, New York, 1996

Chung Min Lee, 'The security environment in Northeast Asia', paper delivered at conference 'Maintaining the strategic edge: the defence of Australia in 2015', Strategic and Defence Studies Centre, Canberra, 1998

J.N. Mak, 'Southeast Asian Security to the Year 2015', SDSC, op. cit., 1998

19

A STRATEGY FOR REVOLUTION
Defence goes on to the front foot

Patrick Walters

HISTORIC CHALLENGES CONFRONT John Howard and his Government in securing the nation's defence and in coming to grips with a profoundly changed strategic environment. As we enter the twenty-first century, the principal task is to complete the fundamental reshaping of our defence force towards a strategy of genuine self-reliance. Another vital, equally demanding responsibility is to materially assist the longer term evolution of a genuine sense of strategic community in Southeast Asia. Without this, ASEAN's stability and Australia's own long-term security cannot be assured.

The lesson of the 1990s is that neither mission will be accomplished easily. Acquiring the capabilities for the defence of Australia will demand a more disciplined focus from the Government on both defence and industry policy. On the one hand, constraints on public sector spending promise to impact negatively on future defence budgets and the capacity of governments to support local manufacture of ships, submarines and other capabilities. On the other, the accelerating information technology revolution promises to transform future war-fighting systems—but these won't come cheaply.

At present, only one country, the US, has the technological base and budgetary resources to bring about the radical changes being discussed by the Pentagon's defence planners. In our immediate region, the Government has a monumental task in assisting the rebuilding of the Indonesian state. And where regional security is concerned, Indonesia remains our most important strategic relationship in Southeast Asia.

The strategic outlook in the Asia–Pacific region is more fluid and uncertain today than at any time since the Vietnam War. Many of the comfortable assumptions upon which our defence planning relied for much of the past 30 years have had to be jettisoned in the face of substantial geo-political shifts in East Asia. In terms of putative military threat, the regional picture, with the notable exception of the Korean peninsula, is more benign. The 1990s has seen an outbreak of peace in Asia–Pacific—Australia confronts no imminent threat of direct military assault, and has not done so for more than half a century. Yet our defence planners are still grappling with the fundamental questions posed by our unique strategic geography, and how best to conceive the independent defence of an island continent and its vast maritime territory.

Recent political and economic developments in Southeast Asia have simply underlined the hazards of predicting how Asia's strategic map will unfold over the next 25 years. In August 1997, the Government's key foreign policy planning document judged that 'economic growth in industrialising East Asia will continue at relatively high levels over the next 15 years' and that the continuing economic rise of Asia would together with globalisation constitute 'the two most profound influences in Australian foreign and trade policy'.[1]

The Government's principal defence planning document, Australia's Strategic Policy, confidently predicted in December 1997 that Indonesia's economy would surpass that of Australia within 20 years. It also postulated a steady decline in Australia's relative strategic standing in East Asia: 'After the turbulence of the late Sukarno era, Indonesia under President Suharto has . . . strengthened Indonesia's cohesion and prosperity.'

These crucial assumptions represent a significant failure in Australia's intelligence assessment processes. Key conclusions in the Government's two principal strategic planning documents were out of date within weeks of being released.

The end of the Cold War also signified the end of the long period of strategic dominance of Asia by Western great powers. In the next 50 years, for the first time in 500 years, Asian security will largely be determined by the region's great powers, including China, Japan and India. Whether the world's remaining superpower, the US, continues a defining role in East Asian security will have a crucial bearing on how the regional power balance evolves.

The post-war global balance of power between the US and the Soviet Union came to a sudden end with the latter's collapse. As Australia's foremost defence analyst, Paul Dibb, has observed, no security system has ever bound Asia together. There is no historical tradition of shared values or common cultures nor any experience of a multi-polar balance of power extending across Asia. 'None of the key players—China, Japan, India, Russia and the US—has any experience of practising balance of power politics across the entire Asian region in such a potentially fluid situation.'[2]

As we enter a new century, there are no clear signs of the likely course of relations between the region's great powers. Will China again seek to become the regional hegemon as its remarkable economic transformation continues, or will it willingly accommodate itself to a new regional balance of power? Will Japan seek to play a more assertive role in East Asian affairs commensurate with its economic strength and in the face of the inevitable decline of America's military presence? Will the US remain as involved in the security of East Asia and fully committed to supporting wider regional stability after the inevitable reunification of the two Koreas? And in Southeast Asia, will the largest ASEAN member states, now assailed by economic difficulties, reach a political accord that will allow common approaches to their external defence to unfold? According to Dibb, the solution for middle powers like Australia is to acknowledge that

> uneven growth among states in Asia will inevitably lead to a new distribution of power that may not necessarily be in their

interests. Middle powers will need to develop strategies of self-reliance as well as co-operation with great powers to preserve their independence of action.[3]

In the twilight of the twentieth century, Australia has been forced to tackle its historical destiny in the Asia–Pacific region. As US influence there gradually recedes, our defence planners must come to terms with our strategic geography and be prepared to largely go it alone in securing the nation's defence. For the first time, the information revolution in military affairs, the so-called Revolution in Military Affairs (RMA), holds the tantalising promise that an island continent with a population of just 18 million can plan its own defence with confidence against the threat of a major military assault on its soil. Our historical dependence on great and powerful friends—first Britain and then the US—for protection from perceived Asian threats has been replaced by a long-term search for security in Asia itself. 'We cannot be secure in an insecure region' and 'We seek security in Asia, not from Asia' have become two standard government refrains as it has sought to build strategic relations with leading ASEAN states as well as North Asian powers. A related objective must be to support the retention of a permanent US military presence in the region.

John Howard's bold new defence doctrine aims not just to ensure the defence of Australia and its territories but to play a leading role in securing the archipelago to our north from external threat. In its redefinition of the scope of Australia's strategic interests and in the more aggressive roles ascribed for our maritime forces, the 1997 Strategic Policy document is the most ambitious defence planning blueprint approved by an Australian government.

Soon after his re-election in October 1998, Howard spoke of the requirement for Australia to play a more assertive political and economic role in the region. His defence ministers have spoken of 'forward cooperation' and even 'forward defence' in articulating the new policy—refrains that echo from another era when our defence forces joined with more powerful friends in fighting wars distant from our own shores. The Government contemplates the possibility of Australian military forces being engaged in high-intensity military conflicts north of the equator, including on the Korean peninsula and in the straits of Taiwan. As the former defence minister Ian McLachlan told Parliament in December 1997:

> We can no longer assume that forces able to meet low-level contingencies in the defence of Australia will be sufficient to handle conflict beyond our territory . . . The Government therefore rejects the argument that we must choose between a defence force to defend Australia and one able, within realistic limitations, to operate overseas.

The Howard Government has redrawn the strategic horizons well beyond Southeast Asia and the South Pacific to cover the whole Asia–Pacific theatre, citing the end of the Cold War and the demise of the superpower balance for its wider Asian focus. As part of this shift, Australia now conducts regular military dialogue with both Japan and China. In Southeast Asia, the Australian Defence Force has developed extremely close defence ties with Singapore and Malaysia, and increasingly important ties with Indonesia's armed forces.

In two important ways, the 1997 Strategic Policy document represents a radical departure from the strategic guidance adopted by the previous Labor governments. It proposes a more potent, offensive role for the ADF in defeating threats to Australia in the northern sea–air gap, as well as providing substantial capabilities to defend 'regional strategic interests' in the Indonesian archipelago and, if required, further north. And it argues that Australia must remain the dominant maritime power east of India and south of China.

This more robust strategic doctrine may prove unsustainable for several reasons. First, there is a danger that the carefully delineated approach adopted in the past decade for determining force structure priorities could be distorted by the Government's apparent enthusiasm for the ADF to be capable of operating in theatres to the north of the Indonesian archipelago. Current strategic guidance says ADF capabilities will be developed to defeat attacks on Australia and to defend regional strategic interests. 'Priority will be given to the first of these tasks but decisions will be influenced by the ability of forces to contribute to both tasks.'[4]

Defending our regional strategic interests inside ASEAN will require a more creative and far-sighted diplomacy than the Howard Government displayed in its first term.

For nearly 30 years, a keystone of Australia's security presence in Southeast Asia has been the Five Power Defence Arrangement under which Australia, New Zealand and Britain have conducted regular defence exercises with Malaysia and Singapore. In August 1998, Malaysia pulled out of the principal annual FPDA exercise, questioning whether the arrangement remained relevant to Kuala Lumpur's defence needs. In earlier days, FPDA performed a useful security function as the Malay peninsula worried about communist insurgencies and events in Vietnam, and it has continued to serve as a useful confidence-building measure. But Malaysia's current attitude should have sent a strong signal to Canberra that the time has come to overhaul the architecture of the post-colonial hangover that is the FPDA. With Malaysia reviewing its future participation by mid-1999, the Government should take the initiative to fold FPDA into a new multilateral defence arrangement that incorporates Jakarta. Indonesia has never been reconciled to FPDA's continuance. Canberra must play a leadership role in devising a new mechanism that initially could include Singapore, Malaysia, Indonesia, Thailand, Australia and New Zealand.

Whatever the Government's present enthusiasm for a more assertive regional role, there are obvious limits to Australia's defence capacity, and to its ability to play a defining role in the future pattern of security arrangements in Southeast Asia. ASEAN sensitivity to Australia's diplomatic and defence roles in the sub-region have been made manifest most recently by Malaysia, with Prime Minister Mahathir working assiduously to exclude Australia from participation in the Asia–Europe (ASEM) summit meetings and from his planned East Asian Economic Caucus grouping. Notwithstanding Mahathir's views, Australia has excellent defence relations with Singapore, Indonesia and Thailand and is possibly the only country that could broker a more inclusive security arrangement that could supersede FPDA.

Extending Australia's strategic focus north of the equator could pose formidable challenges for future governments. Whether Australian forces could participate in a US-led coalition to defend Taiwan, for example, would undoubtedly become a sensitive political issue. As Singapore's Senior Minister, Lee Kuan Yew, warned recently, if the US were to join issue with China over Taiwan, it might not find many supporters in East Asia. 'While nearly all Asian countries support the US presence, no Asian country wants to challenge China on issues falling clearly within China's internal affairs or territorial sovereignty.'[5]

The more pressing problem for defence planners is the level of financial resources available to the ADF as it moves into the next century. The defence budget has steadily fallen to be just 1.9 per cent of GDP—the lowest level in 50 years. Even the path-breaking 1987 Defence White Paper argued that a defence outlay of more than 2.5 per cent of GDP would have to be retained if future governments were to achieve the modest capability levels it outlined. During the 1990s, the defence budget has experienced zero real growth; spending in 1997–98 was just over $10 billion. In absolute numbers, the ADF's regular personnel has shrunk dramatically in the past 10 years from around 74 000 to 54 000; the standing army is now below 25 000. Such stark realities pose the biggest challenge to the Coalition's strategic ambitions.

The latest strategic guidance defines five key interests for Australia in the Asia–Pacific region into the next century by seeking to help:

- avoid any destabilising strategic competition between regional powers;
- prevent the emergence of a security environment dominated by any power(s) whose strategic interests might be inimical to Australia's;
- maintain a benign security environment, especially in maritime Southeast Asia, which safeguards the territorial integrity of all countries in the region;

- block the positioning in neighbouring states by any foreign power of military forces that might be used to attack Australia;
- avert the proliferation of weapons of mass destruction in our region.

Moving away from the defence-in-depth strategy that was embraced by the Hawke and Keating governments, Howard has accepted the argument for greater emphasis on strike forces that could take the initiative and threaten the military assets and installations of an aggressor nation. East Asia's strong economic growth over the past two decades has led to steady increases in defence spending and the military capabilities of Australia's northern neighbours, including key ASEAN countries. While Asia's financial crisis will slow the acquisition of new high-technology weapon platforms, a return to rapid economic growth in East Asia will mean Australia cannot expect to retain a decisive, long-term technological edge over its neighbours.

The US alliance will remain Australia's most important defence relationship, absolutely fundamental to our efforts to achieve a greater level of defence self-reliance. Vital strategic benefits include access to satellite-based surveillance and intelligence systems, leading edge military technologies and support for Australia's own efforts to embrace RMA. Two critically important alliance issues confront our defence planners. One is to determine what level of inter-operability should exist between an increasingly high-tech US defence force and the ADF; the other is how much Australia can afford to adapt to the Pentagon's embrace of the hugely expensive RMA-integrated systems.

The RMA has a particular significance. Its application to surveillance and intelligence gathering would enable the ADF for the first time to know exactly what is going on in the sea-gap at our northern approaches. Together with the Australian-developed Jindalee over-the-horizon radar and satellite-borne synthetic aperture radar systems, the information revolution is expected to transform war-fighting in the next century. It promises to revolutionise command and control arrangements right down to the battlefield, and for Australia—with its relatively tiny defence force and huge territory—could confer huge strategic benefits.

The ADF's objective is to have an integrated surveillance system delivering real-time, all-weather detection of ships and aircraft in our maritime approaches. Defence is also looking at acquiring airborne early warning and control (AEW&C) as a high priority, together with unmanned aerial vehicles that could cover vast distances carrying sophisticated sensors. Over the next 25 years, however, RMA could fundamentally alter the force structure of the ADF. Our strategic planners have already nominated the 'knowledge edge' as the highest priority in developing our defence capability in the next decade. In that time, spending on the 'knowledge edge', with its mix of intelligence, command and communications and surveillance technologies, is expected to account for some 35 per cent of the new capital equipment budget.

Some of the sharpest defence debates in the next few years will revolve around the Government's three other stated priorities for the future defence force structure: defeating threats in the maritime environment; maintaining strategic strike forces to deter potential adversaries; and building a new army structure to deal with hostile forces on Australian soil. By 2005, decisions will have to be made about replacements for the long-serving F–111 strike force, as well as for the RAAF's F/A 18 fighters, which have the key role of achieving air superiority in the sea–air gap and over Australian airspace. The Government intends at present to keep the expensive 30-year-old F–111 bomber fleet in service until at least 2015 by fitting the aircraft with new long-range stand-off weapons and improving their electronic warfare capabilities.

For the navy, the most important addition to its fleet will be the six Australian-built Collins Class submarines that could eventually become the foundation of a strategic strike force. The first boats of the new class have encountered considerable teething problems, but once fully operational will provide a quantum leap in capability over the old Oberon class.

The army is also undergoing a quiet revolution with the abolition of its traditional divisional structures and the wholesale relocation of key units to Darwin. The aim is to create highly mobile task forces equipped with attack helicopters as well as sophisticated land-based surveillance systems and improved Special Forces units. The smaller, more technologically sophisticated army of the future is designed to handle a wide range of military contingencies, including offshore operations. The army also plans to retain a brigade group at a high level of readiness, which could be deployed overseas at short notice.

A significant impediment to the Government's broader defence vision is the lack of political consensus and public support for real increases in the defence vote. Proposed capability changes, particularly the desire to achieve a decisive military edge by adopting RMA solutions, will place huge pressures on future defence budgets at a time when other crucial new platforms will have to be ordered. From 2010, Australia faces the prospect of block obsolescence of key platforms, including its frontline aircraft and FFG warships. State-of-the-art fighters such as the US-made F22 fighter cost around $US180 million a copy.

The Government has trumpeted its defence reform program, which has rationalised command structures and privatised some defence functions, and claims there will be an eventual annual saving to the defence vote of between $770 million and $1000 million. But even if these savings are achieved, they will not preclude the need for a substantial increase in the defence vote over the next decade if the ADF is to be properly equipped for the military task now defined by the Government. On this issue, the 1997 Strategic Policy guidance document issued a timely warning. With ADF personnel having been cut by 20 per cent over the past decade, it concluded Australia is approaching the point at which further cuts to the size of the ADF 'would damage its credibility as a fighting force'. Significant new efficiencies could not be derived from further personnel savings, and relying on generating efficiencies at the 'blunt end' would not be enough to ensure that

> we can continue to achieve the Government's strategic objectives ... Rising personnel costs, preserving and enhancing our

skill base and meeting higher demands for readiness, along with rising investment costs for new capabilities, will place pressure on defence funding. Moreover, the current budget does not make it possible to contemplate developing major new capabilities in the form of new fighter aircraft or new surface combatants.

Defence did not surface as an election issue in the last federal election, and has not done so for many years. The lack of sustained public debate about the future shape and role of our defence force will make it much harder for the Government to convince a sceptical electorate that real increases are needed in the defence vote early in the new millennium. In an unpredictable economic climate, political pressures will build for scarce Budget resources to be earmarked for areas such as education and social welfare at the expense of defence. The Government claims there has been a significant increase in public support for the ADF. A public opinion survey in early 1998 indicated that 67 per cent of respondents were confident of the ADF's ability to defend Australia, compared with 57 per cent three years earlier. But sustaining a national consensus on defence in peacetime is a difficult task for any government.

Above all, there is a real danger the Government's more ambitious defence strategy will lead to a distortion of force structure priorities. The agreed capabilities required to meet the defence of Australia could be lost amid competing claims within the three services for spending on assets of marginal relevance to national defence.

The highest priority remains the creation of a defence force reflecting our unique strategic geography, one capable of matching the evolving military capabilities in our region.

Notes

1 Department of Foreign Affairs and Trade, 'In the National Interest, Australia's Foreign and Trade Policy', p. v, 1997
2 Paul Dibb, *Towards a New Balance of Power in Asia*, Adelphi paper,

Oxford University Press for International Institute for Strategic Studies, 1995, p. 10
3 ibid., p. 73
4 Department of Defence, 'Australia's Strategic Policy', 1997, p. 36
5 Lee Kuan Yew, speech to International Institute for Strategic Studies Conference, Singapore, September 12 1997, p. 5

20

THINK LOCAL, ACT GLOBAL
A return to Fortress Australia is no option

Greg Sheridan

EXCEPTIONALLY NARROW, PAROCHIAL, inward-looking and uninspired as the campaign was, it is still important, if perverse, to try to put the 1998 federal election into an international context. For it was really all about one issue that no one would mention. Globalisation.

This is the most important historical process under way in the world today. It is the defining new paradigm of political economy. Where you stand on globalisation is a much more important policy indicator than where you stand on any traditional Left–Right divide. Globalisation can be compared in its historical effect with the industrial revolution. It will change everything. And because in its current guise it is such a new process, we have not yet worked out the institutions, international or domestic, nor even cultural norms to cope with it.

Electorates around the world have responded to globalisation in different ways. Most affluent Western nations have spawned anti-globalisation parties or movements. Even the US, which in so many ways dominates the global economy and which is experiencing unprecedented economic success, has produced in Pat Buchanan a nationalist rage against the global economy. In Australia, we have spawned our very own anti-globalisation party in Pauline Hanson's One Nation movement. Anti-globalisation parties often have strongly racial overtones because one feature of the global economy is that it's full of foreigners. One manifestation of globalisation is multiracialism.

The sad little secret of the 1998 election is how well our anti-globalisation party did. It is right and praiseworthy that the mainstream parties put One Nation last on their how-to-vote cards, but it still received 8 per cent of the vote nationally and 15 per cent in Queensland. That an outfit like that could get such a vote indicates how managing globalisation remains a profound challenge. In this, of course, we are hardly unique. Take the recent German election. If you add the vote there for the former East German communists to that received by the various parties of the extreme Right, it is clear that about 10 per cent of Germans voted for the spiritual heirs to either the Nazis or the Stalinists. Thus, in the third-biggest economy in the world, in an immensely sophisticated West European nation that, given its history, should be permanently immunised against extremists, a tenth of the population turned to extremists for solutions.

Chicago-based economist David Hale has argued that this level of political alienation arises from Europe's high level of unemployment. In Germany it is well over 10 per cent, as it is in France and Italy. What is fascinating is that continental Europeans have tried to cope with globalisation through high taxes, a high level of bureaucracy (almost a kind of bureaucratic capitalism), an extensive social security system with many universal entitlements and a strong regional association. Despite Mark Latham's jeremiads to the contrary, his Labor leader Kim Beazley was offering a very close Australian replica of the European model. The downside of this model is high unemployment and high taxes.

The American response is the real alternative. The US model rests on a radically deregulated labour market, high geographic labour mobility, high immigration, low taxes and an extremely limited welfare system. The trade-off is this: it gives you an innovative and dynamic capitalism with considerable job opportunities (US unemployment is about 4 per cent), but it means that people at the bottom end of the labour market work for extremely low wages and it is very harsh for the unemployed. This really ought to be the model, somewhat adapted for Australian circumstances, which John Howard and the Coalition offer. It is the model they probably believe in but are too timid to embrace.

Despite all the hype, the GST is not a particularly important structural reform leading towards the American model. The *Asian Wall Street Journal*'s editorial on the election is instructive on this. It praised the personal income tax cuts Howard proffered (which were all but lost sight of in the election) but thought the introduction of a new sales tax just silly. Notably, the US does not have a GST. If Howard and the Coalition were really serious about tackling unemployment, from their ideological point of view and following the international experience they would be championing radical deregulation of the labour market, high immigration and the promotion of an enterprise culture. But there's no chance of that.

International comparisons are complicated by Britain: it runs basically a US model but has a Labour Prime Minister who has promised not to undo the Thatcher–Major revolution. Both Tony Blair and US President Bill Clinton hide their right-wing policies behind the rhetorical cover of 'the third way'. Let's be clear here—the third way is complete baloney. Blair cut benefits for single mothers. Clinton passed welfare reform that severely limited the availability of welfare over time. Such measures would have warmed the hearts of Ronald Reagan or Margaret Thatcher. They have nothing to do with social democracy. Third way-ism is just political cover for the fact that in Britain and the US conservative, free market ideas have decisively won the policy and ideological battle, even if conservative parties are out of office.

In Australia, our system, essentially because of the pro-market reforms of the years when Bob Hawke was prime minister and Paul Keating treasurer, stands between the European and American models. Beazley wants to take us in the European direction, hoping, probably forlornly, that he can have the European bureaucratic security without the European unemployment. Howard and his team, with almost infinite timidity, are nudging us in the American direction. The question is whether the global economy will force our hand, and whether a small, highly indebted economy such as ours, without the basic security of being part of the huge European market, could even afford anything like the European model. That neither side of politics really saw fit to discuss these issues in the campaign was depressing.

In so far as formal foreign policy figured in the campaign, there was overall bipartisanism on basic issues. The Government offered basic continuity with its record, although after the election it became somewhat bolder in supporting reform of the international financial system. On the primary planks of foreign policy—continued support for the American alliance, continued regional engagement as the top priority—Labor took essentially the same position as the Government.

However, Labor—as is the wont of most Oppositions in foreign policy—did go some distance down some seriously irresponsible policy roads. Labor's foreign spokesman, Laurie Brereton, committed a Beazley government to supporting full self-determination for East Timor, elevating human rights to a central focus of Australian foreign policy, appointing an ambassador for human rights and a special envoy for East Timor, and slapping sanctions on Burma. This is all irresponsible, and irresponsible in a way characteristic of Oppositions. It is symbolism politics at best; if it is meant to be taken seriously (a more disturbing prospect), it greatly inflates the role Australia could or should play in these issues. Such moves would certainly do nothing to advance human rights but they would damage us in the region.

Sanctions on Burma are particularly futile. The Burmese Government is very good at isolation—it has practised it as a preferred method of dealing with the world for nearly 30 years. This isolation did not produce any beneficial human rights outcomes. And with China and ASEAN certain to oppose any strategy of isolating Burma, it would be totally unproductive. What is likely to work is economic reform and development, because these almost always produce an increase in political space available to people. But this takes a long time, and does not offer the emotional and political gratification of loud denunciations. Similarly, Australia should be doing everything it can to help Indonesia recover from the regional crisis—not trying to pretend we have a central role in what is bound to be an exceptionally difficult and dangerous political evolution in East Timor.

The only consolation in Labor's approach is that the region is so preoccupied with the economic crisis that it probably would not pay much attention. Moreover, political parties inevitably tend to be more cautious and conservative when they get into office. Nonetheless, the process of ditching the irresponsible ideas from Opposition can be long and costly. Moreover, Labor's approach on human rights cuts across its other policy priority of once again emphasising Australia's close engagement with the region. The regional economy is bound to continue to be the primary focus of foreign policy in the second Howard Government. As it should be. The regional economic crisis is an epoch-marking event in Australia's external environment. The way Australia responds will determine how whole generations of Asians view us.

No East Asian has ever experienced an economic reversal on this scale in their lives. Of course some older Asians have experienced the even worse traumas of war, but short of war nothing represents so fundamental a dislocation, such a profound discontinuity, in modern East Asian history. For many it is the first significant reversal they have encountered since they began practising liberal capitalist economics. As such, the whole orientation of these nations, as pro-Western, free-market and tending towards democracy, is called into question. How these questions are resolved is of profound importance to Australia, and Canberra needs to make every possible effort to see they are resolved in the right way. This will involve using, in an integrated fashion, every available diplomatic resource.

The first Howard Government all but ignored Australia's chief regional diplomatic asset, the APEC forum. The bureaucrats laboured away, Foreign Minister Alexander Downer and Trade Minister Tim Fischer attended relevant ministerial meetings and made useful contributions. But APEC, when it works, is powered at heads of government level. That's where we were lacking energy.

Shortly after the election, Howard gave important indications that he had at last become fully seized of the importance of APEC. In foreign policy, he bore a certain resemblance to Clinton. What? you ask. What comparison could be more far-fetched than one between Howard and Clinton? It works this way. George Bush's greatest strength as president was his command and competence at foreign policy. Clinton, as governor of Arkansas, was inexperienced in this field. But he performed a brilliant political judo trick by using Bush's strength against him, campaigning in 1992 virtually against the very idea of foreign policy. Clinton suggested Bush had been too preoccupied with international diplomacy to the neglect of domestic policy and the real-life concerns of everyday Americans. He promised to focus 'with laser-like intensity' on US domestic issues. As a result, he was a very poor foreign policy president in his first term and probably on purpose appointed a weak foreign policy team. By his second term, he had realised that foreign policy was an absolutely inescapable part of his job description.

Howard in 1996 similarly campaigned against Keating's preoccupation with the 'big picture', of which Asian engagement was so central a part. It is important to get the distinctions right here. Howard did not campaign against the Asian engagement as such but against Keating's preoccupation with issues far removed from the everyday concerns of ordinary Australians. In Howard's early days of his first term, the main message seemed to be limiting, even paring back, the Asian engagement. He and his foreign policy team did reiterate that engagement with Asia was Australia's top foreign policy priority but Howard's early speeches seemed more concerned with placing limits on this. We're not Asian, we're not a cultural bridge between Asia and the West, and so on. Similarly, Hansonism spooked the leading parties.

Nevertheless, the Asian economic crisis did for the Howard Government what the passage of time did for Clinton. Its response was competent, even good, but insufficiently energetic given the scale of Australian interests involved. But by contributing to all three regional IMF bail-outs for Indonesia, Thailand and South Korea, Howard underlined a basic Australian commitment. This was further emphasised by provision of food aid and export credit guarantees for Indonesia, and Australian diplomacy supporting a more realistic and socially-conscious IMF approach to Indonesia.

His second term offers Howard the chance to be much more pro-active, creative, regionally-focused and effective. In two speeches shortly after the election, he gave us reason to think this might be so. The first, to launch a Richness In Diversity exhibition (the brainchild of the Department of Foreign Affairs and Trade) which toured Asia, was perhaps nothing new. But it did offer the most enthusiastic, relaxed and fulsome celebration of Australia's racial diversity as a positive strength, and our cultural heterogeneity as offering opportunities for a distinctive contribution in the Asia–Pacific that we've had from Howard.

The second speech, to an international bankers' conference, offered both a penetrating analysis of the regional economic crisis and a vision for APEC. It was also a significant watershed in the evolution of the official Australian view of the international financial system. In it, Howard acknowledged serious malfunctions in the international financial system, especially concerning the extremely rapid movement of short-term capital, and that as a result Asian nations hit by the regional crisis suffered much worse consequences than their economic fundamentals, or their records of economic management, justified. This was an important political breakthrough in the official view from Canberra. Howard was explicit in arguing that the Asian economies had been punished far more by contagion and panic than was warranted, that contagion and panic became themselves important factors in the equation and not just reflections of underlying economic factors.

His speech was full of ideas. He offered initiatives on improving transparency, changing arrangements for international lending such that the movement of capital is slowed down, setting APEC benchmarks for disclosure requirements, support for the IMF to play a lender-of-last-resort role, and the need for greater assistance, both financial and technical, from countries that can afford it to countries in crisis in the region. He proposed that many of these initiatives should be pursued in the context of APEC. All of this was very good stuff, and very welcome. But its real long-term significance, with regard to Australian foreign policy, lay in two areas. One was the recognition by Howard of the Asian economic crisis as an absolute top priority for Australia. The other was the recognition of APEC as a top priority.

APEC has been Missing In Action for most of the regional economic crisis. This is bad for APEC, bad for the region, and particularly bad for Australia. APEC has always had inestimable benefits for us in terms of promoting regional cohesion and community, and putting Australia at the heart of the region. It is one of the very few regional associations of any consequence Australia belongs to. Australia created APEC and has had something of a leadership role within it. To allow it to wither would be a monstrous waste of a priceless diplomatic asset. Howard needs to make a full-bench-press effort to breathe new life into APEC, even if the Kuala Lumpur APEC meeting last November was more or less a disaster.

More broadly, Australia needs to work towards not only promoting economic recovery in Asia, but also promoting the type of recovery that promotes our interests. Australia needs to work towards a regional recovery in which American commitment to the region is reconfirmed, and in which Japan regains the confidence it needs to resume offering leadership to the region. Japan is an exemplary democracy and a very good friend to Australia. Its overall loss of credibility and prestige in the region is perhaps the single greatest diplomatic consequence of the regional economic crisis. As well, Australia needs to have an influence on the emerging political debate within the region. This will require great dexterity and sophistication, however—a ham-fisted or bombastic tone could easily be extremely counterproductive.

The regional economic crisis will be at the centre of Australian foreign policy for at least the next few years, although there will be other priorities, not least in trade.

The Government will promote a prudent diversification of exports, although even in 1998, in the midst of the crisis, just over 50 per cent of our exports went to East Asia, as opposed to 58 per cent in 1996. This demonstrates the continued overwhelming importance of East Asia to Australia. There will be other important trade priorities as well. The second ministerial meeting of the World Trade Organisation will be held in late 1999 in the US, and it will be a pivotal opportunity for Canberra to push for the establishment of a new global trade liberalisation round. This will remain a very high priority, as it is only in the context of the trade-offs involved in a global round that some areas of traditional concern to Australia, such as agriculture, can be fully included.

The broad direction of Australian foreign policy remains clear—continued high priority regional engagement, a big role in assisting recovery in Asia and in seeking to influence the nature of that recovery, continued affirmation of the American alliance and using our influence with the Americans to try to produce good policy from Washington on East Asia. Bilaterally, Canberra will continue to put maximum effort into several key relationships such as those with the US, Japan and Indonesia.

The bigger challenge, perhaps, lies in convincing the Australian public that continued economic growth will necessarily involve embracing globalisation. Of course we can moderate its extreme effects, but we are much more likely to advance our national interests, and secure our welfare, if we exploit the opportunities of globalisation rather than run from its challenges. We also need to convince the public that foreign policy is not a series of irrelevant junkets but an integral part of the responsibility of government.

One other task transcends foreign policy but involves foreign policy centrally. It is a matter of doctrine with the Howard Government that Australia is not a part of Asia and that our Asian engagement does not involve any change in our cultural identity. Of course it is true that the core elements of our civic identity—such as representative democracy and a free press—are not on the negotiating table with anybody. Nor should they ever be. Nor would any of our neighbours realistically argue that they should be. It is also true that our identity is changing because of our engagement with Asia. Thirty years ago we still followed the White Australia policy and our ethnically Asian population was negligible. Today 5 per cent of our population was born in Asia, and they, like other migrants before them, have made their own distinctive contribution to our evolving national character. This is not much more than stating the obvious. Of course Asian immigration is only one aspect, and not the biggest aspect, of our engagement with Asia. But it is a big development and it does have an effect on our national identity. Similarly, the fact that it is now the policy of state and federal governments to encourage the study of four strategic Asian languages—Japanese, Indonesian, Chinese and Korean—means that tens of thousands of young Australians will make a serious intellectual encounter with at least one of the great Asian civilisations. This is unlike anything in our past. It is really a big change in our national orientation.

Even the prominence APEC enjoys in our foreign policy is a huge development. Before APEC, the only big meetings to which Australian prime ministers were routinely invited were CHOGMs. That meant that the Commonwealth, which does not embody core Australian national interests, was inevitably the focus of much of our foreign policy. Now it is a regional body which is the focus. That, too, represents a change in our conception of ourselves. The 1980s and 1990s have seen a heartening reaffirmation of the American alliance and the centrality of the American relationship. But it too has been re-engineered into a regional alliance, an alliance for Australia in the region rather than part of a global Cold War balance.

Similarly it is instructive that the biggest foreign press corps in Jakarta is the Australian press corps. That signals, and magnifies, a different orientation in the minds of news-consuming Australians. The transformation of the modern global economy into an information and services economy means that at every level our people-to-people contact with Asia has increased dramatically. Life is different, life is good.

The Howard Government is extremely timid about all this, presumably for three reasons. One, it is reacting against

Keating's enthusiasm. Two, it is scared of frightening the Hansonite horses. And three, it is probably itself a little ambivalent about where all these developments are taking us. And that position is not unreasonable. The Howard Government has striven (not always successfully) to be a reassuring government, a calm government. And much of the Australian genius in civic life has been to be the undramatic country, the country of calm good sense. Yet the Government's rhetorical and intellectual timidity has strangely been shared by much of Australia's intellectual community, who seem too discombobulated by the defeat of Keating, the rise of Hanson and the simultaneous Asian economic crisis to challenge the nation any more over questions of identity and regionalism.

Of course the way the life of the Howard Government has unfolded shows that our national interests, which are overwhelmingly contained in Asia, will pull us ever deeper into Asian engagement whether our political leadership is really comfortable about it or not. But the Australian people deserve to be told the truth by someone. There is a process of Asianisation going on in Australian life, such that every important area of national life is coming to have an Asian dimension. The conclusion is inescapable—Australia is part of Asia and will find its destiny in the Asia–Pacific.

This does not imply walking away from the American alliance or other old associations. Our history and geography are assets. We are of more interest and use to the Americans because of our comprehensive Asian engagement. We are of more interest and use in Asia because of our access and influence in Washington. But when *The Economist* or the *Wall Street Journal* run stories about Australia, they place them in the Asian section. When our foreign and defence ministers attend annual AUSMIN talks, their American interlocutors are all ears for Australian perspectives on Indonesia, or even China. They really couldn't care less what our views are about the Balkans or the Middle East. We now participate in the Asian Games. We seek to belong to the Asia–Europe summit process as part of the Asian delegation. The world recognises, even if we don't, that this is where we live and breathe.

As a nation we are going through an Asianisation process that will not undermine our identity but fulfil it. What part of Asia do we belong to? The Australian part, of course.

Our leaders, political and intellectual, need to be bolder and more forthright in telling us the truth about our national circumstances, which remain much more exciting than dangerous, much more appealing than vexing. The Asianisation of Australia is part of globalisation. For us, going global meant going regional. The Asian crisis doesn't make this any less real or less important.

INDEX

Abbott & Costello versus Random House 227
Aboriginal Australians 55, 79
  affront to Howard 176
  Constitution to acknowledge original ownership 161, 178
  dispirited 189
  Mabo Case 177, 179–80, 181, 184, 210
  poverty 177
  reconciliation 13, 31, 45, 46, 82
    and national identity 78
  Senate representation 78
  sense of unfairness 42–3
  Sorry Day 185
  stolen children 81–2, 179, 187, 188
    pressure for apology 185–6
  Wik native title bill 12–13, 15, 17, 180, 181, 196, 197
  Wik-Mungkan culture 180–1
  see also native title
Aboriginal and Torres Strait Islander Commission (ATSIC) 184, 186
Access Economics 27
A.C. Nielsen 218, 220
advertisement, about intolerance (1998 campaign) 67
affliction of the spirit 6–7
aged pension 112–13
Agenda, The 24
agriculture 192, 193, 194, 198–9, 200, 201
Aitkin, Don 133

Alston, Margaret 195
Amcor Ltd 70
American Academy of Cosmetic Surgery 225–6
Anderson, John 196, 202
anti-globalisation movements 256–7
Anwar Ibrahim 239, 242
Apps, Professor Patricia 147
Argus, Don 74–5, 76
Arthur Andersen 71
Asia Pacific Economic Cooperation (APEC) 239, 240, 260–1, 265
  Howard's vision for 262–3
Asian economic crisis 4, 24, 64, 94, 260, 261–2, 263, 266
  consequences 238–41
  cross-border capital flows 22–3
  economic causes 233–5
  lessons from 231–43
  other reasons 235–7
  powerful shock 231
Asian languages 265
Asprey inquiry into tax system 99
Association of Southeast Asian Nations (ASEAN) 239, 240, 241, 244, 246, 247, 249, 251, 259
attack, on Lakemba police station 2
Australia 37–8
  Asianisation 264–7
  defence 244–54
  divisiveness 228
  lucky country 4–5

mood of pessimism 1–2, 3, 5, 6, 23, 83, 143–4, 227
population 114, 166, 265
power of Senate 159
a tribalised nation 36–7
US alliance 241, 247, 251, 259, 264, 265, 266
vision-free zone 57–66
vulnerability 166
Australian Broadcasting Corporation (ABC) 12
Australian Bureau of Statistics 85, 142, 147
Australian Chamber of Commerce and Industry (ACCI) 69, 174
Australian Competition and Consumer Commission (ACCC) 26, 123
Australian Conservation Foundation 201
Australian Council of Social Services (ACOSS) 70–1
Australian Defence Force (ADF) 248–9, 254
funding 250, 252, 253, 254
and RMA 252–3
Australian Democrats 18, 38
break from economic liberalism 8
on immigration 166
third force 49, 59
Australian Education Union 135
Australian Gourmet Traveller 217
Australian Institute of Family Studies (AIFS) 142, 149
Australian Institute of Health and Welfare 118, 122
Australian Labor Party (ALP) 8, 20, 49, 52, 72
branch-stacking 172
crisis for social democracy 20–1, 22
few policies 39
gains votes via One Nation 14
gulf between middle/working class 11, 54
human rights approach 259, 260
and immigration 163, 171–2
inadequate strategy in NSW 101
outpolls Coalition (1998) 16, 17, 100
a party with ideas 22, 45
pro-native title 15
response to One Nation 53–4, 171
result in 1998 election 58–9
returns to opposition (1996) 14
special interests party 38

strategy for 1998 election 54–5
tax package (1998) 53–4
Australian Medical Association (AMA) 123
Australian Medical Workforce Advisory Committee 121
Australian Republican Movement 157, 158, 160
Australian Vice-Chancellors Committee (AVCC) 125

baby boomers 221–2
different family values 150
focus on quality of life 7, 219–20
midlife crisis 217–29
selfish generation 219, 221
stressed generation 220, 227
turning 50 7, 218
Bacon, Jim 154
banking system 3–4, 21, 26
bank mergers 25
Barton, Edmund 153
Beattie, Peter 154
Beazley, Kim 22, 53, 54, 58–9, 257, 258
attacks GST 73
common touch 63
has little effect on One Nation 67
leads ALP 8, 14–15
listens to the people 61
moral victory 17
policy adjustment 59
population policy 170–1
on republic 155, 156
supports immigration 166
tax package 15–16
unemployment target 16, 65, 93–4
Beazley, Mrs (mother of Kim) 62, 65
Beer, Gillian 147–8
Bennelong, seat of 99
Berri fruit juice company 68
Betts, Katherine 164
Bhagwati, Jagdish 232–3
BHP 74
Birrell, Bob 170, 173
biscotti 219
Bjelke-Petersen, Joh 99
Blair, Tony 12, 21–2, 258
'reciprocal responsibility' 25
Boraine, Alex 176
Borbidge Government, opposed to native title 181
Brambles Industries 74
Brennan, Father Frank 79
Brereton, Laurie 259

Britain 249
  breaking ties with 152, 156
  economic policy 258
British Telecom 19
Brotherhood of St Laurence 71, 84, 130, 147
Buchanan, Pat 256
Budget, federal 64–5, 100, 112, 114
  cuts in education 125–6
  in surplus 3
  tough (1996/97) 11
Burma, sanctions 259
bush communities *see* rural Australia, disadvantaged
Bush, George 221, 261
business
  leadership by 68
  mutual obligation approach 25
  offshore ventures 74
  and tax reform 69, 70–2
  unenthusiastic about Howard 12
Business Coalition for Tax Reform 72
Business Council of Australia (BCA) 69, 71, 72, 73
business cycle 88, 91, 93, 94

Cameron, Ross 165
campaigning, Howard-style 10
capital gains tax 54, 101, 106
capitalism 75
Carr, Bob 2, 154, 166, 210
Catchlove, Barry 111–12
Centre for Economic Studies (SA) 193
Centre for Population and Urban Research (Monash) 149
Century Zinc (CRA) 181–2
childcare 145–6, 150–1
Chin-Ning Chu 227
China 241, 242, 250, 259
  Chinese language 265
  Chinese students, given refuge in Australia 172–3
  manufacturing 236
  many seek immigration 5
  military dialogue with 248
  in near future 238, 246
Chipman, Professor Lauchlan 134
Chung Min Lee 240
Clark, Andrew Inglis 153
Clash of Civilizations and the Remaking of the World Order, The 242
classless society, myth 109
Clean Up Australia 79
Clements, Kirstie 225
Clinton, Bill 4, 12, 217, 221, 261
  immigration policy 33
  new position for Democrats 24
  'the third way' 258
Coalition 9, 10, 38
  appeasing the bush 197
  fails to mould opinion 60
  fears backlash from bush 62
  grudging mandate for tax reform 64, 65
  inexperienced after 13 years in opposition 11
  loses votes to Labor 14
  loses votes to One Nation 50
  majority halved in 1998 election 58
  primary vote (1998) 16
  see also Howard Government
coastal living 198
Cold War 238, 242, 246, 248, 265
Coleridge, Samuel Taylor 81
Colston, Mal, defects from ALP 11
Committee for the Economic Development of Australia (CEDA) 74
common touch, important in leader 61, 63
Commonwealth Government
  extension of powers 203–15
  customs and excise duties 207
  High Court decisions 205, 206–7
  income taxes 206
  Special Purpose payments 207–8
Commonwealth Grants Commission 210–11
Commonwealth Heads of Government Meeting (CHOGM) 265
communism 231, 238, 242
competition policy 61, 69
  complexity 73–6
  and rural Australia 193, 197–8
  and schools 131–2
complaint, culture of 5–6, 7
Connell, Bob 136
Connors, Lyndsay 132
conservative politics 186, 258, 260
  alternatives to tax reform 70–1
  and baby boomers 220
  realignment 48–9
Constitution 153, 154–5, 160
  attempts to amend 154–5, 203
  Commonwealth responsibilities 208–9
  double majority provision 154
  new preamble 161, 178
  original intentions 204–5, 211–12
  state responsibilities 209

INDEX

Constitutional Convention (1998) 154–5, 157–9, 159, 161, 220
   supports republic 158
corporatism, basis for allocating capital 24
cosmetic surgery 225–6
Costa, Dr Con 119
Costello, Peter 61, 74, 104, 166
   pleased with tax package 70, 97, 213
   on society's unhappiness 6–7
Costello, Tim 79
cotton 197, 198–9
Council for Aboriginal Reconciliation 176, 184
Council of Australian Governments 199
Country Party 50, 51, 53, 195–6
courage, needed for tax reform 106
Court Government, opposed to native title 182
Court, Richard 44, 204, 209
Craik, Dr Wendy 191–2, 194
Crane, Winston 196
Crean, Simon 22
Crosby, Lynton 52–3
culture building 77–83
Culture of Forgetting, The 81
Curtin, John 14
cynicism 227, 229

dairy industry 199
Davies, Paul 82
Davis, Carol 220, 224
Davis, Mark 221
de Q. Walker, Professor Emeritus Geoffrey 214
Deakin, Alfred 36, 153, 205–6, 214
Deane, Sir William 46, 152–3
defence 244–54
   budget 250, 252, 253, 254
   Collins Class submarines 252
   forward cooperation 247–8
   key interests 250–1
   Revolution in Military Affairs (RMA) 247, 251–2, 253
   strategic community in Southeast Asia 244
   Strategic Policy document 245–6, 247, 248, 253–4
   strategy of self-reliance 244, 247, 251
deflation 236–7
Demidenko/Darville, Helen 81, 82
democracy 28, 158, 243
Democratic Labor Party 49

democratisation, in Southeast Asia 239, 240–1
Dennis Hotels Case 1958 207
deregulation 193
Dessaix, Robert 79–80
   defines a public intellectual 82
Dibb, Paul 246–7
Dictionnaire des Intellectuels Francais 82
Diogenes 124
discontent 7, 42, 64
diversity, in Australian society 5, 13, 36, 38, 45
   see also multiculturalism
divorce 142, 149, 219–20
Djerrkura, Gatjil 186
doctors (GPs)
   co-payment suggested 122
   fee-for-service 121–2, 123
   oversupply 121, 123
   shortfall in regions 194
Doctors' Reform Society 119
Dodson, Mick 79
Dodson, Patrick 79, 176–7, 179, 185
Doing The Right Thing 227
Dombrovskis, Peter 79
Downer, Alexander 59, 157, 166, 260
   on self-determination 183
downsizing 221–2
Dunghutti people 188
Dylan, Bob 99

East Timor 259, 260
Easytax 104–5
economic growth 19, 34
   and quality of life 6
   superior in Australia in 1990s 3–4
economic liberalisation 109, 110, 114
economic liberalism 8, 17, 19, 34–5
economic rationalism
   bogy 19–20
   destructiveness 41–2
   questioned in *Quadrant* 82
education 30, 110, 134
   Dawkins reforms 134
   Enrolment Benchmark Adjustment 129
   export earner 130
   funding 228
   less funds 125–6, 128, 130
   post-compulsory 126
   sponsorships 130–1
   in a state of growing anxiety 124–37
   user-pays 128
   voucher funding system 131
   West review 131, 135

electorate
    antagonism towards immigration 164
    conservative 165, 166
    cynicism/hostility towards politicians 59, 67, 104
    ethnic vote 172
electorates, world, response to globalisation 256–7
electronic commerce, effect on GST 107–8
Ellis, Bob 227
employment 20
    job losses/gains 29
    research by Treasury 88
    for young people 126–7
    see also unemployment
End of History and the Third Man, The 232, 242
Engineers' Case 1920 209
enterprise bargaining 86
equity debate 27–9
Ervin, Lorenzo 169
Europe 257, 258–9
European Union 239
Evans, Ted 28
executive salaries 28
exports 29, 103, 264
    education 130

families 139–51
    fathers and domestic duties 142
    pessimism/fear 143–4
    self-reliance 148
    sexual division of labour 140, 141, 149
    sole parent 149, 219–20
    structural changes 139–40, 141–2
    supermums 141–2
    tax proposals 146, 147–8
    traditional 140–1
Farley, Rick 201
farmers 192, 193, 195, 200
federal election 1993
    Coalition pledges GST 8–9
    Keating's win 9
federal election 1996
    ALP returns to opposition 14
    Coalition wins rural support 194
    Howard's victory 10–11
    Labor loses rural support 194
    Nationals lose seat of Murray 50–1
federal election 1998 51, 67, 69
    'boring' campaign 15
    dearth of enthusiasm 57
    electoral watershed 48–56
    and globalisation 256–67
    Government out of touch 61
    Howard wins 16–17, 39
    Howard's mandate for new tax 98, 100, 101–2, 105
    Labor's tax package 97–8, 101–2, 105, 106
    polarised tax debate 106–7
    race-based election 2, 17, 55, 182, 183, 197
Federal Finance 210–11
federalism 203, 205, 211
    virtues 214
    see also Commonwealth Government
Federation 152, 153–4, 155, 156, 203, 204–5, 211, 212, 213
    dissatisfaction 210
    original intentions 208–9, 214
    White Australia 30
Federation of Ethnic Community Councils 171
Ferguson, Martin 166
Ferris, Senator Jeannie 196
fertility, decline 140
Fightback! 8–9, 10, 69, 72
financial crisis, global 237
financial system
    global 22
    market supervision 26
Fischer, Stanley 233
Fischer, Tim 13, 51, 52, 155, 198, 260
    press release to Asian press 51–2
    on Ten Point Plan 182
Fish, Stanley 82
Fitzgerald, Robert 70–1
Fitzgerald, Stephen 168
Fitzgerald, Vince 223, 224, 225
FitzRoy, Governor Charles 180
Five Powers Defence Arrangement (FPDA) 249–50
Flannery, Tim 79
foreign policy 256–67
franchise fees 207
Franklin Dams Case 1983 210
Fraser Government 113
    open door for Vietnamese migrants 170
Fraser, Malcolm 11, 99
French, Robert 188
Frost, Robert 78, 83
Fukuyama, Francis 232, 241–2, 243

Ganglands 221
Generation Next 222, 228

Generation X 222, 223, 224–5, 228
generational friction 228
Germany 257
Gibbs, Sir Harry 208
Gilbert, Alan 30
Gittins, Ross 82
Glezer, Helen 142, 150
globalisation 55, 61, 241
   an established fact 35, 67–76
   challenge 18, 20–1, 22–3, 24
   complexity 69, 73–6
   election issue that went unmentioned 256–67
   and inequality of wealth 27–9, 109, 114
   and need for security 7
   new paradigm of political economy 256
   winners and losers 1, 240
Good Citizen: A History of American Civic Life, The 81
Goodman Fielder Ltd 68
goods and services tax (GST) 12, 16–17, 40, 73, 258
   Costello proposes 10 per cent 70
   Hewson pledges 15 per cent 8–9
   impact on conservative losses 58
   impact on education 125
   initial confusion 102–3
   little merit as tax reform 97–108
   radical solution 213, 215
Goot, Murray 164
Gorbachev, Mikhail 78
Goss, Wayne 203–4, 214–15
government
   governing well 23–4
   relationship with markets 26–7
governor-general 152, 159, 160
Gray, Edith 142
Gray, Gary 53, 54
Gray, John 227
Great Depression 16
Green Party 18, 180, 201
   on immigration 166
Greenspan, Alan 234
Grey, Earl 180
Griffith, Sir Samuel 153
gun laws 194, 196
   response after Port Arthur 2

Ha & Hammond Case 1997 207
Hale, David 257
Hamilton, Alexander 208, 212
Hand That Signed The Paper, The 81
Hanson, Pauline 13, 34, 44, 50, 100
   benefits from media attention 52
   break from economic liberalism 8
   claimed to lower migrant intake 169
   common touch 63
   and Easytax 104–5
   family life 62–3
   leadership mistake 64
   listens to constituents 197
   loses seat 17–18, 39, 59
   nationalism 46
   phenomenon 144, 165–6, 228
   provocative statements 67
   racism 43, 69
   on UN draft declaration 183
   vision 39, 40
   see also One Nation Party
Hansonism 39, 45, 227, 261, 266
   drawcards 13
   effects on Howard 14
   rise of 2
Harding, Ann 222–3, 224–5
Harradine, Brian 182–3
Hass, Aaron 227
Hawke, Bob 14, 20, 99, 104, 212, 258
Hawke Government 251
   and Aboriginal reconciliation 184
   economic reforms 4
   pro-jobs policy 89–90
   refuge for Chinese students 172–3
   tactics 10
   Wages Accord 89–90
Hayden, Bill 153, 182
health care 110, 121, 223, 224
   Coalition allocation 112
   funding priority 228
   health costs scheme proposed 225
   ultimate test 118
   Whitlam's policy 117
Health Care of Australia 112
Health Insurance Commission 111–12
hedge funds 234
Henderson, Gerard 81
Herbert, Xavier 177
Herron, John 185
Hewson, Dr John 8, 10, 114
   family life 62
   on GST 8–9
   tries for tax reform 69
Higher Education Contribution Scheme (HECS) 125, 128
Hill, Heather 51
Hogg, Bob 72
Honeywood, Phil 134
Hong Kong 235
Hopevale Aboriginal community 188
Horsham, VIC 198

hostility, towards politicians 44
hotel bed tax 98
Howard Government
  Asianisation of Australia 265–7
  attitude to APEC 260–3
  change in family/women policy 145, 148
  defects 12
  defence planning 247–9, 251–2, 253–4
  economic reforms 4
    bring no votes 61
  and global economy 258–9
  and Hansonism 14
  health spending reduced 122
  helps jobseekers 93
  immigration policy 163–4
  little cheer for jobless in 1998 campaign 93–4
  Minister for the Bush 201–2
  no debate on national priorities 46
  no education policy 124–5
  opposition to self-determination 183–4
  and reconciliation 78, 176–89
  rewards child-rearing 115
  tax reform 12, 16, 55, 70, 71, 213–14
  welfare reforms 110–12
  see also Coalition
Howard, John 36, 58, 104
  and Aboriginal society 184, 185–6
    his view on Mabo 181
    mistrusted by Aborigines 187
    pressure to extinguish native title 182
    visits to black Australia 186
  approach to economic reform 20
    courage over GST 65
    economy gets priority 11
    oversells GST 105
    tax reform essential 208
    unfortunate promise 70, 99–100
  difficulties in power centres 12–13
  and families 139
  family life 62
  on financial system 26–7
  lack of vision 44–5, 59
    semblance of a vision 100
  leadership 10, 12, 16, 99, 167
  'mutual obligation' 25
  NSW marginal seat strategy
    secures re-election 100–1
  and One Nation
    has little effect on 67
    loses votes to 63–4

Packer endorsement 68–9
personal traits 63, 99, 100
  determined politician 107
  dislike for multiculturalism 166–7
  ordinariness 63
  promises to be different 59
  re-election (1998)
    victory speech 45–6
    wins despite GST 16–17
  on republic 154–6, 156–7, 159
  on rural Australia 62
  uniform gun laws 2
Hughes, Robert 82
human rights 259, 260
  in rural/remote Australia 195
Human Rights and Equal Opportunity Commission (HREOC) 185, 202
Hume, seat of 51
Huntington, Samuel 242, 243

IBIS Corporate Services 68
idealism 228–9
immigration 43, 163–75
  Asian 30, 164, 165, 167, 265
  bipartisan consensus 163
  bleak outlook 168–9
  cost of migrant welfare 173
  emerging migrant underclass 175
  family reunion 169, 170, 172, 173–4
  foreign doctors' qualifications 174
  'Many races:one Australia' 32–3
  party differences 55
  positive approach needed 174–5
  refugees from former Yugoslavia 173
  skilled 169, 174
  sought by many Chinese 5
  Special Assistance Program 170, 172
  welfare benefits crackdown 168, 169, 171
imports 29
income levels 6
income tax 206, 213
  paying a fair share 103–4
India 246
Indigenous Land Fund 189
individuals
  as independent units 81
  relationship to state 25
  responsibilities 25, 32–3
  rights 25, 32

Indonesia 235, 239, 248, 265
  in deep depression 4
  and FPDA 249
  help to rebuild 55, 245, 260, 262, 264
  unrest 75, 240, 242
Industrial Relations Commission 93
Industrial Relations, Department of 86
Industry Commission 201
  inquiry into competition policy and rural Australia 198
inequality
  caused by unemployment 85, 86
  of income/assets 1, 6, 27, 27–9, 109, 110, 114, 115
inflation rate 3, 88, 98, 103–4
information technology 22
infrastructure 29
insecurity, in society 144
intellectuals 78–80, 80
  defined 82
  intellectual capital 80
  leading thinkers 136
  mistrust of 79–80
  nation's identity 77–83, 266
interest rates 3, 21, 193
  cuts 11
International Monetary Fund (IMF) 233, 262
internationalisation 3, 18, 113
Internet, and GST 107–8
irrigation 199, 200
Isaacs, Sir Isaac 152
Israel, population growth 30

Japan 238, 239, 242, 246, 264, 265
  deflation 237
  economic crisis 4, 24, 236
  exemplary democracy 263
  help from US 236
  military dialogue with 248
  original successful economy 4, 235, 236
Jay, Robert 211
job insecurity 87, 222
job losses 193, 194
Job Network 93
jobs crisis *see* unemployment
John Singleton Advertising 72
Jones, Clem 158
Joon-Num Mak 240–1
Judis, John B. 218–19, 228

Kalgoorlie (WA) 193
Kasper, Professor Wolfgang 211

Keating Government 10, 91, 251
  arrogance 61
  compulsory superannuation 112
  economic recovery brings no votes 60–1
  economic reforms 4, 11
  Native Title Act (1993) 179–80
  welfare reforms 111
Keating, Paul 13, 20, 44, 72, 99, 104, 212
  arrogance 9
  attacks Packer 68–9
  constructs new position for ALP 8
  consumption tax option 99
  enthusiasm for Asia 261, 266
  intelligent pragmatist 20
  pro-marketplace 8, 9, 258
  pro-republic 156, 157
  speech at Redfern Park 184
  tries for tax reform 69
  vision 9–10
Kemp, Dr David 128–9, 132
Kennedy, John F. 23, 78, 83
Kennett Government, education reform program 128
Kennett, Jeff 44, 154, 166, 213–14
Kernot, Cheryl 53
Kerr, Sir John 159
Kiernan, Ian 79
Kimberley Land Council 178
Kingston, Charles 153
knowledge-based industry 30
knowledge workers 41
Koowarta Case 1982 209–10
Korea 236, 238, 248, 265
  unification 238–9, 242, 246
  see also North Korea; South Korea
Krugman, Paul 84, 90–1

labour market, reform 92
Labour Party (UK) 21–2
Landcare 200, 201
Latham, Mark 22, 257
Launceston College 128
Lawrence, Professor Geoffrey 200–1
leadership 61, 65, 80
  adherence to values 66
  Australia's greatest need 47, 55–66, 229
  disappointment in Howard's 12
  Howard gets it right 10
  intellectual 78–80, 82–3, 136
  Keating-style 10
  political, defined 60
  study in failure 13–14
learning 30, 124, 127
  jobs-oriented 133

learning culture 134, 136
Lee Kuan Yew 250
Lees, Meg 59, 67
leisure time, no increase 85
Lend Lease 74
Lester, Yami 186
Liberal Party 38, 40, 51
   directs preferences against Hanson 14
   losses to One Nation 52
   primary vote (1998) 16
   restores Howard as leader 10
   return to centre ground (1993) 9
   schizophrenic aspects 38–9
   see also Howard Government
Liberal Party (UK) 21
liberalisation 240
liberty 25
life expectancy 118
literacy 127, 129, 132
Littler, Craig 222
living standards 6, 98
   sacrificed to buy votes 75–6
Lyons Forum 147

Mabo Case 1992 177, 179–80, 181, 184, 210
Macarthur, NSW 193
Macdonald, Fiona 85
Macfarlane, Ian 232–3
Mack, Ted 158
Mackay, Hugh 219–20
   on baby boomers 226
   birth rate 220
   community cynicism 81
   siege mentality in society 3, 144
MacKenzie, Bill 180
MacLeish, Archibald 77
Mahathir Mohamad, Dr 233–4, 239, 242, 249
Malaysia 235, 239, 240, 242, 248, 249
   riots 75
Manne, Robert 78–9, 81–2, 83
marginal tax rates 115–16
Marginson, Simon 125–6
market economics 23, 34, 231–3, 235
Martin, Ray 186
Maryborough 42
Mason, Sir Anthony 160
Mathews, Russell 211
Mathews v. Chicory Marketing Board 1938 206–7
Mayo, seat of 59
Mayson, Dr George 225–6
McAllister, Ian 164
McClelland, Alison 85

McEwen, John 'Blackjack' 51
McGarvie, Richard 160
McGauchie, Donald 181, 196, 197
McGregor, Malcolm 167
McLachlan, Ian 196, 248
McMahon Government 16
Medibank 111, 117
medical graduates, numbers limited 122
Medicare 111, 112, 117–18, 119, 120
Melbourne Anglican Synod 132
Melbourne High School 132
Menzies, Sir Robert 10–11, 16
middle class 97–8, 101
   shrinking 2
MIM 74
Minchin, Nick 161, 166, 174
Mind and Mood 144
ministers, scandals and resignations 12, 100
Moir, Anne & Bill 227
monarchists 155, 156, 157, 161
Morgan, Hugh 166
Morrisey, Patrick 200–1
multiculturalism 165
   basic policy guide 168
   defined 31–2
   out of fashion 163
   reinventing Australia 5
   resentment of difference 43
multiracialism 257
Murphy, Chris M. 226
Murray, Les 77–8
Murray, seat of 50–1
Murray–Darling Basin 191, 192, 199

Narrogin, WA 198
National Agenda for Multiculturalism 31
National Australia Bank 74, 76
National Centre for Social and Economic Modelling 147
National Farmers Federation (NFF) 181, 191, 192, 195, 196–7
National Health Service (UK) 117, 119
national identity 78, 265
   and intellectual activity 80
   'nagging disquiet' 177
   search for 36–47
National Native Title Tribunal (NNTT) 179, 180, 188
National Party 27, 38, 50–1, 53, 155, 196
   decline 49, 58, 62
   fairly limited vision 201

INDEX

opposed to native title 182
primary vote in 1998 16
see also Country Party
National Railways 194
nationhood 153–4, 204–5
centenary 5, 155
native title 179–80, 185, 187, 194, 201
claims with the NNTT 180, 188
and farmers 192
Ten Point Plan 182–3, 197
see also Wik native title bill
Native Title Act (1993) 179–80, 197
Natural Heritage Trust 200
New Zealand 249
Newman, Jocelyn 110
North Korea 238–9
Northeast Asia 239, 240
nostalgia 226–7
numeracy 127, 129, 132
nursing homes
levy 112
reforms 145

Office for the Status of Women 145
Olsen, John 154
Olympic Games 2000 5, 178
One Nation Party 36, 40, 58, 100, 166
anti-globalisation 256–7
conservative appeal 40–1, 49–50
effect on, of unemployment 28–9
nostalgia for past 34
one Senate seat 59
race-based election 183
rise of 13, 66
strong poll in 1998 2, 17–18, 49
themes of disappointment and hurt 61–2
a third force 39, 48, 50, 52–3
wins in state election 13, 197
O'Neil, Michael 193–4
Optus, Packer proposal 68–9
Organisation for Economic Cooperation and Development (OECD) 94, 110, 135
Australia's health care system 121–2
Organisation for Petroleum-Exporting Countries (OPEC) 89

Pacific Dunlop 74
Packer, Kerry, endorses Howard 68–9
Parkes, Henry 153
Parton v. Milk Board 1949 207
Passages for Men 227
Patterson, Mark 69, 70, 73
Pearson, Noel 185, 189
Pease, Allan & Barbara 227
Pederson, Alan & Karen 189
Perelman, Lewis 135, 136
pessimism, in Australia 1–2, 3, 5, 6, 23, 83, 143–4, 227
pharmaceuticals, co-payment 122
Philippines 235, 239
Pitjantatjara 186
politicians
hostility towards 59
longing for immortality 99
population, ageing 114
Port Arthur massacre (1996) 2
poverty
and Aborigines 177
and unemployment 84–5
Powell, Dr Roy 198, 201
power, centralisation since Federation 209–10
Premiers' Conference 206, 210
private health insurance 111–12, 119, 120–1
community rating 121
extra bills 121
subsidisation 119
private medicine
lucrative 119–20
more expensive 118–19
Probert, Belinda 141
Productivity Commission 26
public opinion, on immigration 164
publishing 80
Punch, Gary 197, 198, 199, 201
Pusey, Professor Michael 143–4

Quadrant 77, 82

racial chauvinism, in politics 13
Racial Discrimination Act (RDA) 182, 183
racism 67, 69, 165
radio 226
station 2SM 226
talkback 5, 79
Ralph, John 69
Rapson, Virginia 170, 173
Ray, Robert 173
Reagan, Ronald 78, 113, 167, 221, 258
Recasting the Stone 227
recession (early 1990s) 7–8, 89, 91
reconciliation 187–8
apology 185, 188
self-determination 183–4
struggle for 176–89, 196, 197

Yu's principles 179
see also Wik native title bill
Reconciliation Convention (1997) 176, 178
referenda, to amend Constitution 154–5, 203
referendum (1999) 152, 158, 159–60, 161
republic
　1999 referendum 152, 158, 159–60, 161
　ALP commitment 15
　Australia moves towards 5, 46, 79, 152–61
　dismissal of president 160–1
　minimalist 154, 156, 158, 159
　support from baby boomers 220
Republican Advisory Committee 156
Reserve Bank, interest rate cuts 11
responsibilities, of individual 25, 32–3
retirement provision 142, 148–9, 223
　privatisation 109–10
revenue redistribution 210–11
Revolution in Military Affairs (RMA) 247, 251–2, 253
Reynolds, Henry 79, 177
Richness In Diversity exhibition 262
rights, of individual 25, 32
Robb, Andrew 72–3, 196
Robinson, Martin 222, 223
Rubin, Robert 75
Ruddock, Philip, skilled immigration minister 168–9, 171
rule of law 4
rural Australia, disadvantaged 191–202
　inadequate services 193, 194, 195, 201
　unemployment 192–3, 194
Russell, Don 10
Russia 246
　deflation 237
Ruthven, Phillip 68, 75
Ryan, Fergus 72
Ryan, Peter, on Lakemba police station attack 3

Saatchi & Saatchi 72
sales tax 206
salinity 200
Salt, Bernard 198
Samuel, Graeme 70–1
saving (as opposed to spending) 29, 223–4
Scales, Bill 26
schools
　fund-raising 130
　private schools 126, 129, 132
　public schools 129–30, 132, 135
Schudson, Michael 81
Scullin, Jimmy 16
Seas and Submerged Lands Case 1975 209
Secrets of the Rainmaker, The 227
self-fulfilment 7
Senate 12, 16, 59, 161, 215
　power to block supply 159
Senate Inquiry into the Status of the Teaching Profession (1998) 127
share ownership 27
Sharp, John 51
Shears, Doug 68, 69
Sheehy, Gail 222, 227
Sidoti, Chris 195
Singapore 235, 239, 248, 249
single-parent households 149, 219–20
Singleton, John 72–3
Smith Family 130
Snowy River 192
social democracy 20–1
social engineering 146
social inclusion 34–5
social security, spending high 25, 27
socialism 75
society
　diversity 5, 31, 34–5
　　diversity with harmony 30–1
　fragmentation 1
　general wellbeing neglected 42
　losing confidence in leaders 3
　social inclusion 31–2
Sorry Day 185
South Australian Riverland 200
South Korea 235, 238–9, 262
　economic turmoil 75
'South Park' 99
Southeast Asia 235, 239, 240, 241, 246
　in deep recession 4
Speaking their Minds 79
stakeholding, in globalised economy 28
stamp duty 107
states, de facto abolition of 203–4, 207–8, 214–15
Stewart-Hunter, David 218, 220–1, 222, 226
Stirton, John 220, 228
Stockdale, Alan 212, 213
Stolen Children report 81–2
stolen generations, apology to 185–6, 187
Stone, Sharman 51

students, overseas fee-paying 130, 131
Subhuman Redneck Poems 77
suicide 194–5
superannuation 110, 224
    compulsory 112, 116–17
Surplus Revenue Act 1908 206

Taiwan 235, 236, 248
talkback radio 79
    medium of complaint 5
tall poppy syndrome 5
tax reform 12, 29, 40, 64
    business divided 69
    crucial 69
    key to 1998 election 15–16, 70
    needs courage 106
Tax Reform Forum 71
Tax Summit (ACOSS/ACCI) 71
taxation 224–5
teachers 133, 136–7
technical and further education (TAFE) 125, 131, 134
technology, take-up rate 4
Telstra 195
    backlash over sale 62
    Beazley fights privatisation 16
    Packer proposal 68–9
    part-sale of 11, 200
    rural job losses 194
terra nullius principle 179, 188
Textor, Mark 167
Thailand 235, 239, 249, 262
    economic turmoil 75
Thatcher, Margaret 72, 113, 258
Thompson, Frank 80
Torres Strait Islanders 178, 184, 185, 186
    Constitution to acknowledge original ownership 161
tourism 192
trade 263–4
transport infrastructure 29
Treasury, research into unemployment 88
Trebeck, David 196
Tuchman, Barbara 229
Turnbull, Malcolm 79, 156, 158, 160–1
Tybingoompa, Gladys 180, 183

Uncle Tobys 68
unemployment 28–9, 33, 82
    4 per cent in US 257–8
    Beazley's 5 per cent target 16, 65, 93–4
    benefits (dole) 92–3, 111, 114
    creation of underclass 110, 115
    elements of a jobs policy 95–6
    in Europe 257
    and families 115
    high levels in Australia 1, 11, 86–7, 89, 114
        exceeds 11 per cent 7–8
    ill effects 84–5
    and immigration 43, 169, 174
    inter-generational 115
    job creation scheme 90
    job shortfall 87
    long-term 110, 111, 113–14, 115
    macroeconomic policy 87–9, 90
    and marginal tax rates 116
    mutual obligation approach 111
    natural rate of 92, 94
    OECD advice 94
    in rural areas 192–3
Uniform Tax Case 1942 206
United Nations, rights of indigenous peoples 183
United Nations Association 75
United Nations Development Program 110
United States 29, 236, 242
    assertiveness/self-promotion 80
    defence capability 244–5
    economic policy 3, 84
    global economy 256, 257–8
    health spending 118–19
    immigration idealised 170
    income tax policy 105
    job creation 94–5
    no GST 258
    presence in East Asia 238–9, 246, 247, 263
Unity Party 171
universities 133, 133–4, 135
    ANU 142, 164
    Canberra 133
    Central Queensland 134
    Charles Sturt 195
    fund-raising 130–1
    James Cook 130
    Monash 133, 149, 170
    Murdoch 130
    Swinburne University of Technology 164
    Sydney 130, 133, 164
    tuition fees 128
    Wollongong 133
University of Queensland Press 80
utilities, failures 2

value adding 29–30
values 1, 43–4
   required for leadership 66
Vanstone, Amanda 128, 129
vasectomy 226
vertical fiscal imbalance (VFI) 207, 208, 213–14
Victorian Secondary School Principals Association 131
Vietnam War 228, 236, 245
vision 46, 78, 100
   Keating's 9–10
   lack of 44–5, 57–66
   prime requirement in a leader 58
Visy Industries 22
Vizard, Steve 79
vocational education and training (VET) 125, 131
Volkswagen 226

Wages Accord 89–90
wages, minimum 94
wages policy 90, 92
Wagga Wagga, NSW 198
Wallis, Stan 69, 70, 72, 73
Wasserstein, Wendy 217–18
water 192, 200
Watson, Don 184
wealth
   inequality 27–9
   and satisfaction 6
welfare groups, and tax reform 70–1
welfare system 42, 109–23
   benefits 114–15
   'mutual obligation' 25
   passive welfare 115
   policy of self-provision 109–10
   privatisation 116–17
   supports one-quarter of Australians 1, 114
   universal 113
   welfare fraud 110–11
Wells, Patricia 217
Wertheim, Margaret 82–3
West review, of higher education 131, 135
West, Roderick 134
Western Australia, referendum on secession 210
Western Yalangi people 188–9
wheat 193, 196
White Australia Policy 30, 164–5, 265

White, Dr John 22
Whitlam, Gough 23, 99, 112–13, 159
Whitlam Government 79, 99
   removal of aged pension means test 112–13
wholesale sales tax 103
Why Men Don't Iron 227
Why Men Don't Listen and Women Can't Read Maps 227
Wik native title bill 12–13, 15, 17, 180, 181, 196, 197
Wik-Mungkan culture 180–1
Williams, Daryl 161
Williams, Rosemary 227
Wilson, Harold 23
Wilson, Sir Ronald 185
wine industry 199
Winterton, Professor George 160, 161
Wolcott, Ilene 142, 150
women
   further education 140
   married, in workforce 140
   as mothers 141, 149, 150
   part-time work 142–3
   taking strain in families 143–4
   workforce participation 145, 146–7, 148, 149
Women's Policy 145
Wood, Alan 60
Woodward, Bob 24
wool 193, 196
work
   demand for professionals 127
   hours of 85–6
   job creation 84–96
   part-time 142–3
   for young people 126–7
work experience programs 87
work-for-the-dole 110–11
workforce, highly educated 4
Working Nation 91–3
workplace
   family-friendly 150–1
   rapidly changing 85, 86
World Bank 110
World Trade Organisation (WTO) 239, 264

youth unemployment 126–7
Yu, Peter 178–9
Yunupingu, Galarrwuy 183